THE NOVEL OF WORLDLINESS

THE NOVEL
OF WORLDLINESS

Crébillon

Marivaux Laclos

Stendhal

BY PETER BROOKS

PRINCETON UNIVERSITY PRESS
PRINCETON, NEW JERSEY
1969

Publication of this book has been aided
by the Whitney Darrow Publication
Reserve Fund of
Princeton University Press

Printed in the United States of America
by Princeton University Press, Princeton, New Jersey

This book has been composed in Linotype Granjon
with Centaur display type

For E. B. and M. S. B.

FOREWORD

AT THE TERM of a study which has led me
toward a wide range of problems and periods,
it is a great pleasure to acknowledge the
much-needed help, advice, and encouragement I have received: first of all from Harry
Levin, under whose sympathetic and ju-
dicious guidance the study first took shape,
as a doctoral dissertation at Harvard University: whatever merit it may have is in large
measure owing to him; from Edward P.
Morris, who provided vital encouragement
and argumentation at the project's inception;
from Dante Della Terza, Henri Peyre, Victor
Brombert, Georges May, and W. M. Frohock,
who read the manuscript at various stages and
contributed both further information and
pertinent criticism. A shortened version of
Chapter VI was presented as a lecture at
Marlboro College in April, 1967, on the kind
invitation of Thomas B. Ragle, President of
the College. The manuscript was completed
while I was beneficiary of a Morse Fellowship
from Yale University, and travel to France
was aided by an American Council of
Learned Societies Grant-in-Aid; for both of
these I am deeply grateful. Finally, to my
wife, for her unceasing support and interest,
at last a public thanks.

CONTENTS

THE NOVEL OF WORLDLINESS

INTRODUCTION

LIKE all such labels, "The Novel of Worldliness" claims only heuristic value. It seems to me the term that most accurately characterizes a kind of fiction written in eighteenth-century France which demands understanding on its own terms. Most study of the novel has in fact consciously or unconsciously shared an outlook formed by the great tradition of nineteenth-century bourgeois realism and its modern transmutations; attention to the eighteenth century has been directed and filtered through this optic in a search for origins. While such an approach has given a fine and subtle account of the major eighteenth-century English novelists in Ian Watt's *The Rise of the Novel*, it can only falsify and distort the French fiction which interests me in this study. Crébillon, Duclos, Marivaux, Laclos, and certain aspects of Stendhal simply do not reveal their full meaning, significance, and value when viewed retrospectively from the later tradition: critics tend to look for the wrong things, to emphasize the rudiments of a "realism" which was not these writers' concern (or criticize its absence), and often fail to take account of their distance from us, the assumptions which informed their work and are now alien.[1] The aim of this study is to make their assumptions our

[1] For the traditional discussions of eighteenth-century French fiction see: André Le Breton, *Le Roman au XVIIIᵉ siècle* (Paris, 1898); Servais Étienne, *Le Genre romanesque en France depuis l'apparition de la Nouvelle Héloïse jusqu'aux approches de la Révolution* (Paris, 1922); F. C. Green, *French Novelists, Manners and Ideas, From the Renaissance to the Revolution* (London and Toronto, 1928), and *La Peinture des moeurs de la bonne société dans le roman français de 1715 à 1761* (Paris, 1924); and the useful statistics and studies in the first volume of Daniel Mornet's massive critical edition of *La Nouvelle Héloïse* (Paris, 1924). Étienne's book, which does in fact give a brief account of several novelists before Rousseau, seems to me the most subtle and accurate; but none of these studies does justice to the novelists I shall discuss. More recently, Georges May has given an important account of the

optic, and to attempt to discover and articulate the sense and
value of their stance and techniques.

By "worldliness," I mean an ethos and personal manner
which indicate that one attaches primary or even exclusive
importance to ordered social existence, to life within a public system of values and gestures, to the social techniques
that further this life and one's position in it, and hence to
knowledge about society and its forms of comportment. The
"literature of worldliness" is then a literature directed to
man's self-conscious social existence—to know, assess, celebrate,
master and give meaning to man's words and gestures as they
are formed by his consciousness of society. The "novel of
worldliness," finally, is a fictional exploitation of the drama
inherent in man's social existence, the encounters of personal
styles within the framework and code provided by society.

Society is to these novelists a concept we have now lost. It
embraces the two distinct senses we give to the word—society,
the whole of organized human existence, and Society, the self-
conscious "being together" of an élite—because both senses are
virtually one for them. There is no human community worth
considering (hence which demands expression in language)
outside the circumference of the élite. Society is known as
le monde, the one World that counts; reader, writer, and characters are all members of this *monde,* and the object of their
attention—as of our critical effort—is man's way of being within its limits and in its terms: what we may call man's worldliness, or *mondanité.*[2] Worldliness is hence a concept at the

---

interaction of critical theory and novelistic practice in *Le Dilemme du
roman français au XVIIIe siècle* (Paris and New Haven, 1963); and
Vivienne Mylne has written a major study, *The Eighteenth-Century
French Novel: Techniques of Illusion* (Manchester, 1965), which, however, seems to me seriously limited by the angle the author has chosen
to consider.

[2] To my knowledge, the only critic who has given serious attention

same time real, moral, psychological, and imaginative: the actual way of life of a milieu, a system of values, a form of personal consciousness and behavior, and a literary subject. And I shall use the term worldliness in all these senses; it will in fact be necessary to do so, since way of life and outlook, system and consciousness, are mutually interdependent.

Since these novelists are directing their attention not so much to the world itself as to worldliness, it is not entirely relevant to ask what correspondence there is between their representations and historical social realities. Yet there is one aspect of social reality that will interest me here at least obliquely: the creation of society's image of itself in the great worldly and literary salons of the seventeenth century. It is evident that the ethos and literature of worldliness can arise only when society becomes an object of conscious cultivation, when it asserts outward closure and inward publicity, when *le monde* ceases to be simply a term opposed to the otherworldly, and becomes a positive entity attended to and cultivated for its own sake. Such a valorization of *le monde* was a product of Renaissance secularism, and in France it received its most important early development in *précieux* circles. Under the direction of women like Mme de Rambouillet and Mlle de Scudéry, an ideal of polite sociability was elaborated, and the literature which responds to it was invented. The salon in fact, like worldliness itself, occupies an ambiguous position between the real and the literary, since the literature it fostered was talked before it was written: what started as conversation illustrating, taking part in worldliness, became the litera-

---

to the literary concept of worldliness is Roland Barthes, in his brilliant essay "La Bruyère," *Essais Critiques* (Paris: Éditions du Seuil, 1964). I read Barthes' essay after completing a first version of this study, and found needed confirmation of my ideas about worldliness in his analysis of *la mondanité*. His remarks on La Bruyère also allowed me to see further implications of the linguistic code of the worldly tradition.

ture celebrating and assessing it. This literature was developed by a line of important *moralistes* who refined and fixed a vocabulary directed to a hard-headed, accurate, penetrating understanding of social man. The eighteenth-century novelists inherit this tradition directly; it informs their stance, tone, attitudes, and expressive tools. This, more than any purely novelistic tradition, can help us understand their conception of the novel and its domain of attention, and therefore deserves consideration.

The seventeenth-century tradition of salons flourished before the refinement of the court was achieved by Louis XIV. In the last decades of the century, Versailles absorbed the attention of good society, and worldliness emanated from a single model of courtliness. But the austere last years of the reign of Louis XIV, then the Regency (when the Duc d'Orléans led the unrefined pleasures of his roués at the Palais-Royal and the infant Louis XV was immersed in boredom at Versailles) brought a decadence of courtliness, which was never to regain its preëminence, and led to a revival of Parisian society. The salons of Mme de Lambert and Mme de Tencin formed the tone and manner of a renewed literature of worldliness, and opened the way to the later drawing rooms of the *philosophes*, those of Mme d'Épinay, Mme du Deffand, Mlle de Lespinasse, and Mme Geoffrin.[3]

This was indeed perhaps the moment of greatest fulfillment in the history of social life. Memorialists like Duclos, Marmontel, and Mme d'Épinay have left a record (as have, obliquely, the novelists) of a life dedicated to sociability, to polite social and intellectual intercourse as a total style of exist-

[3] On these and other historical points, see Georges Mongrédien, *La Vie de société aux XVIIᵉ et XVIIIᵉ siècles* (Paris, 1950); Roger Picard, *Les Salons littéraires et la société française* (New York, 1943); John Lough, *An Introduction to Eighteenth-Century France* (London, 1960); and H. Carré, *Louis XV*, in Ernest Lavisse's *Histoire de France*, Vol. VII, Part 2 (Paris, 1911).

ence. The day passed in the salon listening to music, improvising theatrical performances, composing and reading aloud literary fragments, and primarily conversing. Manners were polished, wit sharpened, tone modulated and refined, language made precise and telling. What this atmosphere could be at its best was given a rare tribute by the man who set himself in violent opposition to his century's worldliness, Rousseau:

> On y parle de tout pour que chacun ait quelque chose à dire; on n'approfondit point les questions de peur d'ennuyer, on les propose comme en passant, on les traite avec rapidité; la précision mène à l'élégance: chacun dit son avis et l'appuie en peu de mots; nul n'attaque avec chaleur celui d'autrui, nul ne défend opiniâtrément le sien; on discute pour s'éclairer, on s'arrête avant la dispute; chacun s'instruit, chacun s'amuse, tous s'en vont contents, et le sage même peut rapporter de ces entretiens des sujets dignes d'être médités en silence.[4]

The literary ideal proposed by such a society valued a style of urbane, unpretentious wit, the unpedantic, elegant, non-specialized exploration of serious subjects of interest to all cultivated ladies and gentlemen. A typical example is Montesquieu's *Lettres persanes*, where social philosophy is put into light and amusing letters, and juxtaposed to a mildly erotic fabulation about a harem.

The company that gathered in such salons was a mixture of true aristocracy, the Robe, and writers recruited almost always from the bourgeoisie (the real aristocrat still did not write, he talked). There was some mingling—severe critics said confusion—of classes; *la bonne compagnie* was larger than in the previous century. Riches were accumulating rapidly. Luxury

---

[4] Jean-Jacques Rousseau, *Julie ou la Nouvelle Héloïse*, ed. René Pomeau (Paris: Garnier, 1960), p. 208. The passage is from one of Saint-Preux's letters from Paris.

was carried to the point where it called forth the fulminations of the clergy and was, ineffectually, regulated by sumptuary laws; it also found apologists like Voltaire. The purity of society was indeed threatened by adventurers, upstarts, gate-crashers, and by a new freedom in the criticism of social institutions. Yet in the novels we will consider, little of this freedom and social mobility is reflected—which is one of the reasons Taine concluded that the eighteenth-century French novel was a less faithful mirror of its times than the English novel.[5] It is as if the novel, the freest form in terms of literary genres, were socially the most conservative. The reasons should become apparent in the course of this study: for those writers concerned to explore modes of social existence, the image projected by *le monde*, the model of sociability it proposed, remained universal and coercive. And it is because of the force of this image that *mondanité*, the worldliness that is our theme, had such imaginative cohesion for the novelists and permitted them to write intelligent and dramatic comedies of manners.

The subject of this study is then a concept both real and imaginative, an ethos and a literary stance, which I will try to discern in its fictional function and evolution. Hence methodologically this study must necessarily be situated somewhere between formalist analysis and literary history or the history of ideas. In fact it is basically "formalist" in approach, because it is only through attention to their literary techniques and linguistic code that we, from our temporal and cultural remove, can grasp the sense and significance of these novelists. Yet by putting together several novelists who in combination span the century, and by extending the study back to the seventeenth

[5] Hippolyte Taine, *Les Origines de la France contemporaine: L'Ancien Régime* (Paris: Hachette, n.d.), Vol. 1, Book 2, pp. 312-15.

century and forward to Stendhal, I am necessarily making some claim to literary history. The claim, however, is really only to the state of an ideal history: not the chronicle of what really happened (for which one would, in the fashion of traditional literary history, have to give an account of hundreds of minor, as well as all the major, works of an epoch, establish trends, lines of influence, etc.), but a selective study of what are the most important events and transformations in terms of an intellectual structure which we impose upon the past in order to understand it.

This intellectual structure is of course the concept of worldliness itself, which was an assumption for the writers studied, but must be articulated as the framework of our study and made our optic on the past. This worldliness is not a "theme" in the sense usually given to that term. A purely thematic study of worldliness, it seems to me, would provide no means for locating and defining the stance central to this literature. Nor will this be the study of a literary type or kind; the novel of worldliness is not that clearly demarcated. I am really most of all attempting to capture an outlook, to show its intellectual and literary dimensions, its field of validity and historical dynamics, and its relevance to our continuing efforts to give meaning to our life together in society.

Such reflections may in some measure serve to justify the organization of the following chapters. They begin somewhat abruptly, with a close consideration of one novel; only gradually will this unfold into larger considerations. The background of the subject—what chronologically would be the first part of this study—comes in Chapter Two, after the initial attempt to analyze worldliness as a system in fiction. In almost all the succeeding chapters, analysis will precede theoretical and historical formulations, and each chapter will define the field of its attention according to the kinds of problems in worldliness presented by each text. I have tried in every case to let the subject emerge as much as possible from direct confrontations with the material, to encounter the outlook of worldliness in the texture of the novels before constructing definitions and attempting evaluations.

CRÉBILLON, DUCLOS, AND
THE EXPERIENCE OF WORLDLINESS

J'ENTRAI dans le monde à dix-sept ans, et avec tous les avantages qui peuvent y faire remarquer.[1] This opening sentence of *Les Égarements du coeur et de l'esprit* is perhaps most remarkable for its lack of detail: there is no date nor place, no indication of setting or historical background. By what it omits as much as by what it includes, the sentence implies a number of assumptions about its readers—that they know what constitutes *le monde,* that they are aware of what might, in its terms, be considered "advantages," that being noticed in this world is an inherently desirable condition, that one's existence in fact is worthy of attention only with entry into society. The author and his reader, it is suggested, share a common social place, an outlook and an understanding dependent upon it.

The subtitle of Crébillon's novel is *Mémoires de M. de Meilcour,* which at once suggests the inevitability of a certain tone and attitude. Giving an account of his youthful first encounter with society, the narrator is detached, hard-headed, witty, epigrammatic, and sophisticated; his voice marks the

[1] Claude-Prosper-Jolyot Crébillon (Crébillon *fils*), *Les Égarements du coeur et de l'esprit,* ed. Pierre Lièvre (Paris: Le Divan, 1929), p. 11. The five volumes of the Divan edition contain most, but not all, of Crébillon's works. All subsequent references are to this edition, and will be given as page numbers in parentheses—a practice I shall follow with all works from which I quote several times. The novel was originally published from 1736 to 1738.

distance between what he was and what he has become. He and the reader participate in an urbane and polite intercourse based on the fact that they are both men of the world and know its characters and their typical comportment. Hence the generality of a statement like, "On s'attache souvent moins à la femme qui touche le plus, qu'à celle qu'on croit le plus facilement toucher; j'étais dans ce cas autant que personne: je voulais aimer, mais je n'aimais point"(13). The statement implies a fund of knowledge about worldly behavior, an accepted view of the ways of young men in their first encounters with women, that is shared by narrator and reader; the narrative will exemplify a generally acknowledged condition.

The tale of Meilcour starts from his "ennui intérieur" at the age of seventeen, the sense of emptiness which oppresses him and which can only be dispelled, he realizes, by a woman. He attaches himself to a woman of his mother's generation, the Marquise de Lursay, who is only too willing, the narrator fully understands, to have Meilcour serve his apprenticeship with her. But Meilcour's timidity is extreme, and even eliciting a declaration of passion from him becomes a major problem for Mme de Lursay: she cannot go so far as to make outright advances, yet Meilcour is easily discouraged by any show of "severe virtue" on her part. The situation is further complicated by the irruption of the Comte de Versac, a fashionable libertine who dislikes Mme de Lursay because she once persuaded an attractive young widow to resist his seductions. Versac undertakes to convince Meilcour that Mme de Lursay is unsuitable, and that he would do better to choose the flamboyant Mme de Senanges. Meanwhile, Meilcour has been struck by the beauty of the young and virtuous Hortense de Théville, and neglects his social responsibilities in romantic daydreaming. The novel finally resolves itself, as it must, by Mme de Lursay's highly artful seduction of Meilcour.

The subject of the novel is, then, first of all Meilcour's sentimental education. But the account of a sentimental education given by a mature and worldly narrator will not itself be sentimental or impassioned, and will display no romantic subjectivity. Rather, he will place this education in its necessary social context, and see it as an initiation in the ways of the world, an experience in the manners and values of worldliness. Hence, for all its chaste economy of line, *Les Égarements* is a comedy of manners, a novel about social beings and ideas dramatized within a social framework. If Meilcour's quest is originally a personal one, its field of operation is to be eminently public.

The sense of an operative public is felt in many ways in the novel. The style, already glanced at, is of a public character in that it calls upon a reader's worldly knowledge and experience. Such sentences as "Une femme, quand elle est jeune, est plus sensible au plaisir d'inspirer des passions, qu'à celui d'en prendre"(39) or "Les conquêtes les plus méprisables sont quelquefois celles qui coûtent le plus de soin; et l'hypocrisie montre souvent plus de scrupules que la vertu même"(96-97) seem to demand judgment on their ability to render with elegance and precision that which has long been known about people, but never so well expressed. More particularly, the portrayal of character reposes on a public act of cognition and rendering which places a person within the social system. Meilcour's chosen tutor, Mme de Lursay, is presented in a lengthy analysis which interrupts the movement of the narrative:

> Coquette jadis, même un peu galante, une aventure d'éclat, et qui avait terni sa réputation, l'avait dégoûtée des plaisirs bruyants du grand monde. Aussi sensible mais plus prudente, elle avait compris enfin que les femmes se perdent moins par leurs faiblesses que par le peu de ménagement

qu'elles ont pour elles-mêmes; et que, pour être ignorés, les transports d'un Amant n'en sont ni moins réels, ni moins doux. Malgré l'air prude qu'elle avait pris, on s'obstinait toujours à la soupçonner; et j'étais peut-être le seul à qui elle en eût imposé. Venu dans le monde longtemps après les discours qu'elle avait fait tenir au Public, il n'était pas sur- prenant qu'il n'en eût rien passé jusqu'à moi. (18-19)

After a description of Mme de Lursay's physical appearance, the account continues:

Elle avait l'esprit vif, mais sans étourderie, prudent, même dissimulé. Elle parlait bien, et parlait aisément; avec beau- coup de finesse dans les pensées, elle n'était pas précieuse. Elle avait étudié avec soin son sexe et le nôtre, et connais- sait tous les ressorts qui les font agir. Patiente dans ses ven- geances comme dans ses plaisirs, elle savait les attendre du temps, lorsque le moment ne les lui fournissait pas. Au reste, quoique prude, elle était douce dans la société. Son sys- tème n'était point qu'on ne dût avoir des faiblesses, mais que le sentiment seul pouvait les rendre pardonnables; sorte de discours rebattu, que tiennent sans cesse les trois quarts des femmes, et qui ne rend que plus méprisables celles qui le déshonorent par leur conduite. (20)

With its multiplication of distinctions to reach the exact label for a form of comportment ("coquette" and "galante," "prude" and "précieuse"), the evocation of scandal ("une aventure d'éclat") and its social consequences ("les discours qu'elle avait fait tenir au Public"), allusions to a "system" designed to mask "pleasures" as sentimental "weaknesses," emphasis on knowing others and their motivations ("Elle avait étudié avec soin son sexe et le nôtre, et connaissait tous les ressorts qui les font agir"), this passage establishes that both the describer and the person described judge personal social style as a function of the image projected by society. Consciousness of this image is indeed the mediating term between social system and personal style; and in its attention to this consciousness, the passage creates an exact definition of Mme de Lursay's place in that *monde* of which the first sentence of the novel made mention.

We must recognize that the passage constitutes a full-length *portrait moral*, a formal and traditional set-piece of rhetoric used by most of the novelists of this period for the presentation of character. In its movement from one defining noun or adjective to another ("Aussi sensible mais plus prudente"), its careful qualifications ("l'esprit vif, mais sans étourderie, prudent, même dissimulé"), its use of abstractions and categories ("coquette," "prude," "les femmes," "un Amant"), its precise distinctions referring to related but significantly different types of social behavior and public being, the portrait makes a claim to rendering an accurate and total physical, psychological, moral, and social account of its subject. A *portrait moral* is indeed the expression of a total public act of knowing by one person of another. It reposes on the belief that all the important characteristics of a person can be apprehended and can be expressed in language. The portraitist takes the measure of his subject from a certain distance; intent to express the relationship of this character to the generality of humanity and the structure of society, he categorizes and abstracts, seeking the typical and socially classifiable. Yet he is careful not to be taken in by social representations, mere seeming, and "penetrates" to the essential nature of his subject, performs an unmasking, lays bare. He may be ironical, even satirical, but he is interested in balanced presentation rather than caricature. He seeks hardness of outline, a permanent reduction of his subject to categories, concepts, and language. As Roland Barthes has pointed out, the static, summary fixity sought by the portrait places the form, in Roman Jakobson's classification of the two basic tendencies of human discourse, on the side of "metaphor" rather than "metonymy":[2] the portrait represents combination and synthesis of discrete details of character into a complete and final representation, a total verbal structure, rather than movement from one contiguous particular to another. The portrait signifies total knowledge about another person, total clarity of perception, total expression in language. It means an arrest of the movement of human life in a stasis of words, the metaphorical expression of an essence rather than a narrative development.

The act of knowing which underlies the composition of a portrait is insisted upon in the novel by the repeated use of verbs *pénétrer* and *fixer*, and the noun *pénétration*. To "penetrate" someone is to find him out, to lay bare his true motives and sentiments: in his first mention of Mme de Lursay, Meilcour remarks that "Malgré mon attention à lui cacher ce qu'elle m'inspirait, elle m'avait pénétré"(18). Immediately following the portrait quoted above, he mentions Mme de Lursay's realization "qu'il lui était important, pour m'acquérir, et même me fixer, de me dissimuler le plus longtemps qu'il lui serait possible son amour pour moi"(21). To fix someone—in the sense of arresting his movement and attaching him with permanence —it is necessary to have penetrated him, caught and held him in definitions, at the same time using disguise to protect oneself. To let oneself be fixed is to sacrifice prestige and freedom of movement. For example, Meilcour, after sizing up Mme de Senanges, comments, "Je me reprochai enfin de donner tant d'attention à quelqu'un qui se définissait au premier coup d'oeil"(148).

To reduce someone to the categories, abstractions, and judgments of the portrait of Mme de Lursay is to be in a position

[2] Roland Barthes, "La Bruyère," *Essais Critiques* (Paris: Éditions du Seuil, 1964), p. 233. See Roman Jakobson, "Two Aspects of Language and Two Types of Aphasic Disturbances," in Jakobson and Halle's *Fundamentals of Language* (The Hague, 1956).

to control that person. And this is an act which cannot be performed by the young, inexperienced Meilcour-as-protagonist, but only by the mature and worldly narrator. Here we seize the ethos implicit in use of a language like that of the portrait: to bring someone to the metaphorical arrest of the portrait implies and in fact proves social superiority and domination. Evident in these opening pages of *Les Égarements* is an ideal of knowing and controlling through knowing which finds expression in the use of a language of hard, precise psychological and social abstractions by those characters socially in control. Mme de Lursay guides her intrigue with Meilcour because of her worldly knowledge, which has acquired the absolute fixity of aphorism: "Elle savait d'ailleurs qu'avec quelque ardeur que les hommes poursuivent la victoire, ils aiment toujours à l'acheter"(21). This is precisely the kind of information that the young Meilcour lacks. He is unable to formulate what appears as an aphorism in the latter part of this sentence: "J'ignorais entre beaucoup d'autres choses que le sentiment ne fût dans le monde qu'un sujet de conversation"(21). This game of penetration to knowledge, and the use of knowledge to control, forms the texture of the novel, and as we advance into this world, we understand that Meilcour's bafflement will lead to his loss of freedom.

Such knowing and controlling of others depends rigorously on a public system—the ethic, conventions, and of course the language, which it has valorized. As we suggested, making a portrait is in itself a social, even a sociable gesture, in that it implies membership in a community, experience of the world, and a thorough familiarity with the concepts and terms one is manipulating. The portrait of Mme de Lursay pointed to a consciousness of the image of society which determines what the behavior and even the self-conception of every member of the community must be. That which does not conform to this image is branded as *ridicule*—a word which, as adjective (ridiculous) or noun (both the general concept, ridicule, or any particular of behavior which is the object of ridicule: *un ridicule*) echoes throughout this novel (and all the literature of this period) as society's final judgment on the individual's style. If this consciousness of society's image has such coercive presence and reality, it is because society is seen as a theater, closed to the outside but utterly public to its members, who are both actors and spectators and must perform their social parts before the eyes of others. The action of the novel is played out in the drawing room, at the Opéra, in the Tuileries Garden at the hour of the promenade, and only ultimately in the boudoir. The drawing room, or salon, entry to which, as Mme de Lursay explains to Meilcour, can be denied to no member of *le monde*, is preëminently the medium of society's sociability, and here Mme de Lursay must maneuver by signs, glances, sighs, rapid whispers, to make herself understood without imprudently revealing herself.

The glance, the look of the eyes, is in fact the central physical and metaphorical expression of the closure and lack of privacy that are the primary conditions of life in society.[3] Near the beginning of the novel, Mme de Lursay seeks to know Meilcour's feelings about her: "Elle n'eut besoin que de me regarder fixement. Je ne pus supporter ses yeux. Ce seul regard lui développa tout mon coeur."(42). The entry of Hortense, at the Opéra, gives us a sense of the inescapable enclosure and publicity of this world: "Cette personne me parut extrêmement jeune, et je crus, à la surprise des spectateurs, qu'elle ne paraissait en public que de ce jour-là" (48). Meilcour, as yet unintroduced to her, seeks to know through a play of the eyes: "Je conduisais, j'interprétais ses regards. Je cherchais à lire dans ses moindres mouvements"(49). Mme

---

[3] These remarks on *le regard* are indebted to Jean Starobinski's essay, "Racine et la poétique du regard," *L'Oeil vivant* (Paris, 1961), pp. 69-90; and of course to Sartre's chapter on the theme in *L'Etre et le Néant*.

de Senanges chooses the Tuileries Garden for her attempt to establish for the public that Meilcour is her property: "le jardin était rempli de monde. Mme de Senanges qui ne m'y menait que pour me montrer en fut charmée, et résolut de se comporter si bien, qu'on ne pût pas douter que je ne lui appartinsse" (217); in this situation, a meeting with Mme de Lursay and Hortense becomes a tortured hazarding and withdrawal of glances. The glance is used to gain knowledge and control of another; the other can attempt to refuse the act of possession: "Je la regardai fixement, mais mon attention la gênant sans doute, elle baissa les yeux en rougissant et me quitta"(205). Crébillon exploits the three related meanings of the verb *fixer*: to attach, to capture in arrest, and to gaze at fixedly. Hence Mme de Lursay delivers her final appeal to Meilcour "en me fixant toujours"(316). Seeing, knowing, and controlling form the nucleus of a system of values shared by the novelist and his characters.

"Connaître les êtres pour agir sur eux": the phrase was found by Stendhal in one of the Idéologues,[4] but already it has a large and explicit application in this novel; it even has its theoretician in the Comte de Versac. Versac, as the narrator presents him in a formal portrait,

... joignait à la plus haute naissance, l'esprit le plus agréable, et la figure la plus séduisante. Adoré de toutes les femmes qu'il trompait et déchirait sans cesse, vain, impérieux, étourdi: le plus audacieux Petit-Maître qu'on eût jamais vu et plus cher peut-être à leurs yeux par ces mêmes défauts, quelque contraires qu'ils leur soient. Quoi qu'il en puisse être, elles l'avaient mis à la mode dès l'instant qu'il était entré dans le monde, et il était depuis dix ans en possession de vaincre les plus insensibles, de fixer les plus coquettes et de déplacer

---

[4] Cited by Jean-Luc Seylaz, *Les Liaisons dangereuses et la création romanesque chez Laclos* (Geneva: Droz, 1958), p. 129.

les Amants les plus accrédités, ou s'il lui était arrivé de ne pas réussir, il avait toujours su tourner les choses si bien à son avantage, que la Dame n'en passait pas moins pour lui avoir appartenu. Il s'était fait un jargon extraordinaire qui, tout apprêté qu'il était, avait cependant l'air naturel. . . . Il avait composé les grâces de sa personne comme celles de son esprit, et savait se donner de ces agréments singuliers qu'on ne peut ni attraper ni définir. (119-120)

The categorical vocabulary of this portrait points not only to the narrator's penetration, but as well to its subject's thorough knowledge and definition of others: to be able to "vaincre les plus insensibles" and "fixer les plus coquettes," one must have performed a lucid census of social types. It is a portrait of a voluntary self-creation, a man who has composed a social being which has had immense success, who has systematically used women in a public manner in order to dominate society.

To dominate others, one must be fashionable, the center of the public's attention, the object of its collective glance; and since fashion is controlled by women, it is through them that a man reaches prominence. Hence Meilcour needs Mme de Senanges, who (unlike Mme de Lursay) will publicize a liaison and "put him in the world." Versac's exposition of this truth to Meilcour provides some of the great pages of the novel, for when Meilcour has made himself thoroughly ridiculous by his failure to profit from either the marked tenderness of Mme de Lursay or the outright provocation of Mme de Senanges, when he is hopelessly discountenanced by the social situations with which he must deal, Versac undertakes his paternal instruction, and reveals the "science du monde." Versac systematically takes up all the subjects essential to a knowledge of the world: his science may seem, he admits, a web of minutiae, but a mastery of women is dependent on knowledge of all the usages, tastes, and errors of one's century.

One must conform to the tone demanded by society—"Il vaut mieux . . . prendre les erreurs de son siècle, ou du moins s'y plier, que d'y montrer des vertus qui y paraîtraient étrangères, ou ne seraient pas du bon ton"(277)—and one's personal style should thus be an artful exaggeration of those *ridicules* which are in fashion. If to know is to control and deprive others of their freedom, conversely to avoid being known is to preserve freedom, virtuality, and pleasure; hence Meilcour should seek to be a totally artificial creation whose disguise protects the self and aids in the unmasking of others. "Vous devez apprendre à déguiser si parfaitement votre caractère, que ce soit en vain qu'on s'étudie à le démêler. Il faut encore que vous joigniez à l'art de tromper les autres, celui de les pénétrer; que vous cherchiez toujours sous ce qu'ils veulent vous paraître, ce qu'ils sont en effet"(266). It follows that the study of man is not the disinterested pursuit of the moralist: "Si nous étudions les hommes, que ce soit moins pour prétendre à les instruire, que pour parvenir à les bien connaître. . . . Paraissons quelquefois leurs imitateurs, pour être plus sûrement leurs juges"(267). The final judge is the *homme à bonnes fortunes*, who holds within his grasp the reputations both of women and of his rivals in conquest.

Versac's system, like any seducer's, is essentially misogynistic, and one senses that what may originally have been a set of maneuvers to the sole end of pleasure is now at the service of the will to power. The significance of his libertinage is indeed suggested by the word's derivation from *libertas*: the libertine, who pursues, seduces, then brings a rupture to recommence the process of pursuit and seduction, remains unfixed and free, while his "victims" are deprived of freedom by his control of their psychological movements and their reputations. For a master of society like Versac, libertinage is a necessary expression of the voluntarization of self, the creation of self as a completely controlled and controlling—limiting, fixing—entity and force, for in the erotic situation as it is conceived by this society there must always be one master and one slave. In fact, from Versac's exposition to Meilcour, and also from Crébillon's two "moral dialogues," *Le Hasard du coin de feu* and *La Nuit et le moment*, it is apparent that society sees the erotic situation as the limit term in human social relationships, a final confrontation of two beings, an ultimate metaphor for what people do to one another. The erotic means a final stylization of self, and codification of human psychology—in the two dialogues it has become almost purely a mechanism; hence it is the domain in which the world master's system best operates. Versac's life has been dedicated to erotic power as social power, and Meilcour's rite of initiation into society must be a sexual act.

Versac is lucidly aware of the personal effect of his elaborate stratagems. To this young admirer who is to become his imitator, he asks, "Pensez-vous que je me sois condamné sans réflexion au tourment de me déguiser sans cesse?"(271). This is the necessary counterpart of the lucid and penetrating glance turned toward others, the price one pays to gain the knowledge which enables one to use the vocabulary of the narrator's portrait of Mme de Lursay. Versac's exhortations become a description of the *via crucis* of the libertine, the constant tension required to maintain a conception of self as world master:

> Combien de pénétration ne faut-il pas avoir, pour saisir le caractère d'une femme que vous voulez attaquer, ou (ce qui est infiniment plus flatteur, et ne laisse pas d'arriver quelquefois) que vous voulez réduire à vous parler la première! De quelle justesse ne faut-il pas être doué, pour ne pas se tromper à la sorte de ridicule que vous devez exposer à ses yeux, pour la rendre plus promptement sensible! De quelle finesse n'avez-vous pas besoin pour conduire tout à la fois

plusieurs intrigues que pour votre honneur vous ne devez pas cacher au public, et qu'il faut cependant que vous dérobiez à chacune des femmes avec qui vous êtes lié! (272-273)

"Pénétration," "justesse," "finesse"; concomitant publicity and dissimulation of the self; and, of course, ever-renewed conquests—these are the elements necessary to maintain oneself in the game, to occupy the attention of society and to avoid disastrous failure.

"Playing the game" means essentially manipulating language and gestures, the signs in a code of social intercourse which has been elaborated to serve the system expounded by Versac. The language of this society is apparently frivolous, devoid of content. As Versac explains, one must be able to talk forever without saying anything. Yet it is also a rigorously functional language in that while refusing to mean it constantly acts—obliquely assessing motives, implying judgments, manipulating conventions. As Michel Foucault has expressed it, "Ce qui charge ce langage, ce n'est pas ce qu'il veut *dire*, mais *faire*."[5] Conversation quickly turns to cruel and witty *médisance,* as during the stroll in the Tuileries, where Meilcour is the captive of Mme de Senanges and Mme de Mongennes, the first of whom is attempting to detach him from Mme de Lursay; the group is joined by Versac, and he is asked to give his opinion of Mme de Lursay:

—Vous connaissez Madame de Lursay, lui demanda-t-elle?
—Excessivement, Madame, répondit-il. C'est assurément une personne respectable, et dont tout le monde connaît les agréments et la vertu.
—Madame [de Mongennes] soutient, reprit-elle, qu'on peut encore aimer Madame de Lursay avec décence.

[5] Michel Foucault, "Un si cruel savoir," *Critique*, No. 182 (July 1962), p. 600.

—J'y trouverais pour moi, dit-il, plus de générosité et de grandeur d'âme.

—C'est ce que je dis, répartit-elle, et qu'on ne peut s'attacher à quelqu'un de l'âge de Madame de Lursay, sans se faire un tort considérable.

—Cela est exactement vrai, répartit-il, mais du premier vrai. Il y a mille belles actions comme celles-là qu'on ne saurait faire sans se commettre, et qui ne prennent jamais en bien dans le monde. (225-226)

. . . Je ne connais personne qu'un fait pareil, s'il était avéré, ne perdît à jamais dans le monde. M. de Meilcour a sans doute pour Madame de Lursay de l'estime, du respect, de la vénération même si vous voulez; mais il serait trop dangereux pour lui qu'on le soupçonnât seulement du reste. (229)

The play here, as in the portrait of Mme de Lursay, is on distinction among terms, signs in the code. Each word used is of an acceptable politeness in itself, but the insistent definition and redefinition is pointed: Versac counters "décence" with "plus de générosité et de grandeur d'âme"; esteem, respect even veneration for Mme de Lursay are possible, but love would be "un tort considérable," which then is defined as total loss of reputation in *le monde*.

The manner and matter of this conversation confirm Versac's axioms on the need for disguise, for a successful, impenetrable, social mask: one must preserve the image of what one pretends to be. This indicates the difficulties encountered by Mme de Lursay in playing her role. She must lead Meilcour to a declaration, yet protect herself and keep an avenue open for retreat if he fails to respond. With a partner who knows the rules of the game, this concomitant opening and protection of self follows a prearranged pattern acceptable to both: "Avec un homme expérimenté, un mot dont le sens même peut se détourner, un regard, un geste, moins encore le met au fait s'il veut être aimé; et supposé qu'il se soit arrangé différemment de ce qu'on souhaiterait, on n'a hasardé que des choses si équivoques, et de si peu de conséquence, qu'elles se désavouent sur le champ"(23). In this society, that is, psychological signs —a sigh, a languid look, a gesture—are as rigidly conventional and functional as its language. The exterior manifestations of psychological behavior can indeed function as a code and a language because their signification is fixed and accepted by all participants in the social game (most rigidly and un-equivocally of all in the erotic situation, which, we saw, is this society's "ideal" social relationship). Hence the passage from gesture to language is immediate: one can *name* the state of being revealed—whether unintentionally or with conscious artifice—by the psychological sign.

But Meilcour is not yet a real participant; he has not yet learned the code, and Mme de Lursay is forced to overreach the limits of the code to make up for his deficiencies in worldly knowledge, yet must also protect her public self, and maintain in his eyes the image of a respectable woman who has been touched with passion for the first time in her life. At the start, Meilcour is excessively timid and refuses to credit the meaning of a tender look or a sigh, and he is thrown into disarray by any show of severity designed to deceive the public; later, after Versac has informed him that Mme de Lursay's life has not been altogether chaste, he attempts to attack direct-ly, abolishing all the accepted formulae and degrees of seduc-tion, the "gradations" upon which Mme de Lursay is obliged to insist. She must preserve both the rules of seduction and the rules of public comportment; since Meilcour understands neither, he is unable to respond in a socially acceptable manner to the verbal and situational stimuli applied to him. His en-counter with system and code creates a comic drama of man-ners. When Mme de Lursay arranges a rendezvous late at night, and the two are finally alone, a long silence is broken by Meilcour's tremulous query:

> —Vous faites donc des noeuds? Madame, lui demandai-je d'une voix tremblante.
> A cette intéressante et spirituelle question, Madame de Lursay me regarda avec étonnement. Quelque idée qu'elle se fût faite de ma timidité, et du peu d'usage que j'avais du monde, il lui parut inconcevable que je ne trouvasse que cela à lui dire. Elle ne voulut pas cependant achever de me décourager. . . . (106)

The verbal stratagems to which she has recourse to make him bolder are without effect:

> —Mais Meilcour, interrompit-elle, savez-vous bien que ma démarche de ce soir est très hasardée et qu'il faut que je pense aussi bien de vous que je le fais, pour m'y être déterminée?
> —Hasardée? repris-je.
> —Oui, dit-elle, et je le répète, très hasardée. (110-111)

The word is chosen as a token in the code, a disguised yet clear indication of a line of action, but Meilcour is unable to relate it to any system of comportment, and inanely echoes it as simply a word. When finally he cannot fail to understand that he should throw himself at her feet and kiss her hand, her defense is purely formal:

> —Eh bien, me dit-elle enfin, ne voulez-vous donc pas vous lever? Quelles sont donc ces folies? Levez-vous, je le veux.
> —Ah, Madame! m'écriai-je, aurais-je le malheur de vous avoir déplu?
> —Eh! vous fais-je des reproches, répondit-elle languissamment? (112)

But he is evidently insensitive to the sign implied by a "languid" tone, and he continues to lose in self-justifications the time that he should spend in seduction; Mme de Lursay, convinced that there is nothing more to be gained for the evening, finally sends him home.

Whereas the comedy of this scene is generated by Mme de Lursay's attempt to seduce without violating system and code, in other scenes her maneuvers to disarm Versac's interference in her relationship with Meilcour form the dramatic center. One of the most comic, and cruelest, episodes in the novel is a dinner for which Versac has unexpectedly appeared; from his opening remarks, Mme de Lursay "ne pouvait pas douter qu'il n'eût pénétré son amour pour moi, et qu'il ne fût tout occupé du soin d'en instruire le public et de la perdre peut-être dans mon esprit"(153). Versac has brought with him a side-kick, the Marquis de Pranzi, an exaggerated imitation of himself who, the two of them let it be understood, was once Mme de Lursay's lover:

> Eh, paix! interrompit Pranzi, Madame connaît, ajouta-t-il d'un air railleur, mon respect, et, si je l'ose dire, mon tendre attachement pour elle. Je me souviens de ses bontés, et je n'aurais point résisté à Versac, si j'avais pu croire qu'elle me les eût conservées. (154)

Imitating Versac, Pranzi here manipulates terms which are unexceptionally polite and even vapid in their meaning, but unequivocally compromising in their contemporary social acceptation; "respect" is what a suitor promises a woman before he has been honored with her "tendresse"; "tendre attachement," coming from someone she does not meet on familiar social terms, is too intimate; finally, "bontés," in the plural form, from a woman to a man, suggests clearly as possible without overt vulgarity that Mme de Lursay once belonged to Pranzi. Faced with these two artful enemies, Mme de Lursay loses control of her social presence, and fails to impose upon Meilcour, the member of her audience who most

27

matters to her: "Je l'en vis rougir sans y répondre, et je conclus sur-le-champ de son silence, et de son air humilié que Pranzi était infailliblement un de mes prédécesseurs" (153).

The scene, whose actors are Meilcour, Mme de Lursay, Versac, Pranzi, the virtuous Mme de Théville and her daughter Hortense, and the ogling Mme de Senanges, quickly becomes a complex and witty comedy of manners, an interplay of words and gestures, where each person is trying to show up another and to protect himself, all within the formal frame of a dinner party which is the stage for their enactments of social roles. It is a scene of maneuvers, from seating at the table to the indirection of *médisance*, most of which, though ostensibly directed at one Mme de ***, falls on Mme de Lursay. The control of the conversation displayed by Versac is the product of his intelligent estimation of relations between Meilcour and Mme de Lursay, his intimate knowledge both of her and of Mme de Senanges, and his unscrupulousness in turning what he knows into witty persiflage. One has the impression that social forms are always on the verge of explosion. When Mme de Senanges admonishes Versac that he has less reason than any other man to criticize women, because their greatest *ridicule* is the way they treat him, his reply sharpens our sense of the savage contest implicit in the scene: "C'est peut-être à cause de cela, reprit-il en riant, que j'en ai si mauvaise opinion"(168). But social forms never do collapse, since they are the necessary weapons of this battle; with the exhaustion of *médisance*, the company falls into card games, then finally goes home, not without first putting Meilcour in such a position that he must, in all politeness, call on Mme de Senanges the following day.

The scene creates for the reader the illusion that he is himself penetrating within a society; he is made to feel the pleasure of apprehending ironies and self-betrayals in the characters' language, of seeing through social self-representations, of evaluating the effect of words and the success of roles. The world the narrator has told him about, which he presumably has himself experienced, and which Versac will explicate, has been dramatically realized. From the narrator's liminary analytical descriptions of society and its characters, the novel develops into a series of scenic representations of the drama of manners, scenes which demonstrate Meilcour's perceptual problems and force us to use the narrator's language of penetration and definition to come to terms with the world.

From attention to such a scene, we can in fact grasp the source and the significance of Crébillon's drama of manners. We move from the stasis, definition, and metaphorical summary of the portrait, its language of total assessment and fixation, to represented drama, because the characters themselves use this language as tool and weapon in their social encounters. Their language, which we have qualified as functional rather than signifying, is directed to a demonstration of social control, and social control both employs and is expressed by this language, which demonstrates that reality has been transmuted into a psychological and social system of which one is perfectly the master—hence master of external reality, in a position, like Versac or the narrator, to make the world move according to one's manipulations of its laws. The seemingly undramatic uses of language we found in the portrait in fact imply a social drama, and lead to it in the hands of a masterful novelist. The drama realized in the scenes set in the Tuileries and Mme de Lursay's drawing room finally refer us back to the essential drama of the act of portraiture itself, the kind of things one tries to do to others with the language and conventions of such a device.

The ultimate drama, the final comic scene of the novel, arrives with perfect inevitability when Meilcour, enlightened, he believes, by the analyses and aphorisms of Versac, makes a last appearance in Mme de Lursay's drawing room with the intent

of punishing her for "the falsity of having tried to appear respectable." Armed with his new-found worldly wisdom, with
the "new" portrait he has composed of Mme de Lursay, and
convinced that she has at least one lover hiding in her closet,
he proceeds to what is to be her discomfiture in a language he
believes to be penetrating and wittily ironic:

> — . . . Je sais que je remplis des moments que vous aviez
> destinés à des plaisirs plus doux que celui de m'entendre et
> que, sans compter l'impatience que je vous cause, vous avez
> à partager celle de quelqu'un qui, peut-être, en gémissant de
> l'obstacle que j'apporte à ses plaisirs ne vous croit pas absolu-
> ment innocente du chagrin que je lui fais.
> —Voilà sans contredit, s'écria-t-elle, une belle phrase! Elle
> est d'une élégance, d'une obscurité et d'une longueur ad-
> mirables! Il faut, pour se rendre si inintelligible, furieuse-
> ment travailler d'esprit. (304)

Mme de Lursay's reply on the form, rather than the matter,
of Meilcour's torturous accusation, is a stroke of social genius.
It denies his control of the social forms he is trying to use as a
weapon, and prepares us for what we, as urbane readers,
should have been awaiting—the reversal of roles, and the
showing-up of Meilcour. She asks, "N'était-ce pas à vous à
connaître et saisir mes mouvements?"(309), and he is forced
to admit that his lack of penetration, his insufficient knowledge of the world caused him to fail to perceive what was implied by Mme de Lursay's manipulations of conventions. It
was for him to discover her sentiments, and his failure to exploit the male role permits her to turn his own phrase against
him: "c'est à vous, et non à moi, *qu'il a plu de faire une belle
résistance*"(314). The description she is able to give of the
stages of her love—innocent interest in his sentimental per-
plexities, followed by an unwilling emotional involvement—
is our indication of how well she has preserved an image of

innocence while expressing a desire to be seduced. In admitting to one (but only one) previous lover—a sign of sensibility, not debauchery—in pretending to congratulate herself on having escaped Meilcour, Mme de Lursay alters Meilcour's whole perspective on the past two months' action, and she finally obtains the sigh of regret for which she has been waiting. From here to the final moment it is only a step; she is willing to rewrite the past, and Meilcour becomes "as guilty as I could be."

It is significant that Meilcour's final emphasis falls on how a superior knowledge of the workings of human personality enabled Mme de Lursay to escape the fixed, limited category to which, after enlightenment by Versac, he had attempted to assign her, and to reassert her control over him:

> Il était . . . extrêmement simple que Madame de Lursay, qui joignait à beaucoup de beauté, une extrême connaissance du coeur, m'eût conduit imperceptiblement où j'en étais venu avec elle. Ce que j'en puis croire aujourd'hui, c'est que si j'avais eu plus d'expérience, elle ne m'en aurait que plus promptement séduit, ce qu'on appelle l'usage du monde ne nous rendant plus éclairés que parce qu'il nous a plus corrompus. (329)

A last knowing irony concedes that superior worldliness leads to the same dénouement, if not by the same routes; knowledge of society leads to the systematic comportment of Versac. Judging his adventure with Mme de Lursay, Meilcour has estimated that there was "moins de fausseté dans son procédé, que de sottise dans le mien"(125). This worldliness of tone measures the journey accomplished by the protagonist-become-narrator, and it indicates the only possible attitude on our part. Our feelings about Meilcour at the end of his itinerary include amusement, perhaps a nostalgic regret at his corruption, but most strongly an ironic and realistic assent to the "way things are."

The narrative structure of the novel closely controls our reactions as readers. Not only does the narrative tone preclude any provincialism, sentimentality, or naive moralism on our part, the structural distance between Meilcour-as-narrator and Meilcour-as-protagonist defines the distance at which we must hold characters and action, determines that we shall view them with the distanced, defining, and evaluative language of the portrait. Furthermore, the presentation of a character like Mme de Lursay in a formal portrait, in concepts and language which are clearly beyond the protagonist's grasp, not only reminds us that the protagonist will gain the narrator's worldly knowledge, but indicates the need for such knowledge, the importance of Meilcour's history. While such a use of the portrait at first seems undramatic to the modern reader, since it violates movement toward discovery by at once presenting all knowledge about a person, thoroughly processed and set in hard outline, it does, we have seen, possess its own drama, since it evokes the necessity of the knowledge and language it exploits and represents a certain kind of act in relation to other members of society. In the game of knowing and controlling, mastery of a certain language is mastery of the world. To use portrait and aphorism in the manner of Versac is to prove one's ability to transmute reality into an intellectual system through which one controls the outside world. And since the narrator's adoption of a similar language and tone is implicitly the end result of an experience of which these "memoirs" give us only the first chapter, there is in the novel what we might call an inherent structural drama: the drama implied by the use of a form, a language, and a tone, necessarily attached to them and the ethos they represent.[6]

[6] Vivienne Mylne, in her chapter on Crébillon in *The Eighteenth-Century French Novel: Techniques of Illusion* (Manchester, 1965), argues that the total retrospective clarity of the narrator in regard to Mme de Lursay violates realism: without omniscience Meilcour could

In *Les Égarements*, this drama is not simply inherent; it is also realized. From a static, formal presentation of character, from metaphorical stasis, the novel unfolds into scenic representations of the experience on which the language of definition and fixation depends, and where it has an active role, the public acts of social beings on a lighted stage governed by a fixed set of rules. The kind of behavior valorized on this stage—the system whereby one attempts to penetrate, unmask, fix, and control others, where disguise of self and artifice in the staging of one's social role are necessary to gain dominion over others, and where the worst fault is appearing ridiculous and the worst *ridicule* being a dupe—elicits from the individual a tense, voluntary acting that is the matter of effective social drama, where the abstract, categorical language of the portrait acts as a weapon in interpersonal relations, where the portrait itself is perhaps the ultimate weapon to be used against others. Like Meilcour, we must come to terms with a world in which people are maskers, words are weapons, and social encounters are combats where the contestants manipulate social conventions to reduce the other to less enviable roles, to fix and dispose of the potential rival, while preserving their own freedom of movement. For us as for Meilcour, the drama is first epistemological and then evaluative: we must find out in order to size up, we must move toward the total clarity, definition, and arrest of the portrait.

The ethos of the society evoked in the novel, then, in conjunction with the narrator's attitude toward the ethos (his acceptance of its language and its system) entail the novelist's effort to represent the drama of manners, and the book turns on remarkable scenes of social comedy. Crébillon's arrival at

---

not know so much about the inner life of another. This argument seems to me to miss the point: that Meilcour has gained a position of worldly knowledge from which he is able totally to *reconstruct* Mme de Lursay's past psychology. This is indeed what his education has been about.

this kind of novel is not the result of any attempt to be a "realist," in the sense of one who attempts to give a comprehensive account of the manners of his time, but rather of his concern with the experience of worldliness, his posing of the question, "What is life in society about?" This distinction will perhaps become clearer if we look at Crébillon's preface to *Les Égarements*, where he carefully detaches his novel from the tradition of the adventure novel, which was popular but had never been held in critical esteem, and argues instead its affinity with comedy, a genre of greater moral seriousness:

> Le Roman, si méprisé des personnes sensées, et souvent avec justice, serait peut-être celui de tous les genres qu'on pourrait rendre le plus utile, s'il était bien manié, si, au lieu de le remplir de situations ténébreuses et forcées, de Héros dont les caractères et les aventures sont toujours hors du vraisemblable, on le rendait, comme la Comédie, le tableau de la vie humaine, et qu'on y censurât les vices et les ridicules. (3-4)

In seeking to attach his novel to a form in which a serious assessment of social behavior had long been possible, Crébillon seems to be calling for the kind of novel of manners that we associate with the names of Stendhal, Jane Austen, or Henry James. When Crébillon refers to his narrative as the "histoire de la vie privée"(7), he seems to situate it within the central tradition of the modern novel; when he continues "des travers et des retours d'un homme de condition," however, he poses the necessity of the public and "sociable" mode of his novel in a manner that needs further attention.

His story is of a private life—not the life of kings or extraordinary heroes—and turns on such ordinary questions as love and youthful inexperience. But the life is that of a gentleman, a member of good society, and this implies that these questions will necessarily be treated within a certain context, as the experience of a system. Hence in all Crébillon's major novels—the one-voiced epistolary novels, *Lettres de la Marquise de M*** au Comte de R**** and *Lettres de la Duchesse de*** au Duc de****, as well as *Les Égarements*—there is a strong felt presence of society. This "presence" must be distinguished from a representation or description of society, which would entail the situation of his characters and his drama through the detailing of setting, the description of accessories and exterior qualities, all the elements of the effort we generally call "realism." Crébillon's realism is of a different variety; it involves, not the exploration of a created society— Yonville L'Abbaye, the Pension Vauquer—but of Society itself, a system of relationships and values whose image is present to narrator, "homme de condition," and reader alike.

The point of tangency of this image with the individual is his consciousness of society, or imagination of society: the way he sees the system as determinative of his own and others' behavior. Crébillon's efforts at rendering are directed to this imagination of society. He need not reproduce the world in his novel, he rather situates his novel in the world—the one World that counts—and uses its manners as the significant terms of his representations, though not the object of his representation, since he is writing always as an "insider," assuming that his reader knows the meaning of the conventional gestures that are the stuff of his drama. The reality that concerns him, then, is the detail of social gesture, primarily verbal gesture; these are the tokens with which Meilcour must work to solve his epistemological problems, and the foundations of our eventual assessments. Hence the texture of *Les Égarements* is fabricated from a rich interplay of gesture and tone, of the various enactments of people's self-created social representations. It is perhaps the first wholly social novel—concerned totally and exclusively with life in society, with a kind of experience we can most pertinently call the experience of worldliness.

35

Crébillon's last novel, the *Lettres de la Duchesse de*** au Duc de****, was published in 1767.[7] It is a curious work, 470 pages of letters from a Duchesse to a Duc who would have her love him, but never even obtains permission to appear on the scene. Perilously close to the Flaubertian ideal of a "book about nothing,"[8] the novel is the purest of lessons in listening to tones of voice, of penetrating to the truth about a character from the slenderest, most fragmentary evidence. The enterprise has a ring of defiance about it, which is further affirmed by the preface, where Crébillon states flatly that his novel will not appeal to those who enjoy the imitators of Richardson, who seek "facts" in a novel, rather than the "connaissance du coeur" and "usage du monde"—together they form the experience of worldliness—which he offers.

We suddenly realize that by 1767 Crébillon feels his kind of novel somewhat of an anachronism. Why this is so we will discuss in a later chapter. The point that should be made now is that at the time of *Les Égarements*, the opposite was true: there is a whole body of literature which, by its techniques and concerns, could be labelled "the novel of worldliness." Works by Mme de Tencin, Antoine Hamilton, Mme Élie de Beaumont, Mme Riccoboni, the Marquis d'Argens, and some of Prévost, all belong to a degree to the same enterprise. Without attempting detailed exploration of the mass of this fiction,[9] it might be useful to glance at the work of one man, a writer of considerable contemporary fame and some novelistic skill (though indeed not genius) who shows all the elements of the worldly attitude with particular clarity and simplicity. This is Charles Pinot Duclos, historian, memorialist, moralist, gram-

[7] This novel is not included in the Divan edition. See instead, *Oeuvres complètes* (London, 1777).

[8] This similarity was also remarked by Clifton Cherpack in his study, *An Essay on Crébillon fils* (Durham, North Carolina, 1962), p. 123.

[9] For a general typology of this fiction, see Chapter Two, pp. 87-88.

marian, academician, and novelist. One of the first of the eighteenth-century professional men of letters who were to mix freely with aristocratic society in a manner impossible a generation earlier, he was an habitué of the literary cafés and of Mme de Tencin's salon. His two novels, elegant and witty accounts of two careers in society, are evidently extensions of his social role.[10] The first, *Les Confessions du Comte de****, presents itself as a reply to a friend who has written to ask why the Comte has withdrawn from society into the solitude of the provinces. His answer is a paradigm of worldweariness: "J'ai usé le monde."[11] His book will be, he continues, a "faithful confession" of the errors of his youth, which will serve as a lesson to his young correspondent.

The Comte goes on to contrast his formal education which, since he was an aristocrat, was totally neglected, to his initiation into the world, his education through experience. "Experience" is in fact the central theme of the novel: the Comte is formed by a series of women, each of whom furthers his education in worldly values and codes of behavior. Experience of the world is commanded and directed by women, and the Comte's story is essentially a series of portraits. The narrative is linear, episodic, and static; compared to *Les Égarements*, there is far less of an effort to represent the drama latent in the social encounters described. Yet each of the narrator's mistresses is really a social type, a "character" in the sense of La Bruyère: each is important as an aspect of the Comte's developing consciousness of society, and by the time he has moved through all his definitions and evaluations, he has created a

[10] On Duclos' life and works, see the fine study by Paul Meister, *Charles Duclos* (Geneva, 1956).

[11] *Les Confessions du Comte de****, in *Romanciers du XVIIIe siècle*, ed. Étiemble (Paris: Bibliothèque de la Pléiade, 1965), II, 199. Étiemble prints the text of the original edition of 1741, with variants from the edition of 1767, which most editors of Duclos have used.

complex picture of social forces and attitudes that corresponds in almost every detail to that drawn by Versac.

In a summary but effective paragraph the narrator describes
the maneuvers of a new mistress, Mme de Rumigny, and the
woman with whom he has just broken, the Marquise de
Valcourt:

> Madame de Rumigny ne me fit pas languir davantage; le
> lendemain elle voulut que j'allasse avec elle à l'opéra en
> grande loge; j'y consentis, son triomphe était le mien. La
> marquise s'y trouva le même jour; elle était fort parée, et
> n'y venait que pour démentir les discours du public: une
> telle démarche est un coup de partie, le jour qu'on a été quit-
> tée; mais je remarquai son chagrin caché. (205-206)

As in *Les Égarements*, the Opéra is a privileged public space
in a world seen as a theater, an illuminated stage demanding
a performance the falsity of which is apparent to the penetrating and informed spectator who sees through the representation to the dissimulated emotion. The role of world
master as seducer in this theater is put into sharp relief in
an analysis of his situation by the Comte, who has just returned to Parisian society after a time spent in England, and
must turn his attention to the important question of which
woman he is to use to regain public attention:

> Cependant une conquête nouvelle m'était nécessaire; et je
> me trouvais dans un assez grand embarras. Après un an
> d'absence, c'était une espèce de début; on était attentif au
> choix que j'allais faire: de ce choix seul pouvait dépendre
> tous mes succès à venir. Madame de Limeuil me parut
> d'abord la seule femme digne de mes soins; mais la réflexion
> sut réprimer ce premier transport. Elle était jeune, elle pas-
> sait pour sage, et il fallait qu'elle le fût, car on n'avait point
> encore parlé d'elle. L'attaquer et ne pas réussir, c'était me

38

perdre; un homme à la mode ne doit jamais entreprendre que des conquêtes sûres. (247)

To hold society in this flattering attention, to fix it in expectant arrest, one must create and maintain the illusion of irresistibility. Once one is cast in this role, the rest of society will play theirs in relation to it: system will continue to function smoothly if one respects its code.

What failure can mean in this world is given a remarkable representation in the episode involving the Comte's friend Senecé and Mme de Dornal—an episode which inevitably reminds one of Proust's account of Swann's love for Odette. For the libertine Senecé allows himself to be fixed by a woman without birth, beauty, or wit, a woman unworthy to hold the public stage; and being fixed, he loses his faculties of penetration, he reaches a perceptual impasse in which he cannot perceive the true visage of Mme de Dornal, and fails to see that he is himself on the verge of passing from being *ridicule* to becoming *méprisable*(258). When the Comte details for him an accurate portrait of Mme de Dornal, Senecé is forced to give it credence—yet still cannot bring the liberating rupture. The Comte's attempts to free his friend are then pushed to the point of seducing Mme de Dornal before Senecé's eyes—in vain, since she reëstablishes her control, detaches Senecé from the Comte, and eventually becomes Senecé's wife. This "shameful slavery" brings Senecé's destruction: he is lost from *le monde*. And the Comte concludes with the aphorism, "la femme la plus méprisable est celle dont l'empire est le plus sûr"(266).

The Comte's successive portraits represent at each stage, at each new conquest and rupture, a stocktaking of what one has come to know about a person, an effort to arrest a total evaluation in a formally complete verbal structure, a transformation of human social presence into language. As with

Crébillon, so here libertinage is not merely, not even essential-ly, the search for pleasure. As Duclos speculates in a critical essay,

> Je ne sais pourquoi les hommes taxent les femmes de faus-seté, et ont fait la Vérité femelle. Problème à résoudre. On dit aussi qu'elle est nue, et cela se pourrait bien. C'est sans doute par un amour secret pour la Vérité que nous courons après les femmes avec tant d'ardeur; nous cherchons à les dépouiller de tout ce que nous croyons qui cache la Vérité; et, quand nous avons satisfait notre curiosité sur une, nous nous détrompons, nous courons tous vers une autre, pour être plus heureux. L'amour, le plaisir et l'inconstance ne sont qu'une suite du désir de connaître la Vérité.[12]

Duclos here seizes the close interdependence of the will to knowledge and the will to power, and the relation of both to the unremitting pursuit of erotic conquest and erotic knowl-edge. The statement captures perfectly the sense of the liber-tine's quest to uncover, find out, define—then to fix, dismiss, and move on. If it indicates the male need to know in order to conquer, and to conquer in order to know, it also estab-lishes the necessity of the woman's effort to attach and fix, to break the chain of seduction and infidelity in order to over-throw a system of violation and subjugation.

*Les Confessions du Comte de*** ends with the Comte's reasonable marriage to a virtuous woman, and their retreat to a country estate. We are made to sense the emotional ex-haustion of someone who has used up and worn out the world, and for whom it only remains to impart his worldly wisdom to others. This worldly didacticism, the sense of a lesson ex-tracted from and applied to social conduct, is stronger still in Duclos' other novel-as-memoir, the *Mémoires sur les moeurs*

[12] *Oeuvres complètes de Duclos* (Paris, 1820-21), IX, 424. Subsequent references to Duclos are to this edition.

de ce siècle. It is in fact the stance of the moralist which is central to Duclos' fiction: moralist not in the modern acceptation of the term—that which gained currency later in the eighteenth century—but rather in the seventeenth-century sense of the *moraliste*, a social observer who scrutinizes human social experience for its profound significance. "J'ai vécu, je voudrois être utile à ceux qui ont à vivre. Voilà le motif qui m'engage à rassembler quelques réflexions sur les objets qui m'ont frappé dans le monde"(I, 5). Duclos casts himself in this role of paternal guide to the world in the first sentence of what is probably his best-known work, the *Considerations sur les moeurs de ce siècle*, where he distilled what he calls his "science du monde." He distinguishes between the study of man, for which self-analysis is sufficient, and the study of men, for which it is necessary to frequent society. From specific examples of social experience, he works to a general analysis of motivation and comportment. In a loosely-organized series of chapters, he considers the experiential meaning of such terms as virtue, honor, reputation, consideration, *le ridicule, la mode*. His categories and his judgments constantly remind us of Versac's exposition to Meilcour: "La méchanceté," he assures us, "n'est aujourd'hui qu'une mode"(I, 104). Fear of ridicule is the chief determinant of behavior: "Le ridicule est le fléau des gens du monde, et il est assez juste qu'ils aient pour tyran un être fantastique"(I, 111). He confirms Versac's observation that exaggeration of a well-chosen *ridicule* is the surest means of becoming fashionable (I, 117).

The tone is characterized by the directness, even abruptness, for which Duclos was celebrated; but it would be totally wrong to conclude that he rejects the world toward which he is directing his satire. On the contrary, he believes, that "sociable man is the citizen par excellence"(I, 99). Duclos' effort, like Versac's, is one of definition rather than prescription or moralizing. Nor is he descriptive: his considerations are not accumulations of details; each is rather a penetration, a laying-bare of an essential characteristic of motivation or comportment. Stylistically, this implies a constant effort toward precision and concision—toward choice of the proper sign and the presentation of the right conjunction of signs in rapid, definitive ellipsis. Many of Duclos' developments strive for a terminal aphorism: "Il n'appartient pas à tout le monde de vendre son nom" (I, 126); "L'orgueil est le premier des tyrans ou des consolateurs" (I, 129); "L'amour ne dépend pas de l'estime; mais, dans bien des occasions, l'estime dépend de l'amour" (I, 180). The same tendency to aphorism was found in *Les Égarements,* and in Duclos' novels; the reason is of course always the same: the aphorism marks a limit term in the reduction of external reality to language, the movement of human life to the complete stasis of total verbal metaphor. The linguistic code which we note with particular clarity in Duclos' final presentation of his "science of the world" is the necessary tool and weapon of the system of comportment expounded by Versac, the Comte de ***, and their creators.

In reading Duclos, we feel we are receiving a rather prosaic, occasionally pedestrian, but lucid and unambiguous exposition of what Crébillon's enterprise is all about: he can in fact help us to define "worldliness." The field of Crébillon's and Duclos' attention is *le monde,* an entity and a system defined by its internal publicity and closure to the outside. The object of their attention is the totality of man's being within this enclosure, his worldliness or *mondanité* which, as Roland Barthes points out, exists only in function of closure: exclusion of outside realities and exclusive valorization of the gestures which enact one's role within *le monde.*[13] A novel directed to an exploration of this worldliness will, from a formal and technical point of view, necessarily show the same exclusions. It will not

13 Barthes, pp. 226-27.

describe objects, detail settings, or particularize the world, but rather will focus on language and gesture within a code, and will value forms like aphorism and portrait which transmute experience into language and permit final estimation of the individual's sociability, his adaptation to the image projected by society. Yet these forms of arrest, these metaphorical, summary presentations of reality, imply a drama in their social use—the drama of worldliness. We have a language of clarity and fixation operating within an enclosure, directed to estimating man's presence in the enclosure, yet at the same time forcibly becoming the terms of a drama enacted there.

The novel of worldliness depends on a concept, worldliness, which is simultaneously real, moral, psychological, and literary: the way of life of a social group, a system of values, an individual consciousness and personal style, an object of literary attention which allows the writer to concern himself with the image of society rather than society itself. And this worldliness depends on an idea of exclusion and enclosure, the medium for social representations and the source of the language responding to them. We are led to ask how the enclosure, the concept of *mondanité*, the language and the literature of worldliness emerged to provide the system we have seen at work in the novels of Crébillon and Duclos. The line of investigation toward an answer is suggested by the repeated echoes in Crébillon and Duclos of writers like La Rochefoucauld and La Bruyère: it is to the seventeenth-century *moralistes* that we must turn, and beyond them, to a literature of sociability extending back to the Renaissance.

43

THE PROPER STUDY OF MANKIND

· I ·

THE literature of worldliness responds to man's social presence, to a certain man-in-situation within the organized system of manners and values called society, whose rules and goals govern his ideals and endeavors. Such a man-in-situation is of course important in some forms of classical literature (satire, comedy), and in the courtly literature of the Middle Ages. Yet a modern tradition of worldliness directly relevant to the novel would seem surely to be the product of Renaissance secularism, which permits man to consider the world without the cosmos, the world as the exclusive medium of his existence. The Renaissance attached a new value to man's non-metaphysical earthly presence, to a cultivation of his worldly being, and to the self, the individual personality in its interplay with other personalities within the human community. In a hierarchical society, the ideal center of such a community is the court, a closed and ordered hypercommunity. The behavior the court demands is an intensification and codification of individual social presence, a new valorization of the cultivated social personality, of the self as a voluntary, artistic creation judged on its style. Our first image of the worldly master is a courtier, and Castiglione's *Il Cortegiano* is in fact the necessary first term in any consideration of the literary tradition of worldliness—a tradition I will attempt to sketch in a rather sinuous argument, touching on some points of intellectual and literary history and analyzing the texts of major relevance to the eighteenth century novel of worldliness.

The conversations in Urbino's Ducal Palace recorded by Castiglione work toward a definition of the new man-in-society, the studied, artistic self-creation who must adapt himself to the demands of the social medium, which has become the essential fact of his existence, and whose individual comportment should be dictated by a consciousness of the manners which further social intercourse. While the chief avocation of Castiglione's courtier may still be the practice of arms, in his daily social existence he should nurture above all else "that certain grace which we call an 'air,' which shall make him at first sight pleasing and lovable to all who see him"[1]—a manner which artfully conceals art through the assumption of *sprezzatura* (nonchalance) and *disinvoltura* (ease).[2] What counts is total social presence and manner, one's "way of being" in society. In Castiglione and the Italian moralists who imitated and ramified his enterprise, we have a complete picture of man who has chosen to dedicate himself to giving meaning to his worldly existence.

Il Cortegiano was translated into French in 1537, and its concerns and precepts entered a milieu where they were of immediate relevance—the Valois court, dedicated to an Italian ideal of civilization, a refinement of culture and personal relations most fully elaborated in the circle of François Ier's sister, Marguerite de Navarre. This flowering of court civility was to a degree interrupted by the strife and barbarism of the Wars of Religion, and it is in fact in the early years of the seventeenth century that we come upon a spate of French imitations of Castiglione (some of them also influenced by the Spaniards,

[1] Baldesar Castiglione, *The Book of the Courtier*, trans. Charles S. Singleton (Garden City: Anchor Books, 1959), p. 29.
[2] *Ibid.*, pp. 43-44.

Guevara and Gracián, and by certain ideals of education found in Montaigne). Du Souhait wrote *Le Parfait Gentilhomme* (1600), Nervèze a *Guide des Courtisans* (1606), Nicolas Pasquier *Le Gentilhomme* (1611), Eustache de Refuge *Le Traité de la cour* (1616), Guez de Balzac *Aristippe ou de la cour* (1618), Nicolas Faret *L'Honnête Homme, ou l'art de plaire à la cour* (1630), a book which had seven editions in the course of the century.[3] Most often, these treatises are manuals of recipes for success in society; they all emphasize the need to perfect manners, to refine words and gestures, to modulate the voice, and give grace to the movements of the body. The perfect courtier creates his social style, his public representation of himself. Indeed, to some of these writers (and here the influence of Machiavelli, of Gracián, and of Torquato Acceto's *Della Dissimulazione onesta* has served to put into relief a theme latent in Castiglione) the courtier is by essence a dissimulating being, one whose social presence is a mask, an act played to a particular audience with certain ends in mind. As the Chevalier de Méré was to sum things up: "Je suis persuadé qu'en beaucoup d'occasions il n'est pas inutile de regarder ce qu'on fait comme une comédie, et d'imaginer qu'on joue un personnage de théâtre."[4] With its emphasis on

---

[3] There are two major studies of this literature: Pietro Toldo, "Le Courtisan dans la littérature française et ses rapports avez l'oeuvre de Castiglione," *Archiv für das Studium der neuren Sprachen*, 1900, No. 104, pp. 75-121, 313-30; No. 105, pp. 60-85; and Maurice Magendie, *La Politesse mondaine et les théories de l'honnêteté en France au XVIIe siècle, de 1600 à 1660* (2 vols.; Paris, 1925). See also Claude Papin, "Le sens de l'idéal de 'l'honnête homme' au XVIIe siècle," *La Pensée*, Nouvelle Série, No. 4 (1962), pp. 52-83. Giovanni Macchia has discussed the drama inherent in this literature in "La Scuola della dissimulazione," in *Il Paradiso della ragione* (Bari: Laterza, 1960), pp. 175-90. On the influence of Montaigne see Alan Boase, *The Fortunes of Montaigne* (London, 1935).

[4] Antoine Gombaud, Chevalier de Méré, *Oeuvres*, ed. Charles-H. Boudhors (3 vols.; Paris: Les Textes Français, Éditions Fernand Roche, 1930), III, 158.

manner and gesture, social masks and the game of society, this didactic court literature already suggests the drama exploited in the novel of worldliness.

The first literary exploitation of this drama, though, did not come from the court, but from an equally enclosed and self-conscious milieu, the salon—or *ruelle*, as it was originally called—and must be credited to the *précieuses*. No longer the brilliant creation of the first Valois, not yet the well-mannered and policed milieu of Louis XIV, the court at the start of the century was still infected by an uneducated, warlike, and rather gross nobility that had much to learn about civility. The *Chambre Bleue* of the Marquise de Rambouillet, a gathering self-consciously removed from the court, was the first laboratory of seventeenth-century sociability and the literature which responds to it. Mme de Rambouillet, descended from the Roman house of Savelli, indeed had an Italian ideal of social life. She preached refinement of manners, respect for women, delicacy of expression, and cultivation of sociability. As Erich Auerbach describes it,

> . . . the Hôtel de Rambouillet was the first home of the atmosphere which foreigners, down to our own century, have looked on as typical of French society, an atmosphere compounded of cultivation, equality, social warmth, and ease, adaptation of the individual's inner life to the socially appropriate, and the concealment of all unseemly depths.[5]

In this community, men of letters, almost always of bourgeois

[5] Erich Auerbach, "La Cour et la Ville," trans. Ralph Manheim, *Scenes From the Drama of European Literature* (New York, 1959), p. 164. On the *précieux* milieux, see also René Bray, *La Préciosité et les précieux, de Thibault de Champagne à Giraudoux* (Paris, 1948); Georges Mongrédien, *la Vie de société au XVIIe et XVIIIe siècles* (Paris, 1950); Mongrédien, *Madeleine de Scudéry* (Paris, 1946); and Roger Lathuillère, *La Préciosité, Étude historique et linguistique* Vol. 1 (Geneva: Droz, 1966).

origin, mingled with aristocrats; in this interchange, the former polished their manners, the latter their wits. Literature was a parlor game, a light, witty, charming, reiterated celebration of the community and the individual's adaptation to it. But more important to our subject than the sonnets, madrigals, metamorphoses, and letters of the Hôtel de Rambouillet is a later development, the novels of Madeleine de Scudéry. Her manners were formed in the *Chambre Bleue* from 1630 to 1645; then, after the Fronde, she became mistress of her own salon. In *Le Grand Cyrus* and *Clélie*, she dramatizes her heroic contemporaries of La Fronde (Cyrus is Condé, Mandane, the Duchesse de Longueville), and her intimates in *précieux* circles. And for this dramatization, she invents a way of presenting character: the *portrait moral*.[6] The introduction of each new character is the occasion for a full-length rendition; and in these portraits we rediscover almost all the attitudes and procedures we found to be important to Crébillon and Duclos—because the very act of portraiture necessarily implies and dictates a certain stance and a certain language.

The whole *problématique* of the portrait is in fact discussed by Mlle de Scudéry when she comes to her self-portrait, under the *précieux* code name of Sapho, in the last volume of *Le*

---

[6] Description of persons was a recognized category in the rhetorics of Antiquity; and many of the techniques of the *portrait moral* can undoubtedly be found in the earliest literature. But there seems to be general agreement that the formal set-piece—deriving perhaps from the contemporary popularity of collections of pictorial portraits—first makes its appearance in *Le Grand Cyrus*. See Magendie, *La Politesse mondaine*, II, 584; Victor Cousin, *La Société française au XVIIe siècle d'après Le Grand Cyrus de Mlle de Scudéry* (Paris, 1858); Édouard de Barthélemy, preface to *La Galerie des Portraits de Mademoiselle* (Paris, 1860); and Roger Picard, *Les salons littéraires et la société française* (New York: Brentano's, 1943), p. 190. On various sources and precursors of Mlle de Scudéry, see J. D. Lafond, "Les Techniques du portrait dans le 'Recueil des portraits et éloges,'" *Cahiers de l'Association Internationale des Études Françaises*, No. 18 (1966), pp. 143-44.

Grand Cyrus. Démocède has undertaken to tell the story of Sapho; before he begins, his listeners beg to know exactly "what she is like." This calls for a portrait, and also for a disquisition on the subtleties of portraiture:

> . . . car à mon advis il n'est pas aussi aisé de faire une Peinture fidelle, du coeur, de l'esprit, & de toutes les inclinations d'une Personne, que de son visage: puis qu'il est vray qu'à moins que d'avoir un certain esprit de discernement, qui sçait trouver de la difference entre les choses qui paroissent semblables, à ceux qui ne les examine pas bien, il n'est pas aisé de faire une Peinture bien ressemblante. En effet il faut sçavoir distinguer tous les divers degrez de melancolie, & d'enjouement: et ne se contenter pas de dire en general, c'estoit une Personne serieuse, ou une Personne enjouée, comme il y a beaucoup de gens qui font: car il est certain qu'il y a mille petites observations à faire, qui mettent une notable différence, entre les temperammens qui ne semblent pas opposez . . . il faut . . . sçavoir l'art de mettre de la difference entre la melancolique et la serieuse; entre la divertissante, & l'enjouée; quand on veut faire une de ces Peintures, où les Pinceaux & les Couleurs n'ont aucune part.[7]

Discernment, distinction among discrete characteristics which the inattentive observer apprehends only in a general impression, intelligent categorization in a vocabulary of moral and psychological abstraction, an effort toward the total representation and definitive fixity of a painted image—these are, for Mlle de Scudéry as for the eighteenth-century novelists, the essential characteristics of, and also the reason for, the portrait. And already there is the implication, without the use of the word, that penetration is the key to portraiture—the

---

[7] *Artamène, ou le Grand Cyrus* (10 vols.; Paris: Chez Augustin Courbé, 1649-53), x, 549-51.

discovery, the laying bare which provides one with the right category, the right tone, nuance, and word. After this preface, Démocède's listeners exclaim that they will know Sapho better than they know themselves when he has done.

Démocède's portrait starts with elaborate preliminaries about Sapho's homeland, her genealogy and childhood. Then he moves to her physical appearance, and his description fixes on her eyes: the eyes are important to the *précieuses* (as, of course, to the Petrarchists before them) because it is there that the junction of exterior and interior qualities, soul and body, is made visible, explicit, and a person's totality expressed. These "mirrors of the soul" are made to reflect a subtle and complex emotional being through their very appearance; the nouns and adjectives are so chosen that physiognomy leads us directly to the inner person. In a particularly striking example, in her portrait of Mme de Rambouillet (Cléomire), Mlle de Scudéry notes: "Au reste, sa physionomie est la plus belle & la plus noble que je vy jamais: & il paroit une tranquilité sur son visage, qui fait voir clairement qu'elle est celle de son ame" (VII, 491). Moral and physical realms are seen as necessarily interacting: the calm of Mme de Rambouillet's face *is* that of her soul; the portrait has captured an entire moral being, language has reached total truth.

As it draws to a close, the portrait of Sapho (like that of Mme de Rambouillet) expands into a consideration of her relations with others, her manner in social life:

Au reste elle a un esprit d'accomodement admirable: & elle parle si également bien des choses serieuses, & des choses galantes, & enjouées, qu'on ne peut comprendre qu'une mesme Personne puisse avoir des talents si opposez. Mais ce qu'il y a encore de plus digne de louange en Sapho, c'est qu'il n'y a pas au monde une meilleure Personne qu'elle, ny plus genereuse, ny moins interessée, ny plus officieuse.

De plus, elle est fidelle dans ses amitiez; et elle a l'ame si tendre, & le coeur si passioné, qu'on peut sans doute mettre la supreme felicité, à estre aimé de Sapho: car elle a un esprit si ingenieux, à trouver de nouveaux moyens d'obliger ceux qu'elle estime, & de leur faire connoistre son affection, que bien qu'il ne semble pas qu'elle face des choses fort extraordinaires, elle ne laisse pas toutesfois de persuader à ceux qu'elle aime, qu'elle les aime cherement. (X, 564-65)

As we unfolded from the physical realm into the psychological and moral, here we advance into the social. Sapho's most admirable qualities, her true claim to superiority, are her capacity for love and friendship, the social consciousness and manner (and the portrait continues to detail it) which make her the leader of a society of intelligent and refined beings.

Démocède's portrait is a formally complete set piece giving a total account and final definition of Sapho's appearance, psychology, moral being, and manners; it summarizes and fixes her whole life, and finally places her amidst her society by its celebration of those qualities she has cultivated to make life in the community agreeable. In fact, the portrait and the language it uses can be said to have been invented and elaborated by Mlle de Scudéry in order to perform a critical census of her society. With the psychological, moral, and social analysis of the portrait, she estimates, criticizes, and celebrates her contemporaries and their capacities for sociability, their readiness for life in the salon. The census indeed has an important didactic function. Mlle de Scudéry is intent to propagate the social virtues her contemporaries should cultivate—kindness, refined manners and refined friendship, an elaborate gallantry toward women, the art of *conversation,* which in French at this time still had the full range of the Italian *conversare*: talking, and being together, frequenting the same group. If the enduring interest of her novels, as Victor Cousin first among modern readers perceived, resides principally in the related techniques of portraits and conversations, it is because these are both social forms, directed to an understanding of man-in-society, and the appropriate vehicle for the didacticism of the "Reine du Tendre." *Cyrus* and *Clélie* in fact contain a complete guide to etiquette, a programmatic dissertation on manners directed to the education of their readers. A selection of conversations was even extracted from the novels and published separately as *La Morale du Monde*, a portable guide to social behavior.[8]

Social didacticism is hence possibly the starting point from which Mlle de Scudéry moves to a remarkably extensive representation of her society through a gallery of portraits of individuals whose social personalities are carefully estimated. If her novels were so popular throughout the seventeenth century, and even the eighteenth (Voltaire and Rousseau both admit to having devoured them) it is because she does succeed in giving us the sense of a milieu which is real for her characters and for her readers. There is a "realism" here, located not in the plot or the narrative, not in what is most "novelistic" about the novels, but in the conversations and portraits, static forms which she invented to give meaning and significance to her society. Compared to an earlier romance like *L'Astrée*, where the pseudo-medieval society is essentially a philosophical construct, *Cyrus* and *Clélie* give us a vital interplay of people within a social system whose values are felt as determining factors in individual behavior. Despite the external machinery of the heroic romance, the moral, psychological, and social universe of these novels is surprisingly live and real.

One should not, however, simply dismiss the heroic machinery; its use sheds light on the whole enterprise of Mlle de Scudéry, the *précieuses*, and those who were influenced by

---

[8] *La Morale du Monde, ou conversations* (Amsterdam, 1686); published in Paris the same year as *Conversations morales*.

them. To Boileau, and probably almost all succeeding critics, this machinery (found in Gomberville, La Calprenède, and other novelists as well as Mlle de Scudéry) seems perfectly ridiculous, wholly at odds with the tone and ethos of these novels. Yet, isn't the use of an epic structure, and more particularly the baptism of modern courtly heroes with the names of classical heroes (the tendency to "paint Cato as a gallant and Brutus as a fop," to use Boileau's terms)[9] perhaps a more or less conscious attempt to reinterpret heroism from a moralistic and sociable point of view, a reinterpretation similar to that found in the medieval romance, or in Pope's "heroi-comical" *Rape of the Lock*? To give an ancient hero modern, social virtues, to call a character Alexander and then make him a model of courtly, rather than military virtues, is a way of stating that true heroism has more to do with comportment in the drawing room than with one's stance on the battlefield. As in *The Rape of the Lock*, there is evidently a discrepancy between the machinery and the reality of modern concerns; but as Clarissa's speech to Belinda in Pope's poem clearly shows, the qualities by which one emerges victorious in social engagements— good humor, wit, imperturbable manners, urbanity—are possibly more admirable than those involved in duels under the walls of Troy.

This reinterpretation becomes most evident in the didactic and theoretical writings of the Chevalier de Méré. Like Castiglione and many other authors of treatises on court life, Méré frequently refers us to a number of sources in Antiquity— Cicero, Seneca, Quintilian, Plutarch—who provided models of heroism. His own perfect gentleman—whom he usually refers to as a "prince"—is modelled on Achilles, Alexander, and Caesar. The Achilles that interests him, however, is not a fierce warrior, but a young man tutored in right action and

---

[9] "Peindre Caton galant et Brutus dameret," *L'Art poétique*, Chant III. See also Boileau's "Dialogue sur les héros du roman."

excellent expression by Phoenix (an interpretation which he, like Castiglione before him, found in Cicero's *De Oratore*).[10] His Achilles is similar to the one Chapman gave to Elizabethan England in his translation of the *Iliad*: a gentleman of educated reason, faced with essentially moral choices and dilemmas. It is curious to notice how the historical reality of someone like Caesar (for instance, his order that all the inhabitants of a conquered province have one hand amputated) sometimes annoyingly intrudes to trouble Méré's vision of the magnanimous prince (III, 141).

The central effort of *précieux* circles was to define and propagate a modern ideal of social heroism—an ideal which also pervades Corneille's conception of the "generous" hero and is to an extent abstracted in Descartes' ethical philosophy. To describe this new hero, Chapelain coined the word "urbanité," but the terms more commonly used for the desirable social manner were "le galant homme" or "l'honnête homme." The latter, from its original, literal acceptation, came to mean, in Richelet's definition, he who possesses "toutes les qualitez propres à se rendre agréable dans la société."[11] It is of course Méré, whose doctrines were elaborated in conversations in *précieux* circles, who made himself the theoretician of "hon-

---

[10] Méré, *Oeuvres*, i, 5, and 142n; i, 78. My subsequent references to Méré's *Oeuvres* will be given in the text. Castiglione judged that Phoenix must be Homer's portrait of the perfect courtier since he is charged by Peleus with teaching Achilles "how to speak and act, which is nothing but the aim we have given our courtier" (*The Book of the Courtier*, pp. 331-32).

[11] See also Furetière, who defines the "honnête homme" as "qui a pris l'air du monde, qui sçait vivre, qui a du mérite et de la probité"; and the *Dictionnaire de l'Académie* which mentions "civil, courtois, poly" and goes on: "Quelque fois on appelle . . . *Honneste homme* un homme en qui on ne considère alors que les qualitez agréables et les manières du monde; et en ce sens, *honneste homme* ne veut dire autre chose que galant homme, homme de bonne conversation, de bonne compagnie." All these definitions are quoted by Lathuillère, *La Préciosité*, i, 591.

nêteté." Of his many definitions and redefinitions of the term, perhaps the most pertinent is this:

> . . . si quelqu'un me demandait en quoi consiste l'honnêteté, je dirois que ce n'est autre chose que d'exceller en tout ce qui regarde les agrémens et les bienséances de la vie: Aussi de-là, ce me semble, dépend le plus parfait et le plus aimable commerce du monde. (III, 70)

Social manner is a total style of life, its cultivation man's sole study: "Cette science est proprement celle de l'homme, parce qu'elle consiste à vivre et à se communiquer d'une manière humaine et raisonnable" (III, 72). Méré insists upon the generality of the "honnête homme," who must eschew all professionalism or specialization and present himself not as a writer, a captain, or a magistrate, but as something which transcends these functions: as purely man, which for Méré means a man who has subordinated the particular and individual to the social community, devalued all that does not advance worldly commerce, and elevated all that serves to further a pleasant social existence. This should not be taken as a recommendation of "naturalness" or "simple humanity." We saw earlier that Méré considered the successful courtier to be essentially an actor playing a role agreeable to others, and like the eighteenth-century novelists, he sees as a necessary corollary the ability to penetrate appearances, to find out what forces animate society and its members:

> C'est ce génie qui pénètre ce qui se passe de plus secret, qui découvre par un discernement juste et subtil ce que pensent les personnes qu'on entretient, et je suis persuadé qu'on ne sauroit être honnête homme ni d'une aimable conversation sans cette adresse de savoir deviner en beaucoup de rencontres. (III, 72)

55

It is natural, as well as notorious, that the search to refine manners, to redefine and subtilize the notion of heroism, and to propagate a new ideal of social style, should have entailed an effort to redefine the concepts and vocabulary of social intercourse, to discover terms for expressing a hypersensitivity to modes of social behavior. *Préciosité* starts as a private language elaborated to celebrate the sociability of a closed milieu. Yet it must also be seen as part of a general movement to make French a more flexible, subtle, and clear instrument of expression. From their concern with the manners of an inner circle, the *précieuses* contributed to the reform and refinement of the language of moral, psychological, and social analysis. The multiplication of distinctions in Sapho's portrait, her desire to delimit the exact connotation of every appearance, gesture, and word (one *précieuse* is indeed reputed to have distinguished twelve basic categories of sighs, each with numerous subdivisions); the use of moral and psychological abstractions, the manufacture of new words (real neologisms, and the creation of nouns from adjectives and infinitives) and the invention of new metaphors to define inner states of being; the effort to link inner and outer selves in one image, related in turn to the structure of images which is society; even pastimes like the "Carte du Tendre" and the more ridiculous games of language recorded by Somaize in his *Grand Dictionnaire des Précieuses* work to impart new clarity, subtlety, and significance to the tokens and code of social intercourse.

By their creation of a closed and self-conscious milieu and their attention to the forms of its sociability, the *précieuses* are the most important source of the seventeenth-century's ideals of worldly behavior. By their cultivation of the literary language and techniques which respond to these ideals, they are the first term in a literature of worldliness that would be developed by the *moralistes*, social observers and worldly psychologists who directed their scrutiny to the motives and gestures of man-in-society and refined the tools of analysis invented in the first salons of the century and given their first novelistic trial by Mlle de Scudéry. Preëminent among these tools is the *portrait moral* because it provides the means for a public, total act of knowing, a way to represent social beings.

It is notable that after its appearance in the novels of Mlle de Scudéry, the portrait became a society game. In the third important worldly and literary drawing room of the century, the highly aristocratic circle of Mlle de Montpensier ("La Grande Mademoiselle"), during the seasons of 1657 and 1658, portraits were the rage; all the members of good society attempted to paint themselves and one another. In 1659, an anthology of their efforts, the *Divers Portraits* (known later as the *Recueil des Portraits*, and finally as the *Galerie des Portraits*)—the first of several such collections in this period—was published in a strictly limited edition (thirty copies) for circulation in *le monde*; it includes the work of Segrais, La Rochefoucauld, Mme de Sévigné, Mme de Lafayette, and Mademoiselle herself, to name only the most famous. The preface to the anthology (doubtless written by Segrais) praises the invention of the form by Mlle de Scudéry, but also finds precedent in Plutarch, whose psychological art is the same:

> Enfin, c'est par son entremise que nous les connaissons [les sujets des *Vies* de Plutarque] à fond, et qu'ils n'ont rien de secret pour nous. Les portraits produisent un effet semblable, et nous en tirons un profit considérable. Nos peintres ne s'arrêtent pas seulement à l'extérieur et à tout ce qui paroit à nos yeux; ils font bien plus, et leur plume a beaucoup d'avantage sur le pinceau. Ils découvrent l'intérieur et s'attachent à l'âme. Ils déclarent si nous avons de l'esprit, du jugement et de la mémoire. Ils ne déguisent point notre tempérament, nos moeurs, nos sympathies et nos apathies, notre foible et notre fort, tellement qu'on les peut appeler des historiens

57

en raccourci, des abrégés de notre vie, et des espèces de confession générale, s'il m'est permis de me servir de cette com-
paraison. Ainsi, l'on ne sauroit trop les vanter....[12]

What is most interesting here is the pairing of "general confession" and "condensation of our life": the form of confession
which we reach through the agency of the portraitist is in
fact a fixation and concentration of what is essential about
each person. The portraitist makes himself an "historien en
raccourci" to reach the arrest of a total verbal form in order
to evaluate, compare, and pass judgment. The *mondain* di-
version is a serious means to knowledge, and an implement in
social relations.

This preface strikes an appropriately aristocratic and unprofessional pose. The assembled portraitists are not authors,
but simply men and women endowed "only with good common sense," who have not read "either the Rhetoric or the
Poetics of Aristotle."[13] Their enterprise cannot be attributed
to that of Theophrastus, for they are all "moderns," and regard the novel as their favorite literary form. This conjunction
of attitudes is significant: it indicates at the same time the relation of portrait to novel and the relation of both portrait and
novel to the milieu of aristocratic sociability and to *préciosité*.
Mademoiselle herself, in collaboration with Segrais, wrote two
novels based on the life of her salon, and on the whole the
précieuses, and more generally those engaged in the life of
mondain drawing rooms, took the novel more seriously than
did critics and professional men of letters. We have, for
instance, Méré's testimony that he would rather read *L'Astrée*
than Roman history.[14] The *précieuses* were perhaps the first of

[12] *La Galerie des Portraits*, ed. Barthélémy, pp. xvi-xvii.
[13] *Ibid.*, p. xix.
[14] The remark is made in a letter from Méré to Balzac, *Oeuvres*, I,
xxxiv.

the "Moderns," and when the famous Quarrel erupted at the end of the century, we find their attitudes echoed by Perrault, who considers the *Iliad* and the *Odyssey* inferior to *Cyrus* and *Clélie*.[15]

In a way, a gallery of portraits is already almost a novel, in that it represents and dramatizes a society. When we consider the *Galerie* as a total structure, we find that it illuminates the social sense of the gesture one makes in composing a portrait in the first place. It is clear, from the individual portraits of the *Galerie*, as from those of *Cyrus*, that the portraitist takes his own stance as a member of society and places his subject in relation to society. Further, in the *Galerie* the social structure is defined by the collection itself, by the presence of other members of society, by their names, by the gesture they are all performing, and by the desire to be presented as one of this structure, as contained within the enclosure. Outside the enclosure, one has no "right" to the portrait, no claim to celebration, no being in language; he is a non-person as far as *le monde* is concerned. Within, on the contrary, one is given a character, an individual personality worth careful attention. The portrait implies both an investigation of this individual personality, and an exploitation of many individuals living together in a system of manners: it is a form which gives meaning and significance to their "being together." And in this sense, its function is similar to that of the novel of manners itself. In the portrait and its social origins, we discover not only an important novelistic tool, but a kind of concern and enterprise which have much to do with the genesis of the novel itself—or at least a certain kind of novel. This novel would have its first realization with Mme de Lafayette, then develop into a whole fictional mode in the early eighteenth century.

[15] Lathuillère, *La Préciosité*, 1, 468.

But before returning to the eighteenth-century novel, it is important to consider what happened to the literature of sociability adumbrated by the *précieuses*, and to the tools—especially the portrait—they invented to express their conception of social man. A complete history of the seventeenth-century literature of sociability—or even a history of the portrait in all its uses—is not possible. What seems to me essential is to discern the form that this literature takes, the tradition it creates, and how this tradition leads to a certain kind of novel. We could call this the *moraliste* tradition, using that term in its most general sense: the line of worldly literature, conversational and social in its origins, hard-headed in its attitudes, directed toward an exploration and definition of man in the social medium, which was pursued in memoirs, letters, aphorisms, reflections, histories, and on the stage in the 1660's and 70's. The attitudes and techniques of such literature proliferated in this period—as did the portrait, which Méré finds was positively abused by good society (I, 63)—and it would be interesting to follow its various metamorphoses in history (which was becoming more psychological and analytical), in the memoirs of Retz and Tallemant des Réaux, in the letters of Mme de Sévigné, or the *contes* of La Fontaine. But the names that seem to me to represent this tradition most importantly are those of Molière, La Rochefoucauld, Mme de Lafayette, and La Bruyère, and through a brief examination of their enterprise, we can follow the development and transformation of a *précieux* literature of sociability into the literary stance that was inherited by the eighteenth-century novelists.

Portraits would seem to have no place in the theater. We think of theatrical characters as revealing themselves by words and actions through the medium of time, in a kinetic form which has no need for the static, summary knowledge of the portrait. But Molière in fact assigns them an important role: in his *comédie de caractère*, where individual characteristics which differ from the social norm are offered to the ridicule of society, the portrait becomes an important set-piece in which one character publicly "exposes" another. The most famous instance is the "scène des portraits" in *Le Misanthrope*, where the social personality of several members of her circle are rendered in a performance by Célimène. Her procedure is to start from a phrase, furnished by her listeners, which gives an accepted assessment of the person in question, then to refine, elaborate, define, or reverse the set definition. When, for example, Clitandre remarks that Cléonte appeared "ridicule achevé," Célimène continues:

> Dans le monde, à vrai dire, il se barbouille fort,
> Partout il porte un air qui saute aux yeux d'abord;
> Et lorsqu'on le revoit après un peu d'absence,
> On le retrouve encor plus plein d'extravagance.

(II, iv, 571-74)

The essential word here is "extravagance," which marks the degree of deviation from acceptable normality in "le monde." And this stigmatization of the socially non-conformist underlies Alceste's outburst when Clitandre applauds Célimène's perception as a portraitist: "Pour bien peindre des gens vous êtes admirable." Alceste replies, "Allons, ferme, poussez, mes bons amis de cour!"

This reaction is significant, and we will return to it, since Rousseau's most telling attack on the attitudes and techniques of the *moraliste* tradition is embodied in his critique of Molière's treatment of the Misanthrope. Portraits are the tools of a Célimène or a Philinte, and the whole system of values which they imply is inimical to Alceste. His reaction and his fate in the play indicate the extent to which the social ideal elaborated by the *précieuses* has, by the year 1666, become a prescriptive and coercive pattern. In Molière we feel the influence of a hierarchical society where prestige and power emanate from the court and eventually from the king alone. As Erich Auerbach has observed, for Molière *ridicule* "means deviation from the normal and customary,"[16] and from about 1660 the normal and customary depends on the court, which gained an ascendancy, an absolutism, and a centrality which tended to concentrate all sociability in itself, to impose a uniform pattern of comportment, and to bring the decadence of those salons which had been the original source of the ideal of sociability. *L'honnêteté, l'air galant*—those terms which describe the accepted worldly attitude—have become more and more identified with a pattern of courtly behavior in a society revolving about its earthly sun king.

The practice of worldliness hence begins to take on more and more the hard-headed absolutism of tone, the cynical authority, and the sharp judgment that we found in the narrative voices of Crébillon and Duclos and in the formulations of a master worldling like Versac. Philinte, whom post-Rousseauian critics have often considered a rather vile *complaisant*, is in fact quite representative of this new tone. Although his stance is obviously determined by Molière's dramatic and satiric necessities, given a comic *charge* (and for this reason neither he, nor Molière's comedy in general, can validly be called "worldly"), he is in essence an "honnête homme" who finds "extravagant" views incompatible with his experience of society. His well-known advice:

Il faut, parmi le monde, une vertu traitable;
A force de sagesse on peut être blamable. . . . (I, i, 149-50)

reminds us of one of his contemporaries' lapidary statement,

---

[16] *Mimesis*, trans. Willard Trask (Garden City: Anchor Books, 1957), p. 318. See also "La Cour et la Ville," *Scenes From the Drama of European Literature*.

"C'est une grande folie de vouloir être sage tout seul."[17] With La Rochefoucauld, we have reached the mature note of worldliness, the tone which, *mutatis mutandis*, will dominate the early eighteenth-century novel.

The *Maximes* are placed under the emblem of penetration: the frontispiece, with its engraving of Seneca unmasked, is entitled "L'Amour de la vérité," and the liminary aphorism, "Nos vertus ne sont le plus souvent que des vices déguisés," indicates the kind of search for truth La Rochefoucauld has in mind. Like Versac, La Rochefoucauld holds this penetration to the truth to be his essential enterprise; and he is also aware that, like everything else, the desire to penetrate psychologically can be assimilated to our self-regard: "La pénétration a un air de deviner, qui flatte plus notre vanité que toutes les autres qualités de l'esprit"(425). This "demystification" of our seeming virtuousness, of our complacent morality, our psychological and social satisfactions, operates, as Jean Starobinski has so well shown, by a decomposition of moral qualities into their component parts.[18] When, for instance, La Rochefoucauld announces, "Pendant que la paresse et la timidité nous retiennent dans notre devoir, notre vertu en a souvent tout l'honneur"(169) the value of the statement comes from its analysis of *devoir* as a restrained form of behavior which appears the result of something called virtue, but is in fact determined by such simple and unexalted emotions as laziness and timidity. He has denounced the false

---

[17] La Rochefoucauld, *Maximes et Mémoires*, ed. Jean Starobinski (Paris: 10/18, 1964), No. 231. Subsequent references will give the number of the *maxime* between parentheses in the text. The *Maximes* were first published in 1665. It is interesting to note that one of the court treatises discussed by Magendie contains the same maxim, in less hard and polished form: "Il vaut mieux être fou avec tout le monde que sage tout seul" (Chevigni, quoted in Magendie, *La Politesse mondaine*, p. 79).

[18] In his introduction to *Maximes et Mémoires*.

"seeming" of an accepted moral category and given a truer, more profound motivation to the behavior originally referred to the category.

This is similar to the procedure of the portrait, where the portraitist must go beyond accepted descriptions of a character to a deeper analysis. Like the portrait, the aphorism records a penetration, a knowing, a finding out. It resembles the portrait in its definitive formal hardness and arrest; it is a similarly final statement about men, but further stripped of any picturesque exterior, any contingent detail, and more typological—a pure metaphor, a final fixation of the movement of life. Many of the *Maximes* read as condensed, essential statements of the experience of life found in novels like *Les Égarements* or *Les Confessions du Comte de****, for example: "L'esprit ne saurait jouer longtemps le personnage du coeur" (108), or "La sévérité des femmes est un ajustement et un fard qu'elles ajoutent à leur beauté"(204). Their tone is that of Versac: consider the arch and cruel "Il y a des gens qui ressemblent aux vaudevilles qu'on ne chante qu'un certain temps"(211). The statement is final, its appeal to the judgment of society as ultimate arbiter of personal style irrevocable. The coercive system of Versac is evident in La Rochefoucauld's use of the word *ridicule*, fear of which, as Duclos assured us, dominates life in the world: "Le ridicule déshonore plus que le déshonneur"(326); "S'il y a des hommes dont le ridicule n'ait jamais paru, c'est qu'on ne l'a pas bien cherché"(311). And as in the novels of Crébillon and Duclos, it is the clever actor, the *habile homme,* who dominates others.

Both in their subject and their form, the *Maximes* reveal with particular clarity and purity an enterprise implicit in the way all the *moralistes,* and those eighteenth-century novelists strongly influenced by them, use language. La Rochefoucauld finds meaning in his world, and gives meaning to his world, by a language which actively mimes this world's enclosure, which defines and fixes limits. His quest to know man is carried out by discovering and recording what he can and cannot do, the limits of his control of self and others, what can be attributed to his conscious efforts, and what is the work of the emotional forces which control him. The language of the aphorism, and of the portrait, is chosen, elaborated, and refined in order to provide an essential and final definition which is a fixing of limits, a statement of the definitive contours of the question beyond which nothing of truth, relevance, or importance is to be found. When, for example, La Rochefoucauld states, "Cette clémence, dont on fait une vertu, se pratique tantôt par vanité, quelquefois par paresse, souvent par crainte, et presque toujours par tous les trois ensemble"(16), he has absolutely defined and fixed the contours and the frame of an act or a kind of behavior called "clemency"; there is no room for other possibilities. La Rochefoucauld may extend our understanding of the ways language is used by Crébillon and Duclos, and by those of their characters socially most in command. Their definitions of their contemporaries and the society in which they operate find meaning and attribute meaning because they limit and fix. They know in order to fix and control, but they also fix in order to know. The process works, since the whole society sees this language as the only one that rightly interprets and gives significance to its gestures.

The prefatory *Discours* to the *Maximes* strikes the casual, aristocratic, unprofessional pose with which we are familiar from the preface to Mademoiselle's *Galerie*—the *Maximes* lack "order," show no attention to "rules," but instead demonstrate "the negligent manner of writing of a courtier who is possessed of wit" rather than "the stilted regularity of a doctor who has never seen anything but books"[19]—and reminds us that the aphorism, like the portrait, is a social form, and

[19] *Maximes et Mémoires*, p. 48.

that the idea of publishing a collection of maxims occurs only after one has essayed and polished them in conversations in a drawing room. For La Rochefoucauld, this drawing room was Mme de Sablé's, and an understanding of the rôle played by Mme de Sablé and her circle can illuminate the sense of La Rochefoucauld's enterprise, the hardness and limiting pessimism of his tone and attitude, and also give us an indication of the true relationship of the later *moralistes* to the *précieuses* whom we have discussed.

The Marquise de Sablé in fact figured in the three most important *précieux* drawing rooms of the century—those of Mme de Rambouillet, Mlle de Scudéry, and Mlle de Montpensier—and an allegiance to the concerns, spirit, and language of *préciosité* are evident throughout her life. She also entertained relations with the Jansenists, especially Mère Angélique, and in 1659 she retired to a house built for her within the walls of Port-Royal de Paris. Here she opened a small, select salon whose membership included La Rochefoucauld, Mme de Lafayette, Jacques Esprit, Guilleragues, and Pascal. At the center of their conversations was a traditional *précieux* theme: love, and especially the social consequences of love, the relations of ethics and passion. But their discussion of the theme was marked by a certain Jansenist pessimistic determinism—a sense of the injustice of the ego, the destructiveness of the passions, the inevitability of dissimulation, the elusiveness of truth. The conversations of the company, often framed as portraits, reflections, aphorisms—Mme de Sablé considered herself the inventor of the *maxime morale*—are reflected, directly or obliquely, in a number of important works of social philosophy. The enterprise of *De la fausseté des vertus humaines,* by Jacques Esprit, is similar to La Rochefoucauld's in the *Maximes,* and its spirit is the same. The Marquis de Sourdis proposed a number of "Questions" on love which, following debate in the drawing room, probably inspired Guilleragues'

Lettres portugaises,[20] and perhaps, to a degree, *La Princesse de Clèves* as well. The *Discours sur les passions de l'amour,* traditionally attributed to Pascal, perhaps the work of this same Marquis de Sourdis, was almost surely a product of this circle; and the *Pensées* themselves, in their critique of worldliness—and their worldly tone—show the mark of this period of Pascal's life.

It is possible to say, tentatively, that the "Cornelian-Cartesian" ethic of the *précieuses*—their ideal of courtly, generous heroism—underwent a transformation through the influence of Jansenism in the circle of Mme de Sablé;[21] her salon was the central laboratory of the worldly pessimism that dominates so much of the literature of the last third of the seventeenth century. The thought of Jacques Esprit, La Rochefoucauld, and Mme de Lafayette is not religious; rather, it is marked by a Jansenism without Christianity,[22] a secular pessimism, and disillusioned lucidity in the investigation of man's social being. The "demolition of the hero" remarked by Paul Bénichou[23] in the passage from early to later seventeenth century reflects this movement toward a more restricted, skeptical, disillusioned literature—a literature which retains the concerns of the *précieuses* and the tools they developed to define and assess their society, which remains directed to a penetrating scrutiny of man's social existence, but which reveals a new hardness and cynicism, an intensified sense of the drama, and the

---

[20] See Frédéric Deloffre's introduction to his edition of *Les Lettres portugaises* (Paris: Garnier, 1962). It should be noted that not everyone accepts the attribution of this novel to Guilleragues, but Deloffre's arguments in its favor seem to me conclusive.

[21] This point is suggested by Nicolas Ivanoff in *La Marquise de Sablé et son salon* (Paris, 1927), p. 126. On this group, see also Victor Cousin, *Madame de Sablé* (Nouvelle édition; Paris, 1882).

[22] Port-Royal accepted the *Maximes* as an analysis of existence, a preparation for the wager that God exists, but insisted that a further step be taken.

[23] "La Démolition du héros," *Morales du grand siècle* (Paris, 1948).

tragedy, of personal relations, a new skepticism about moral heroism. In the salon of Mme de Sablé, the literature of world-liness takes on its definitive tone and attitude—the limiting, pessimistic clairvoyance of La Rochefoucauld, La Bruyère, Mme de Lafayette, and eighteenth-century novelists.

This transmutation of *précieux* social portraiture into the worldliness of the *moralistes* can help us to understand the complex moral atmosphere of *La Princesse de Clèves*, the one significant contemporary novel of good society, the model to which the eighteenth-century novels of worldliness all implicit-ly refer. It has been pointed out that the immediate antecedents of this novel are to be found more in the *nouvelle historique* —the secret history, the memoir claiming to reveal the hither-to hidden, usually amorous motives of historical acts, works which from a formal standpoint replaced the complex "epic" structure of much earlier fiction with a straightforward chron-ological narrative—than in the realism of the burlesques or in the *précieux* novel.[24] Thus the historical "episodes" of *La Prin-cesse de Clèves*, which have struck some critics as irrelevant, are in one sense its starting point, for it is a novel about an historical way of courtly, public life, and about what happens to love in this way of life. This prototype of the *roman d'ana-lyse* is also insistently about courtliness, or the worldliness of a court. As Mme de Lafayette herself judged: "c'est une par-faite imitation du monde de la cour et de la manière dont on y vit."[25]

It is, however, precisely Mme de Lafayette's development of courtliness as milieu and subject which cannot be explained by reference to the *nouvelle historique* alone. The tales of

[24] On this filiation, see the excellent discussion by Bernard Pingaud in *Madame de Lafayette par elle-même* (Paris: Éditions du Seuil, 1959), pp. 131-42. Mme de Lafayette's first tale, *La Princesse de Montpensier*, is directly in this line.
[25] Letter to Lescheraine, 13 April 1678, *Correspondance* (Paris, 1942), II, 63.

Saint-Réal, Segrais, or Mme de Villedieu (whose *Désordres de l'amour* appeared to contemporaries a source of *La Princesse de Clèves*) are like the "episodes" of Mme de Lafayette's novel without the central situation which develops the social, psychological, and moral effects of the court setting.[26] In these authors, a linear narrative turns on historical events which form the armature of the plot. There is little depth of analysis and no exploitation of a system of manners. While historical events are explained by reference to private motives, there is little indication of how individual behavior is shaped by an historical situation and a type of society. Mme de Lafayette unquestionably profits from the *nouvelle historique*, from memorialists, and in general from the new attention to history, but her primary interest is in how the individual's actions are determined by his consciousness of society. And when she begins her novel, "La magnificence et la galanterie n'ont jamais paru en France avec tant d'éclat . . . ," her hyperbole refers us to the vocabulary and concerns of the *précieuses*, to whom society as the medium of our self-conscious existence was so important. The historical moment she has chosen further confirms this allegiance for, as Giovanni Macchia has demonstrated, the *précieuses* gave a retrospective historical reality to their mythic ideal of courtly heroism by locating it in the reign of the Valois monarchs.[27]

The court, its structure, the conditions it imposes, and the behavior it demands are the subjects of the opening pages of the novel. Inevitably, these pages are filled with portraits of those who, through their prominence, set the tone of the court. The most important is that of the Duc de Nemours:

Mais ce prince était un chef-d'oeuvre de la nature; ce qu'il

[26] This is especially true of *Les Désordres de l'amour*, where four different tales are linked through their connection to the intrigues of the court, but the court itself is never the subject.

[27] Macchia, *Il Paradiso della ragione*, p. 181.

avait de moins admirable, c'était d'être l'homme du monde le mieux fait et le plus beau. Ce qui le mettait au-dessus des autres était une valeur incomparable, et un agrément dans son esprit, dans son visage, et dans ses actions que l'on n'a jamais vu qu'à lui seul; il avait un enjouement qui plaisait également aux hommes et aux femmes, une adresse extraordinaire dans tous ses exercises, une manière de s'habiller qui était toujours suivie de tout le monde, sans pouvoir être imitée, et enfin un air dans toute sa personne qui faisait qu'on ne pouvait regarder que lui dans tous les lieux où il paraissait. Il n'y avait aucune dame dans la cour dont la gloire n'eût été flattée de le voir attaché à elle; peu de celles à qui il s'était attaché, se pouvaient vanter de lui avoir résisté, et même plusieurs à qui il n'avait point témoigné de passion, n'avaient pas laissé d'en avoir pour lui. Il avait tant de douceur et tant de disposition à la galanterie qu'il ne pouvait refuser quelques soins à celles qui tâchaient de lui plaire: ainsi il avait plusieurs maîtresses, mais il était difficile de deviner celle qu'il aimait véritablement.[28]

The portrait starts from a comparison to the Vidame de Chartres, and insists upon Nemours' superiority to all the other exceptional young princes of this elitist society. The typically *précieux* hyperbole—"un chef-d'oeuvre de la nature," "l'homme du monde le mieux fait et le plus beau"—gives the image of a perfectly conceived and executed being. Perhaps the essential point is that in this society of ranks, Nemours is "above the others" because of his "incomparable value," and this value elevates Nemours, the narrator suggests, because it is also an "agrément": it possesses the social public grace that "pleases." His "enjouement," his physical dexterity, his manner of dress result in, and are complemented by, a decisive "air

[28] Madame de Lafayette, *Romans et Nouvelles*, ed. Emile Magne (Paris: Garnier, 1958), pp. 243-44.

dans toute sa personne qui faisait qu'on ne pouvait regarder que lui dans tous les lieux où il paraissait": this "air," as always undefined and not completely definable, has the public result of drawing everyone's attention to him. And since his public representation is the center of attention, it is necessary for the "gloire" of every woman to attach—the eighteenth-century word would be fix—Nemours. The passage ends by reminding us of another essential trait of the courtier: it is difficult to know what his true feelings toward anyone are, for public attention has inevitably elicited individual dissimulation. The act of knowing has, for the moment, reached its limits.

As this and other liminary portraits suggest, the court of *La Princesse de Clèves* is a closed, lighted and gilded stage where nothing can long remain private.[29] The central action of the novel turns on this condition, and the "episodes" confirm it. One thinks, for example, of the Vidame de Chartres' story of his lost letter. The first mention of the heroine is, as with Hortense in *Les Égarements*, simultaneously an introduction to the reader and a presentation to society: "Il parut alors une beauté à la cour, qui attira les yeux de tout le monde, et l'on doit croire que c'était une beauté parfaite, puisqu'elle donna de l'admiration dans un lieu où l'on était si accoutumé à voir de belles personnes" (247). The public appearance, the drawing of all eyes to herself, is a torture to Mlle de Chartres, who must fashion an acceptable public deportment in a milieu described as a precarious equilibrium between elegant order and struggle for pleasure and position: "il y avait une sorte

---

[29] The "closure" of this stage has been discussed by Serge Doubrovsky in "*La Princesse de Clèves*: Une Interprétation existentialiste," *La Table Ronde*, No. 138 (June, 1959), pp. 36-51; and by Pingaud, who analyzes the role of the *regard* within this enclosure (*Madame de Lafayette par elle-même*, pp. 82-90). My reading of this novel has also been influenced by discussions with M. Jacques Bersani of the École Normale Supérieure.

d'agitation sans désordre dans cette cour, qui la rendait très agréable, mais aussi très dangereuse pour une jeune personne" (253). As Mme de Chartres warns her daughter, "Si vous jugez sur les apparences en ce lieu-ci . . . vous serez souvent trompée: ce qui paraît n'est presque jamais la vérité"(265). All this being so, Mme de Clèves could survive only by adopting a mask herself.

But she is surrounded by a play of penetrating glances: the *regard* given and refused, while one is under the gaze of others, is the essential expression of the act of knowing and of possession in this world of voyeurs. The meeting of Mme de Clèves and Nemours, at the ball, is presented as a visual moment: she, like the reader, mentally possesses his portrait, and when she turns her eyes to the stranger advancing toward her, she knows it can only be he. "Ce prince était fait d'une sorte qu'il était difficile de n'être pas surprise de le voir quand on ne l'avait jamais vu"(261-62), and Nemours himself is "surpris" by his first view of Mme de Clèves.[30] Nemours and the Duc de Guise discover their rivalry in love by a careful

[30] One could juxtapose this meeting to a *précieux* game, the playing board for which is preserved in the Bibliothèque Nationale (Estampes, Tf mat.), in which the path that will end (after some ninety moves) at "le Palais de l'Hymen" begins with "la vue," followed by "l'admiration," followed in turn by "l'amour au berceau." This marks clearly the *précieux* (and also the Cornelian) relationship of vision to love. Mme de Lafayette's glance starts from the same premises, but it is radically different, because the active power of the eyes has moved from object to subject, from seen to seer. One could indeed write an "histoire de l'oeil" in the seventeenth century: the *précieuses*, like the Petrarchan poets before them, valued *la vue*, the eyes as expression, the exponents of the soul, a magnetic force which "wounds" and "enslaves" the beholder through love (in the words of a quatrain of the time: "Par son regard toujours vainqueur / Cloris de cent beautés pourvue / Blesse ses amants droit au coeur / Leur ayant donné dans la vue"). For the *moralistes*, for Mme de Lafayette, and also for Racine, while the woman's eyes may initially cause this "wound," the active power of vision has essentially passed to the beholder: *la vue* has become *le regard*, a force consciously and cruelly applied to the possession and enslavement of the object.

watching of one another's glances. The famous scene of the stolen portrait becomes the occasion of a complicated and telling *jeu des regards*:

> Mme la Dauphine était assise sur le lit et parlait bas à Mme de Clèves, qui était debout devant elle. Mme de Clèves aperçut par un des rideaux, qui n'était qu'à demi fermé, M. de Nemours, le dos contre la table, qui était au pied du lit, et elle vit que, sans tourner la tête, il prenait adroitement quelque chose sur cette table. Elle n'eut pas de peine à deviner que c'était son portrait, et elle en fut si troublée que Mme la Dauphine remarqua qu'elle ne l'écoutait pas et lui demanda tout haut ce qu'elle regardait. M. de Nemours se tourna à ces paroles; il rencontra les yeux de Mme de Clèves, qui étaient encore attachés sur lui, et il pensa qu'il n'était pas impossible qu'elle eût vu ce qu'il venait de faire. (302)

This play of the eyes—where actions are performed behind the actor's back and perceived through half-closed curtains; where Nemours sees in Mme de Clèves' eyes that he has probably been seen—suggests the extraordinary complexity and anguish of personal relationships in this milieu. Subject to the glance, Mme de Clèves cannot avoid letting Nemours see that she is aware of his action; she cannot speak against it in public, and she is not permitted to see him privately. Nemours, aware that he has been seen, cannot press his advantage before the eyes of others; he must maneuver by whispers, asides, glances. The scene expresses both the intense, wounding attempt at communication—including communication as possession—which the court elicits, and the irreducible isolation of the characters.

The moment at which this scene occurs is significant: it follows Mme de Clèves' first total recognition of her feeling for Nemours, and her estimation that she must avoid his presence.

The stealing of her portrait, here painted rather than verbal, can be seen as symbolic cause of her subsequent loss of control. She no longer possesses the hard outlines of the portrait, she no longer knows who she is. She will soon discover that she no longer "recognizes" herself(329). She becomes a tracked animal (and there is already some of the cruelty of a Versac or a Valmont in Nemours, in his persistent attempt to obtain an *aveu*); her only hope is to flee the court, into the shadows of a country retreat where failure to control her "appearing" will go unnoticed:

> ... elle fit réflexion à la violence de l'inclination qui l'entraînait vers M. de Nemours; elle trouva qu'elle n'était plus maîtresse de ses paroles et de son visage ... qu'enfin il n'y avait plus rien qui la pût défendre et qu'il n'y avait de sûreté pour elle qu'en s'éloignant. (303)

It is, of course, one of the central ironies of the book that this retreat, the shaded and protected summer house at Coulommiers, should also be subject to the spying presence of Nemours, and that he should there overhear her confession to her husband. His public revelation of this confession leads to the tortured confrontation of husband and wife, where neither can believe that the other has revealed their secret, yet cannot see how the secret might otherwise have escaped. The only practical solution to the dilemma, M. de Clèves tells her, is to dissimulate in public. Another retreat to Coulommiers becomes another occasion for Nemours to track her down: he again sees her in the summer house, now holding a torch to the part of a painting of the Siege of Metz where his own portrait is represented:

> On ne peut exprimer ce que sentit M. de Nemours dans ce moment. Voir au milieu de la nuit, dans le plus beau lieu du monde, une personne qu'il adorait, la voir sans qu'elle sût qu'il la voyait, et la voir tout occupée de choses qui avait

du rapport à lui et à la passion qu'elle lui cachait, c'est ce qui n'a jamais été goûté ni imaginé par nul autre amant. (367)

Here once again, it is the discovery, the laying-bare of the glance—and the verb "to see" is used four times in one sentence—that expresses Nemours' cruelty and Mme de Clèves' victimization by knowing.[31]

After the death of M. de Clèves, during Mme de Clèves' voluntary sequestration, Nemours, renting a room with a view of her apartment, becomes pure *regard*, an insistent visual presence. It is only through the ruse of the Vidame de Chartres that he can overcome the distance of vision and talk to Mme de Clèves. At their interview, the narrator is careful to insist that this is the first time the two have been in a position to see one another without the interference of the vision of others: "L'on ne peut exprimer ce que sentirent M. de Nemours et Mme de Clèves de se trouver seuls et en état de se parler pour la première fois"(382). But the reaction of Mme de Clèves is to reject Nemours' presence. Her decision is based on her sense of integrity, her refusal to be violated by the ethic of worldliness which would denature her sense of duty, and eventually destroy her happiness through Nemours' inconstancy, the inevitability of which has been sufficiently established by the entire narrative: "Ce que je crois devoir à la mémoire de M. de Clèves serait faible s'il n'était soutenu par l'interêt de mon repos; et les raisons de mon repos ont besoin d'être soutenues de celles de mon devoir" (388-89). The repose which Mme de Clèves seeks to guarantee in detaching herself from the world is in fact a state toward which she has been striving through-

---

[31] Not only does this scene show Nemours spying on Mme de Clèves, who is in turn gazing at his image: Nemours is himself followed by M. de Clèves' spy, whose glance, however, is blocked by the garden wall, entailing a failure to penetrate beyond appearances which will be the direct cause of the mortal despair of M. de Clèves.

out the novel: a state of removal from the light of the court, from the eyes of others—an escape from the imposing demands of worldliness. Light and shadows, with the seeing and hiding they express, form the central metaphorical texture of the novel, and its last pages, where Mme de Clèves moves progressively farther from society, and from life itself, are unlighted, obscured, desolate.

This final desolation, in its contrast to the initial hyperbolic insistence on magnificence, gallantry, and heroism, places one before the question debated by several critics: whether the ethic of *La Princesse de Clèves* is, to put it in shorthand, Cornelian or Racinian—the "heroic concept of the *précieux* and Corneille" or the "materialist nihilism of Racine and the Jansenists," as Claude Vigée expresses it.[32] For M. Vigée, the novel is finally "the expression of the unresolved conflict between these two conceptions of human nature, and, to a certain degree, a desperate attempt to resolve their antinomies." But to pose the problem in violent antinomies is to falsify the subtlety of Mme de Lafayette's attitude, which, like that of other members of Mme de Sablé's circle, retains elements of the *précieux* ethic and concerns, but transmuted into the worldly realism of the *moralistes*. If Mme de Clèves' final decision appears to echo *préciosité*—refusal of marriage because marriage destroys love, imposition of trial by distance, the Provençal "amor de lonh," on her suitor, a certain proud feminism—on closer consideration her decision transcends such concerns: it does not involve trial of another, for it does not have reference to Nemours—it is finally a decision which has only to do with herself and her experience of the world. With utter clarity of perception, Mme de Clèves chooses quietism, absence, and desola-

---

[32] Claude Vigée, *"La Princesse de Clèves* et la tradition du refus," *Critique*, No. 159-60 (1960), p. 725. See also S. Fraisse, "Le Repos de Mme de Clèves," *Esprit*, No. 300 (1961), pp. 560-67; and Doubrovsky, *"La Princesse de Clèves."*

tion, a choice based on the realism of the moralist. At the origins of *La Princesse de Clèves* is the *précieux* interest in courtliness, gallantry, "parfaite amitié," heroism, sociability, and the means for knowing and evaluating these qualities; but its point of view is tempered by the ethical pessimism, the hard-headed worldliness of tone, the sense of the limits to action in the world which the *moralistes* of the last part of the century brought to the debate about these qualities. *La Princesse de Clèves* develops fully the social drama implicit in Mlle de Scudéry and the earliest commentators on worldliness, and it mirrors the evolution of worldly moralism in the seventeenth century.

In many respects, the end of this evolution is La Bruyère's *Caractères*, published in 1688. The collection is a *summa* of seventeenth-century portraiture, the end-term of a society's effort to portray, take stock of, and give meaning to itself. La Bruyère's enterprise is, to the modern sensibility, absurdly ambitious: the representation of "les moeurs de ce siècle," of all the typical characters and situations of his time. The project involves the establishment of loose categories of various types —*Femmes, Hommes de Lettres, Esprits Forts, Les Grands, La Mode, La Ville, La Cour*—which make his collection a sort of infinitely expandable accordion file: indeed, part of the power of *Les Caractères* comes from La Bruyère's evident exuberance at the discovery that everyone can be reduced to language, labelled, and assigned to one section or another. The categories are basically social subdivisions (La Bruyère's man is before all else social) of the two primary terms of the human community as his generation knew it: *la Cour* and *la Ville*. The portraits of *De la ville* are the most satiric, because the town is often only a bad copy of the court, its manners marked by pretension and falsity. The town defines the outside limit of La Bruyère's world and his glance; beyond it, nothing exists. The celebrated passage on the peasants, humane and

77

moving as it is, serves as a gesture of exclusion: the status of anything living beyond the theater of society is rendered problematic. La Bruyère is not interested in social classes, but rather, as Roland Barthes terms it, in the "inland" of *le monde* which is defined by its circumference, by the fact that what lies in the "outland" has no status, hence no claim to expression in language.[33] *Les Caractères* thus perfectly images the century's efforts to attain perfect closure, and to represent itself in terms of this closure.

This means that the object of La Bruyère's attention is very consciously *la mondanité*, or worldliness: the totality of the forms of man's social existence as they can be encompassed and formulated by a language and a system which make no reference (to introduce an anachronism as the only way of making the comparison) to sociology, to psychology, etiquette, or any other specialized, partial, or fragmentary sciences of man as such. Worldliness, as point of observation and object of study, is one, a total ethos, the one way of being in the only society that counts. La Bruyère's attention, in whatever domain, is continually directed to the gestures that reveal our place within this total system:

> Il n'y a rien de si délié, de si simple et de si imperceptible, où il n'entre des manières qui nous décèlent. Un sot ni n'entre, ni ne sort, ni ne s'assied, ni ne se lève, ni ne se tait, ni n'est sur ses jambes, comme un homme d'esprit.[34]

At the center of La Bruyère's "inland" is the hyper-enclosure of the court, corrupt, corrupting, but fascinating, to which he, like all the *moralistes* of the second half of the century, is necessarily drawn. "Il faut qu'un honnête homme ait tâté de la cour: il découvre en y entrant comme un nouveau monde qui lui

---

[33] Barthes, pp. 227-28.
[34] Jean de La Bruyère, *Les Caractères ou les moeurs de ce siècle,* ed. Robert Garapon (Paris: Garnier, 1962), p. 108.

était inconnu, où il voit régner également le vice et la politesse, et où tout lui est utile, le bon et le mauvais"(222). The
court is in fact the primary term of reality, the privileged space
in the theater of society, and at the center of La Bruyère's
portrait gallery is the courtier, once again seen as a voluntary,
artistic performer:

> Un homme qui sait la cour est maître de son geste, de ses
> yeux et de son visage; il est profond, impénétrable; il dis-
> simule les mauvais offices, sourit à ses ennemis, contraint
> son humeur, déguise ses passions, dément son coeur, parle,
> agit contre ses sentiments. (221)

Worldliness emanates from a nucleus of courtliness.

It is indeed the concentric hierarchization, closure, and publicity of this world that allows La Bruyère to bring off his ambitious enterprise. Everyone knows everyone else, and because
this is so, La Bruyère, says Barthes, is able to "name" the world
in a manner denied to modern writers. When he calls someone *fat* or *ridicule*, the definition rests on a set of values and
a common experience of society shared by author and reader
—and his readers responded by making keys to the portraits,
to show that they were in fact part of the experience. This
"nomination," to follow Barthes again, does not involve an
abstraction from several real characters to reach an ideal "type"
—as may be the case with the "functional" persons of comedy
—but rather refers immediately to a unity known in relation to
other unities in the "inland" of *le monde*. As a result, La
Bruyère can recite his characters like the successive cases of a
social declension.[35]

[35] See Barthes, pp. 229-35. This may suggest that "portrait" and "character," though distinguished by rhetoricians of Antiquity and by some
authors in the seventeenth century, in practice are virtually indistin-
guishable. In theory, the portrait was assigned to description of the
individual's distinct traits, the character to creation of a type from the
grouping of typical traits in a general social category (on these points, see

The portraits of this declension are undoubtedly more anecdotal and more "kinetic" than those of Mlle de Scudéry, Mme de Lafayette, the *Galerie*, or Crébillon and Duclos, but their quality of narrative is deceptive, since whatever is recounted tends not toward "metonymic" extension, but rather the "metaphoric" encompassment and combination of all traits related to one entity. It is through a series of arrested, total metaphors that La Bruyère puts his world in such a position that he can evaluate it with the principles of Cartesian clarity:

> La règle de Descartes, qui ne veut pas qu'on décide sur les moindres vérités avant qu'elles soient connues clairement et distinctement, est assez belle et assez juste pour devoir s'étendre au jugement que l'on fait des personnes. (365)

La Bruyère performs a "demystification" of experience by giving it hard mental outlines, and his portraiture is in fact the direct antecedent of the novelistic portraits of Crébillon and Duclos.

La Bruyère's collection, then, is a book of total knowledge about society. He may, as Barthes suggests, be the last moralist to embrace total man within one volume: the later eighteenth-century will need the thirty-three volumes of the *Encyclopedia* because its focus has enlarged beyond *mondanité*.[36] And yet the example of the *Encyclopedia* is irrelevant to the continuing enterprise of those intent to describe man-in-society. To them, worldliness remained subject and medium, and La

---

Lafond, "Les Techniques du portrait . . . ," *CAIEF*, p. 144, and the discussion of his article, pp. 274-75). But all portraiture of the individual, we have seen, seeks the typological and socially classifiable, and La Bruyère's "characters" seek the particular, revealing trait. To most of his contemporaries, in fact, the only distinction between portrait and character was in the assumption that the former had a real model, and even this distinction loses its pertinence when we are dealing with novelistic personages.

[36] Barthes, p. 225.

Bruyère's collection remained an example and a source book. These were, basically, the memorialists and the novelists. And before returning to the novelists, it is perhaps worth appending a footnote within the text about another kind of book of total knowledge, conceived at this time and executed later: the *Mémoires* of Saint-Simon.

Saint-Simon is particularly interesting in our context because he carries to the point of exasperation the processes of observation, penetration, and assessment central to the literature of worldliness. Like Nemours at certain moments of *La Princesse de Clèves*, Saint-Simon becomes pure *voyeur*, as in the famous passage describing the death of the Grand Dauphin. "Il ne fallait qu'avoir des yeux," he begins, and he unfolds the problem of trying to veil his glance while reading in the eyes of others their reactions to the event: "on lisait apertement sur les visages."[37] Or the passage on the *Lit de Justice*, where his eyes "fichés, collés sur ces bourgeois superbes" (VI, 168), become the final weapon in his struggle against the *parlementaires*, the ultimate expression of his punishment of those who refused public hommage to his rank. He indeed coined the adjective *voyeux* to describe his stance in life, a stance which is the exacerbated conclusion of his extreme sensitivity to his own social and political position in the world promulgated by Louis XIV. His sense of what the *Duc et Pairs* should be, his opposition to monarchical absolutism and the elevation of the bourgeois (and the Bastards) attuned him to extraordinary powers of observation of every act, word, and gesture at the court. And since he was in fact powerless to change any matter of substance, his attention finally became obsessively fixed on the domain of manners in their most rarefied, non-utilitarian, symbolic mode—etiquette. Psychologically, he moves from an attention to etiquette as a sort of political vindication

[37] Louis de Rouvroy, Duc de Saint-Simon, *Mémoires*, ed. Gonzague Truc (Paris: Bibliothèque de la Pléiade, 1947-61), III, 815 ff.

to a devotion to etiquette for its own sake, as the final expression of personal relationships.

Yet, while Saint-Simon in many ways represents the final, slightly decadent flower of seventeenth-century worldly moralism, in his practice of the portrait he establishes his own rules, breaks with static moralistic character portrayal of the classical period and, as Erich Auerbach has decisively shown, creates a style of a particularity, visual immediacy, narrative movement, and a personal involvement that has no precedent.[38] If we think of the portrait of the Duchesse de Bourgogne:

> Régulièrement laide, les joues pendantes, le front avancé, un nez qui ne disait rien, de grosses lèvres mordantes, des cheveux et des sourcils châtain brun fort bien plantés, des yeux les plus parlants et les plus beaux du monde. . . . (III, 1159)

or his final judgment on the Grand Dauphin—"une boule roulante au hasard par l'impulsion d'autrui, . . . absorbé dans sa graisse et ses ténèbres" (III, 845)—we realize that we are in the presence of a descriptive and narrative art bolder than anything attempted by La Bruyère, closest perhaps to Hamilton's portraits in the *Mémoires du Comte de Grammont*, and quite distinct from the summary, abstract, static portraiture of Crébillon and Duclos. Saint-Simon, had he turned to the novel, might have been the French Fielding, and provided the model for a comic epic in prose. In fact, however, the novel of the first half of the eighteenth century remains closely linked to the enterprise, techniques, and language of the *précieuses* and *moralistes*.

· III ·

The idea of worldliness emerges from a systematic, closed, self-conscious society, a milieu whose closure to the outside

[38] See *Mimesis*, pp. 365-382.

world and internal publicity makes it a theater, a stage for the individual's representations of his social life, and elicits a conception of man as a voluntary artistic self-creation whose social style is the most important fact about him. The literature of worldliness develops in response to this idea, to the act on the stage as it evolved with increasing formality and self-consciousness from the Renaissance court, through *précieux* drawing rooms, to the court of Louis XIV. In France, we have argued, the *précieuses* first posited a modern ideal of social man, and first created the tools to know, represent, and evaluate man in relation to the ideal, to give meaning and significance to social life. The writers whom we can generally class as *moralistes* were animated by the same concerns, and adapted the literary methods and language forged by the *précieuses*, refined them, and imparted to them a new tone which reflects a change in the ethos of sociability, which has become centralized, absolute, prescriptive, conformist, pessimistic, and hard —which means that its language will be remarkable for what it does to its objects, the way it limits, fixes, and controls them. The *précieux* concern with distinction, definition, categorization, and totality becomes a vision intent to define man by fixing his limits. This is the kind of vision we find in Crébillon and Duclos, in their accounts of worldly experience whose interest is epistemological (knowing others) and normative (evaluating others in relation to the system in which they exist).

The period of Crébillon and Duclos was strongly marked by the classical inheritance, probably most strongly of all by the tradition of worldliness that we have described. The greatest of classical literary forms—tragedy and *comédie de caractère*—were exhausted, their inheritors reduced to sterile imitation; but the tradition of worldliness—the tone and the enterprise of the seventeenth-century's aphorisms, memoirs, portraits, and reflections—seems to have been a fruitful influ-

ence. Its spirit in fact pervades the most interesting literature of
the early eighteenth century: Montesquieu's *Lettres persanes,*
Le Sage's portraits in *Le Diable boiteux* and *Gil Blas,* Hamilton's *Mémoires du Comte de Grammont,* and the best tales of
conteurs like La Morlière, Crébillon, Voltaire, or, later, Nerciat
and Vivant Denon.

Behind all these hard-headed commentaries on the game of
social existence is, of course, a new reflective attention given
to society in this period, not yet with revolutionary intent, but
with the aim of defining, evaluating, and questioning the quality of social experience. Most of eighteenth-century literature
is in fact concerned with man's mundane existence, and a good
part of it with his social life. A penetrating assessment of man
in society is one of its essential undertakings, from Crébillon
and Duclos, as well as Montesquieu and Voltaire, to the Idéologues, who would codify in scientific language the psychological system we have seen at work in these novelists and in
the *moralistes,* and who would erect into scientific methods
of investigation their perceptive tools. Indeed, a few sentences
chosen from the Idéologue P. F. Lancelin show what a remarkable continuity there is from the court treatises of
the early seventeenth century to these philosophers of worldly
comportment:

> Pour tirer parti des gens, il faut étudier et connoître à
> fond leur caractère, leurs foibles, etc., épier les occasions, les
> saisir, et ne jamais rien brusquer: pour cela, il faut être doué
> d'un esprit très délié, très flexible. . . .
>
> Pour bien se conduire en société, on est souvent réduit à
> feindre: alors il faut, en pénétrant adroitement dans le carac-
> tère des autres, faire en sorte de rester toujours impénétrable:
> on peut tout penser, mais il faut s'habituer à ne dire et à
> ne faire que ce qui peut nous être utile sans nuire à personne,

et taire tout ce qui pourroit choquer l'amour-propre toujours irascible de nos semblables.[39]

The vocabulary and the whole system to which it refers are evidently still in place, ready for transmission to a contemporary novelist who knew and admired the whole tradition of
worldliness, and will be the final term of our study, Stendhal.

Related to this attention to society—and especially to the
enterprise of novelists like Crébillon, Duclos, and Marivaux—
is the renascence of social life in the 1720's and 1730's. Under
Louis XIV, sociability had been more and more centralized
within a court system, and when the austere last years of his
reign eclipsed courtliness, no important groups outside the
court continued its traditions. Decline continued under the Regency, when there was no real court. Regeneration came from
la ville rather than *la cour*; there was a new flourishing of
Parisian salons, societies dedicated to the art of conversation,
the appreciation of women, and the science of manners. First
in the drawing room of Mme de Lambert, then in the "bureau
d'esprit" of Mme de Tencin—centers, as we shall have occasion
to see, of a new *préciosité*, a new attempt to refine the concepts and vocabulary of sociability—both socialites and men of
letters (La Motte, Fontenelle, Montesquieu, Duclos, Helvétius,
Marivaux, to name only the most famous) gathered to polish
their wits. The result was a fruitful interchange which has
been described by the Abbé Voisenon: the *mondains* gained
much-needed instruction, whereas for the writers, "ce fut
l'usage du monde qui leur donna le coloris et qui leur apprit
que les grâces de la négligence l'emportent parfois sur un style
desséché par l'exactitude."[40] The quotation may incidentally

---

[39] P. F. Lancelin, *Introduction à l'analyse des sciences* (Paris, 1802),
II, 129, 128. I am indebted for these quotations to the perspicacity and
generosity of Victor Brombert.

[40] Picard, *Les Salons Littéraires*, p. 150.

indicate how a provincial bourgeois like Duclos could so quickly attune himself to the style of the best conversation, and write of worldly experience in the tone we associate with social mastery.

With the rebirth of social life, the new critical attention toward social experience, and the exhaustion of the major literary genres of the seventeenth century, the early eighteenth century marks the novel's coming of age: it has often been remarked that this was the one literary form that advanced in the eighteenth century. The classical literature of worldliness had been largely a literature of fragments—reflections, aphorisms, portraits, a literature static rather than kinetic, couched in terms which reflected its aim to fix and define. The novel was not, of course, considered a "serious" genre; it was mainly women—especially the *précieuses*—who were freer from the obligation to conform to the hierarchy of literary forms, who exploited its possibilities; gentlemen, especially aristocrats, did not want to be confused with bourgeois scribblers (the professional writer being in the nature of a superior domestic). The gentlemen tended to talk rather than write, and when they wrote, it was in the fragmentary forms of conversational wit. The novel as a mature and serious form emerges with Mme de Lafayette because she works, not from what was most obviously "novelistic" in Mlle de Scudéry—what we would call most "conventional"—but from what was most profoundly dramatic: the interplay of characters in a structured social system. This drama was implicit in the enterprise of moralists and *précieuses* from its inception, and it is from the worldly *moraliste* tradition that Mme de Lafayette absorbs and modifies what is best in *Le Grand Cyrus*. And it is a worldly *moraliste* novel that she provides as a legacy to the eighteenth century.

Some distinctions are necessary here. One must recognize that *roman*, to authors and readers at this period, suggested the *romanesque,* and there were probably more adventure stories and melodramatic tales published than anything else.[41] The "novel of worldliness" is both a fraction of the total novelistic production of the period, and a more limited (and esthetically more significant) phenomenon than the general body of "literature of worldliness" to which it belongs. There were at this period specific forms of the novel that lent themselves particularly well to an exploration of the experience of worldliness. There was the epistolary novel, made popular by Guilleragues' *Lettres portugaises* (1669), illustrated by Crébillon, Mme Riccoboni, Mme Élie de Beaumont and others; its relation to the forms of social intercourse is evident. There was the *nouvelle historique,* whose early development in Segrais, Saint-Réal, Mme de Villedieu and Mme de Lafayette we glanced at, and which continued, aided by an ever-increasing interest in history, to account for a substantial number of books in which there is usually an attempt to show the relation of private manners—those of the great and powerful—to public events.[42] Most important, there was the novel-as-memoir, the form exploited with greatest success by Crébillon, Duclos, and Marivaux, and appropriate to a novel of worldly experience because of its inherent structural distance between mature, worldly narrator, and young, inexperienced protagonist: a structure where the two terms of the narrative are both the same and different, the gap to be overcome between them the very subject of the story which, while it develops through dramatic encounters, necessarily tends toward a final stasis, a total metaphor of one person's social life. This form is used with success

[41] For a bibliography and classification of the novels published in this period, see S. Paul Jones, *A List of French Prose Fiction from 1700 to 1750* (New York, 1939).

[42] On the importance of this fiction, and its relation to history, see Georges May, "L'Histoire a-t-elle engendré le roman? Aspects français de la question au seuil du siècle des lumières," *Revue d'Histoire Littéraire,* LV, 155-76.

by many of the more interesting novelists of the period—Mme
de Tencin, Mme Riccoboni, Prévost[43]—but the superiority
of Crébillon, Marivaux and (to a lesser extent) Duclos seems
to me clear: it is they who most effectively create a drama of
manners in fictions of dramatized social discoveries and evaluations. This must be our justification for dwelling upon them
and not others.

Everything we have said about the kind of novel they write,
and about the tradition from which it derives, suggests that
some generally accepted notions about the "rise of the novel"
need revision. The common arguments that "realism" in the
novel derives from the picaresque, the burlesque, or more
precisely from the comic epic inheritance of Fielding from
Cervantes, or else (a more persuasive view, I think) from Richardson's patient detailings of private experience, should be
qualified. For the first novels where an image of society, a consciousness of society as a system of values, forces, choices, is a
decisive factor, and hence an object of the novelist's efforts at
rendition, derive directly from the *moralistes*, and indirectly
from a tradition of worldly literature which can be traced back
to the Renaissance court. This tradition has nothing to do with
picaresque or burlesque fiction, or with the mock-epic convention: indeed, as we saw, the literature of worldliness has a very

---

[43] It should be noted that Prévost's *Mémoires d'un homme de qualité
qui s'est retiré du monde* has been set in a false perspective by modern
criticism because it is usually read only in its seventh and last volume,
the *Histoire du Chevalier des Grieux et de Manon Lescaut*, the arche-
typal romantic tale. In fact, *Manon Lescaut* is an addendum which forms
a sort of "double plot," in the sense that William Empson gives the
term in *Some Versions of Pastoral*: an alternative ending to the main
plot, which in this case concerns the Marquis de Rosemont and Nadine,
a young Eyptian girl whom his tutor forces the Marquis to renounce
because she is not of his social "quality." This plot ends in victory for
the forces of social conformity and polite manners, whereas the story of
Des Grieux is an illustration of what happens when one has no tutor and
breaks through all moral restraints, to end up in Louisiana rather than
le monde.

different relation to classical epic, and implies a very different reinterpretation of heroism from that we find in the picaresque, constructed on the rogue, the adventurer, the outsider to whom Society is an object of observation instead of a medium of self-enactment. And the original novels of worldliness considerably antedate Richardson, whose example in fact, as we shall have occasion to see, gives another direction to the novel. Hence when Ian Watt, in his excellent study of eighteenth-century English fiction, *The Rise of the Novel*, feels obliged to state:

> In France, the classical critical outlook, with its emphasis on elegance and concision, was not fully challenged until the coming of Romanticism. It is perhaps partly for this reason that French fiction from *La Princesse de Clèves* to *Les Liaisons dangereuses* stands outside the main tradition of the novel. For all its psychological penetration and literary skill, we feel it is too stylish to be authentic. In this Madame de Lafayette and Choderlos de Laclos are the polar opposites of Defoe and Richardson, whose very diffuseness tends to act as a guarantee of the authenticity of their report, whose prose aims exclusively at what Locke defined as the proper purpose of language, 'to convey the knowledge of things,' and whose novels as a whole pretend to be no more than a transcription of real life—in Flaubert's words, 'le réel écrit.'[44]

we may feel that, although he is surely right about the "main tradition of the novel" as it later came to be understood, his words apply only to a certain novel; that he is neglecting an important convention and tradition.

"Le réel écrit" is in fact a phrase that may point to different conventions. If it is taken to mean the detailing of the material circumstances, the "things" of man's existence, the *épaisseur*

[44] *The Rise of the Novel* (3rd edition; Berkeley and Los Angeles; University of California Press, 1962), p. 30.

de vie surrounding him, this has undoubtedly been at the center of the evolution of a certain kind of novel, from Richardson to Balzac to Joyce to Robbe-Grillet. But in the portrayal of human social relationships, the novel of manners where emphasis falls on the social and moral question "how to be," the evolution, indeed the whole question of descent, is far less clear. One may see the origin of such a novel in the *moraliste* concern for right definition and assessment of worldly behavior; its first successful exploitation in Mme de Lafayette, then in Crébillon, Duclos, and Marivaux; its subsequent high points in Laclos, Jane Austen, Stendhal, Henry James and Proust. The emphasis of historical scholarship has fallen too exclusively on the evolution of external realism, the realism of situation and detail, and not enough on the various stages in the creation of a psychological and moral realism in the representation of man's worldly behavior, the classical sense of the *vraisemblable*.[45]

The modern novel must deal in things, in particulars, because the particular world described in each novel is fragmentary and specialized, and hence must be made visually, sensibly real to a reader who does not necessarily participate in it as ethos and system, who does not necessarily live by his con-

[45] Vivienne Mylne, in *The Eighteenth-Century French Novel: Techniques of Illusion*, argues that "illusion," rather than *vraisemblance*, is the governing esthetic principle in the novel of this period. But I think she is confusing the formal presentation of the novel (as memoir, bundle of letters, true "history," etc.) with its techniques for presenting character and action: the latter still are governed by the concept of *vraisemblance*, whereas the former may indeed be illusionistic, *trompe l'oeil*—though Miss Mylne is rather naive in assuming that the eighteenth-century public was "taken in" by such devices: they were conventional devices, and the enlightened literary public at least knew it, a point to which we shall return in discussing Rousseau. A more subtle argument about the uses of illusion is made by Frédéric Deloffre in "Le Problème de l'illusion romanesque et le renouvellement des techniques narratives entre 1700 et 1750," *La Littérature narrative d'imagination* (Colloque de Strasbourg) (Paris, 1961).

sciousness of it. Richardson, writing in a country where the middle classes early asserted a right to their interpretation of life, and to the novel, may have been the first novelist to need the particular in this sense. With French novelists like Crébillon and Duclos, for whom the World is still one, instead of a concern with the particular we have a search for generality and rightness of an analytical and normative language; their realism depends not on a description of a society, but reflection of the moral consciousness of Society in its point of tangency with the individual. They are concerned with the question of what it is like to live in society, and their approach to the subject is not that of detailing what meets the eye— this would be the view of an outsider for whom good society is only one possible zone of existence, the view of the interloper, the Balzacian hero-as-parvenu—but rather of defining the interplay of social representations, manners and motives, that they find there. Their realism is not of texture, but of tone, attitude, and judgment.

It is evident that the emphasis on the particular of the "Balzacian" novel is related to a novelistic manner that valorizes the "metonymic": as Jakobson asserts, the style of Realism and Naturalism is essentially metonymic, following the path of contiguous relationships, sliding from one particular to another, and the characteristic trope of the realist is synecdoche, which names the general through the particular, and achieves its total effect through linkage by creating a chain of particulars.[46] Crébillon and Duclos, like Mme de Lafayette and the *moralistes*, do not depend for their effects on narrative movement and the creation of a sense of passing time. Rather, their novels resolve themselves into scenes which represent and summarize aspects of human experience in society more than they advance the action—into conversations, and portraits, forms

[46] See "Two Aspects of Language and Two Types of Aphasic Disturbances," *Fundamentals of Language*, p. 78.

that arrest action and fix life in order to permit final knowledge, evaluation, and transmutation of all the particulars of reality into a language valued for its precision, generality, abstraction, and its power of synthesis into total metaphor.

Historically, we must give this form of social "realism" precedence over the "Richardsonian" or "Balzacian" mode, for *worldliness* is in fact a literary object before *realism* in our modern acceptation. Roland Barthes, who contrasts "mondanité" with "réalisme politique" (a term which I think he takes to include any literature which refers us to the total organization of the polis) suggests both this precedence and the continuing attraction of worldliness when he argues:

> Avant que la littérature se posât la question du réalisme politique, la mondanité a été pour l'écrivain un moyen précieux d'observer la réalité sociale tout en restant écrivain; la mondanité est en effet une forme ambiguë du réel: engagée et inengagée; renvoyant à la disparité des conditions, mais restant malgré tout une forme pure, la *clôture* permettant de toucher au psychologique et aux moeurs sans passer par la politique; c'est pourquoi, peut-être, nous avons eu en France une grande littérature de la mondanité, de Molière à Proust. . . .[47]

It is this phenomenon, this literary object which permits a realism which does not proceed through the fragmented details of the real to reach totality, but in fact starts from a given ethical totality, that here interests us—the enterprise of novelists to render the experience of worldliness.

Such an enterprise, we have seen, precisely depends on the existence of an exact, elegant, and general language of psychological and moral analysis (opposed to Watt's language of diffuseness), as well as the constituted, closed, and ordered society which alone can create such a language and give it mean-

[47] Barthes, p. 227.

ing—just as the language gives the society meaning and significance. Hence the original novel of worldliness as we have delineated it was, and at this period of history could only have been, a French phenomenon. The importance and possibilities of the form have to some degree been suggested; its ideological dimensions and historical dynamics need to be more closely examined, but not until we have given close attention to the structure and texture of what is probably the finest novel of this period, Marivaux's *La Vie de Marianne*.

MARIANNE IN THE WORLD

L A SCIENCE du coeur humain, Marivaux argues in a letter to the Academy, is one that all must learn in order to take part in the great confrontation that is social life. This science has no special school:

> C'est la société, c'est l'humanité même qui tient la seule école qui soit convenable; école toujours ouverte, où tout homme étudie les autres et en est étudié à son tour, où tout homme est tour-à-tour écolier et maître.
>
> Cette science réside dans le commerce que nous avons tous, et sans exception, ensemble.[1]

Society is seen as a vast stage where one studies others playing their roles, and is in turn studied by them, where knowledge of the way people behave in social encounters is necessary to further the essential business of life, which is simply living together, partaking of the commerce of society. And it is notable that this letter to the Academy, while ostensibly an essay on Corneille and Racine, develops into a demonstration of the necessity of a novel of manners.

Marivaux, in many ways the most original literary mind of

---

[1] "Réflexions sur l'Esprit Humain, à l'occasion de Corneille et de Racine" (Letter to the Académie Française, 24 August and 24 September 1749), *Oeuvres complètes de M. de Marivaux* (Paris: Chez la Veuve Duchesne, 1781), XII, 86. The second part of the Letter was not included in the Veuve Duchesne edition but was uncovered by Frédéric Deloffre in the *Mercure de France*, and is available, along with the first part, in Mario Matucci, ed., *Marivaux narratore e moralista* (Naples, 1958).

the period we have been discussing, prepared himself for the
novel of manners through a series of apprenticeships, not only
in the theater, but also (the case with many major novelists)
as parodist—doing pastiches of Homer, Fénelon and the adventure novel—and as moral essayist inspired by the example
of Addison and Steele. The succession of pieces that make up
Le Spectateur François, *L'Indigent Philosophe* and *Le Cabinet
du Philosophe*, Marivaux's one-man periodicals, all turn on his
chosen role of "spectator." He is constantly diverted by his
random wanderings in society, and his ability to unmask and
render its characters was to give him the title of "the modern Theophrastus." The gallery of characters assembled in the
pages of the *Spectateur* and its successors does in fact remind
us of La Bruyère; Marivaux seeks to capture all the typical
gestures, expressions, and figures of his society. His portraiture
expands into a manner of speculative reflections on worldly
behavior—a "morale du déshabillé," a "philosophie des vête-
ments." It also shows a marked tendency toward becoming
anecdote and even tale, most notably in "Le Voyageur dans le
nouveau monde," part of *Le Cabinet du Philosophe*, where
the "new world" is identical to Paris, but where the members
of each drawing room reveal their true thoughts and selves to
the hypersensitized protagonist. The new world is "the world
of truth," where the manners of society are immediately and
automatically decoded, its realities stripped of hypocritical
masks. Indeed, Marivaux's essayism, while faithful to the spirit
and concerns of the *moralistes*, is marked by a repeated need
to violate the form he has set for himself, to let his narrative
penchant take control and to carry what was supposed to be
illustrative incident, exemplary anecdote, to a length where
characters and situations begin to exist in their own right,
and to demand a greater amplitude of development. It is not
surprising that Marivaux should have turned to the novel of
manners, and that he should have chosen the loosest of pos-

95

sible forms for his major fictional effort, *La Vie de Marianne*. The history of a life is a form that provides the freest and fullest possible commentary on life itself.

Yet *La Vie de Marianne* is not, strictly speaking, a life at all. Although "Madame la Comtesse de***" starts with her birth, the melodramatic circumstances of her parent's death, and her upbringing by a country priest, she moves rapidly to the point that really interests her: arrival in Paris at the age of fifteen. Some eight books later, when the story of Marianne gives way to that of Mlle de Tervire, not more than two months' time has elapsed, and the reader tends to feel that the period has been even shorter. The classical principle of compression operates, and Marianne's first day in Paris is at least as busy as the night of *Le Cid*. What this suggests, it seems to me, is a confirmation of what we may already have suspected to be the case from the structure of the narrative—where an old woman looks back on her youth—and the tone of the narrative voice. Like Crébillon, whose protagonist begins to exist at age seventeen, Marivaux is exclusively concerned with Marianne's entry into the world, her début in Paris; he wants to record the emergence of Marianne's social consciousness in its given medium, good Parisian society.

This emergence is a learning only in a very special sense: Leo Spitzer very accurately characterized the novel when he called it a "roman d'explicitation" rather than a "roman d'éducation."[2] The aristocratic principle is inherent to Marianne; her primary mental structures seem to incorporate a knowledge of social structure and social forms, though submerged and obscured. Each new situation brings more of this submerged knowledge to consciousness; she consults the aristocratic principle within herself and brings to light the kind of behavior it dictates to her. She is an orphan, but the eight-

[2] Leo Spitzer, "A propos de la *Vie de Marianne* (Lettre à M. Georges Poulet)," *Romanic Review*, XLIV, No. 2 (1953), 108.

eenth-century English translation's title, *The Virtuous Orphan*, with its overtones of bourgeois self-righteousness, sounds the wrong note: never do we as readers question the nobility of Marianne's birth, and a yardstick of the characters in the novel is the length of time it takes them to recognize that Marianne's manners point to her aristocratic origins. Marivaux in some ways seems closer to Molière than to Richardson. We think of traditional scenes of recognition in which the heroine, long a prisoner of the Turks and thought to be a mere soubrette, refinds her noble father, who is of course the best friend of her noble suitor's father. Marianne never does find her parents, and the novel is too realistic to permit the final peripety of comedy, but her story is a series of interior "recognition scenes" in which Marianne discovers in herself aristocratic origins, and an allegiance to the manners of *le monde*. In this sense, the Marivaux of *Marianne* is an "essentialist," and Georges Poulet's contention that the life of Marivaux's characters is a series of fragmented moments, loss and refinding of self under the impulse of passion, does not seem to apply here.[3] What Marianne is, her essence, preëxists, but has been obscured and disguised by the circumstances that made her an orphan. The action of the novel serves to bring this essence to consciousness, for the reader and for Marianne, and the movement of the novel follows this discovery of self.

It is, then, really a literary-historical sleight of hand to see in Marianne, as many critics have done, a sort of delicate, female predecessor of the Balzacian *arriviste*: she arrives only in the sense of becoming able to take the place that is rightfully hers, surmounting the obstacles presented by a lack of positive proof that she can claim the place. Significantly, her arrival in Paris is rendered as a sort of delayed birth, an awakening to what she deserves:

[3] In *La Distance intérieure* (Paris: Plon, 1952), pp. 1-34.

Je ne saurais vous dire ce que je sentis en voyant cette grande ville, et son fracas, et son peuple, et ses rues. C'était pour moi l'empire de la lune: je n'étais plus à moi, je ne me ressouvenais plus de rien; j'allais, j'ouvrais les yeux, j'étais étonnée, et voilà tout.

Je me retrouvai pourtant dans la longueur du chemin, et alors je jouis de toute ma surprise; je sentis mes mouvements, je fus charmée de me trouver là, je respirai un air qui réjouit mes esprits. Il y avait une douce sympathie entre mon imagination et les objets que je voyais, et je devinais qu'on pouvait tirer de cette multitude de choses différentes je ne sais combien d'agréments que je ne connaissais pas encore: enfin il me semblait que les plaisirs habitaient au milieu de tout cela. . . .[4]

If one were to compare this passage with any number of arrivals in Paris in the novels of Balzac—I think especially of Lucien de Rubempré's first walk in the Tuileries, in *Illusions perdues*, where he realizes that his cravat is of a style worn only by butchers' boys—one would find that the feeling of otherness, of alienation is missing here. Instead, after an initial state of semi-awareness in which Marianne merely records impressions, there is a "douce sympathie" between the heroine and the objects that meet her attention, an instinctive knowledge of their potentialities, a warmth which comes from the sense of rightness and intimacy. This is not a question of isolated objects only, but of a whole world, the one World that counts. To explain her instinctive repugnance for Mme Dutour and her shop, Marianne tells us that "mon âme"

. . . avait le sentiment bien subtil, je vous assure, surtout dans les choses de sa vocation, comme était le monde. Je ne connaissais personne à Paris, je n'en avais vu que les rues,

[4] *La Vie de Marianne, ou les Aventures de Madame la Comtesse de****, ed. Frédéric Deloffre (Paris: Garnier, 1957), p. 17.

mais dans ces rues il y avait des personnes de toutes espèces,
il y avait des carrosses, et dans ces carrosses un monde qui
m'était très nouveau, mais point étranger. Et sans doute, il
y avait en moi un goût naturel qui n'attendait que ces objets-
là pour s'y prendre, de sorte que, quand je les voyais, c'était
comme si j'avais rencontré ce que je cherchais. (33)

The World is Marianne's vocation, her natural field of exploration, new to her, but not at all foreign; she finds what
she has been seeking without ever realizing that she has been
seeking. Hence the element of chance in the novel—the "coups
de hasard" such as Marianne's being run down by Valville's
carriage—are not inept dramatic coincidences so much as
metaphors for the fulfillment of an inescapable destiny which
decrees that Marianne, despite her start as a penniless orphan,
will meet the representatives of her class and find a place in
their society.

It is, implicitly, her natural aristocracy that enables Marianne
not only to behave with perfect propriety, but also to detect
in others behavior which is in violation of social norms. Her
reaction to the *faux dévot*, M. de Climal, is the first indication
we have of her sense of right and wrong ways of talking:

Cependant, malgré l'anéantissement où je me sentais, j'étais
étonnée des choses dont il m'entretenait; je trouvais sa conversation singulière; il me semblait que mon homme se mitigeait, qu'il était plus flatteur que zélé, plus généreux que
charitable; il me paraissait tout changé. (30)

This ability to distinguish between bordering moral states
seems to be inherent in the young Marianne, even though we
should attribute the language in which the distinctions are
couched to the mature narrator. The young woman's knowledge is instinctive, and the Comtesse de ***, Marianne grown
older and wiser, and ensconced in a sure social position, pro-

vides the explication of this instinct, recasts her reactions into the fully verbalized forms of society. An example of Marianne's instinct at work is found in her first encounter with good society, in church, where she goes to mass after donning the new dress she has received from M. de Climal. She places herself in the front of the assembly, to see and to be seen, and watches all the young chevaliers bowing, offering salutations to right and to left, less for the sake of politeness or duty than to display their pretty mannerisms:

> Et moi, je devinais la pensée de toutes ces personnes-là sans aucun effort; mon instinct ne voyait rien là qui ne fût de sa connaissance, et n'en était pas plus délié pour cela; car il ne faut pas s'y méprendre ni estimer ma pénétration plus qu'elle ne vaut. (59)

"Instinct" possesses "connaissance"; it leads to immediate understanding of the gestures of others, and to self-possession.

It should be evident that the form of Marivaux's narrative is the perfect vehicle for his theme: the mature woman looking back on her youth, on her début in society, is able to provide a hard-headed, witty, explicit commentary on what in Marianne is a groping toward clarification of worldly behavior. This "structure of the double register," as Jean Rousset has called it,[5] preserves both the first response and the later interpretation (which was much less true in Les Égarements, where the later interpretation dominated); it permits a complex play between the tone of experience and that of freshness, the worldly and the spontaneous, the lucid and the indefinite, what Marianne will become and what she is. The verbal style of the narrator stands as the end term in the evolution of Marianne's personal social style. The "double register" authorizes the narrative manner that has alternately attracted and re-

---

[5] "Marivaux et la structure du double régistre," *Studi Francesi*, No. 1 (January-April 1957), reprinted in *Forme et Signification*.

pelled critics of Marivaux: the constant play of analytical and moralistic "reflections" on the narrative. Contemporary reactions were as strong as those of later critics, and Marivaux felt obliged to come to the defense of his manner in the "Avertissement" to the second part of *Marianne*:

> La première partie de la *Vie de Marianne* a paru faire plaisir à bien des gens; ils en ont surtout aimé les réflexions qui y sont semées. D'autres lecteurs ont dit qu'il y en avait trop; et c'est à ces derniers à qui ce petit Avertissement s'adresse.
>
> Si on leur donnait un livre intitulé *Réflexions sur l'Homme*, ne le liraient-ils pas volontiers, si les réflexions en étaient bonnes? Nous en avons même beaucoup, de ces livres, et dont quelques-uns sont fort estimés; pourquoi donc les réflexions leur déplaisent-elles ici, en cas qu'elles n'aient contre elles que d'être des réflexions?
>
> C'est, diront-ils, que dans des aventures comme celles-ci, elles ne sont pas à leur place; il est question de nous y amuser, et non pas de nous y faire penser. (55)

The evocation of the *moralistes*, and the anticipated objection that the *moralistes* have nothing to do with the novel, indicates Marivaux's awareness—an awareness shared by Crébillon and most of the better novelists of the period—that *roman*, to the reader of his time, still meant the *romanesque*, the tale of adventures, that *histoire* meant the simple narrative of events, and that the novel of moral observation, despite the prestigious example of *La Princesse de Clèves*, was still the exception rather than the rule. Marivaux feels the need to close the gap between narrative and reflection, action and commentary upon the examples of human behavior found in the action. To justify his procedures, he insists that his novel is neither novel nor history, nor indeed any accepted literary genre. His argument is based on another aspect of the narrative structure he has adopted: the Comtesse de*** is giving an account of her life to a friend:

> Marianne n'a aucune forme d'ouvrage présente à l'esprit. Ce n'est point un auteur, c'est une femme qui pense, qui a passé par différents états, qui a beaucoup vu; enfin dont la vie est un tissu d'événements qui lui ont donné une certaine connaissance du coeur et du caractère des hommes, et qui, en contant ses aventures, s'imagine être avec son amie, lui parler, l'entretenir, lui répondre; et dans cet esprit-là, mêle indistinctement les faits qu'elle raconte aux réflexions qui lui viennent à propos de ces faits: voilà sur quel ton le prend Marianne. Ce n'est, si vous voulez, ni celui du roman, ni celui de l'histoire, mais c'est le sien: ne lui en demandez pas d'autre. Figurez-vous qu'elle n'écrit point, mais qu'elle parle; peut-être qu'en vous mettant à ce point de vue-là, sa façon de conter ne vous sera pas si désagréable.
>
> Il est pourtant vrai que, dans la suite, elle réfléchit moins et conte davantage, mais pourtant réfléchit toujours; et comme elle va changer d'état, ses récits vont devenir aussi plus curieux, et ses réflexions plus applicables à ce qui se passe dans le grand monde. (55-56)

Perhaps the most striking phrase here is the author's description of Marianne's life as a "tissue of events which have given her a certain knowledge of the human heart and character," for it again indicates, in its very syntax, Marivaux's attempt to establish a possible and necessary relationship between the novel and the moralist's enterprise of knowing and evaluating men. The "tissue" of events finds its justification in the illumination of men that it provides, and this illumination will come to us, perceptually, through our involvement with the tissue of events. The reflections are Marivaux's way of dealing with the complexity of commentary that social life demands, the necessary elucidation of social encounters; when he in large measure abandons them in the ninth, tenth, and eleventh sections of *Marianne*, the result, as we shall have occasion to see, is a very different sort of novel.

The structure of Marivaux's novel, his tone and style, and his attention to evaluative commentary on the narrative imply that he, like his contemporaries, will fill his novel with portraits. In fact, he was of two minds about portraiture. One of the alternatives he adopts is quite frankly and openly to paint his portraits even if they interrupt the narrative for some fourteen pages, as is the case with that of Mme Dorsin. The two central portraits—those of Mme de Miran, Marianne's adoptive mother, modeled on Mme de Lambert, and Mme Dorsin (who would undoubtedly have played a larger role than she does had the novel been finished), based on Mme de Tencin, stand out as elaborate set pieces in the middle of the novel. The portrait of Mme de Miran, the more successful of the two, begins—as did that of the *précieuse* Mlle de Scudéry, with whom Marivaux has a real spiritual affinity—with a protestation of the impossibility of achieving total accuracy:

> On ne saurait rendre en entier ce que sont les personnes; du moins cela ne me serait pas possible; je connais bien mieux les gens avec qui je vis que je ne les définirais; il y a des choses en eux que je ne saisis point assez pour les dire, et que je n'aperçois que pour moi, et non pas pour les autres; ou si je les disais, je les dirais mal. Ce sont des objets de sentiment si compliqués et d'une netteté si délicate qu'ils se brouillent dès que ma réflexion s'en mêle; je ne sais plus par où les prendre pour les exprimer: de sorte qu'ils sont en moi, et non pas à moi.
>
> N'êtes-vous pas de même? il me semble que mon âme, en mille occasions, en sait plus qu'elle n'en peut dire, et qu'elle a un esprit à part, qui est bien supérieur à l'esprit que j'ai d'ordinaire. (166)

103

This passage goes to the heart of the question of knowing and of rendering in Marivaux. Spitzer has dealt very well with the question of the "objets de sentiment" in commenting another phrase in the novel, "Je pense, pour moi, qu'il n'y a que le sentiment qui nous puisse donner des nouvelles un peu sûres de nous . . ."(22). This is not a "pre-Romantic" or "pre-Rousseauian" argument for the rapport of souls, the natural affinity of *les belles âmes* who know themselves and others instinctively, but rather an argument for the value of intuitive psychological knowledge: as Spitzer contends, this *sentiment*— which Marianne will equate with "goût naturel" in her description of Mme de Tencin's drawingroom—resembles Pascal's intuition, the cognitive faculty which constructs on the basis of intuitive perception. Spitzer talks of Marivaux's "glorification of feminine intuition, an organ of knowledge" and points out that while Marivaux may be, as Marcel Arland has called him, a "feminine soul" his theme is that of "la connaissance," the eminently masculine faculty, as our consideration of Crébillon and Duclos should have indicated.[6]

Marivaux's acute awareness of problems of knowing and rendering is suggested in his "Pensées sur la clarté du discours," where he writes:

En fait d'exposition, d'idées, il est un certain point de clarté au delà duquel toute idée perd nécessairement de sa force ou de sa délicatesse. Ce point de clarté est aux idées ce qu'est à certains objets le point de distance auquel ils doivent être regardés pour qu'ils offrent leur beautés attachées à cette distance. Si vous approchez trop de ces objets, vous croyez rendre l'objet plus net, il n'est rendu que plus grossier. Un Auteur va-t-il au delà du point de clarté qui convient à ses idées, il croit les rendre plus claires;

[6] Spitzer, p. 121.

il se trompe, il prend un sens diminué pour un sens plus net.[7]

If this passage raises many questions about the art of portraiture—and to these we will return in a moment—it finely indicates the need for, and the sense of, the style known as *marivaudage*, a style which seeks to move from a state of semi-awareness and confusion to a clear and total knowledge of the self (Silvia's "Ah! que je vois clair dans mon coeur!"), while concomitantly refusing to verbalize that which cannot be spoken without a resultant loss of subtlety. Both aspects are simultaneously present in most of Marianne's phrases: for instance, when she righteously decides to return the dress given her by M. de Climal, she reports:

> Je me levai donc pour l'aller prendre [la robe]; et dans le trajet qui n'était que de deux pas, ce coeur si fier s'amollit, mes yeux se mouillèrent, je ne sais comment, et je fis un grand soupir, ou pour moi, ou pour Valville, ou pour la belle robe; je ne sais pour lequel des trois. (132)

Evidently, the answer is "for all three," but the proportion of each, the relative dosage, remains unclear—as it must, if the analysis is to be fine and accurate. Further elucidation would bring, not true clarity, but a falsification of reality. Yet recognition of the coexistence of three motives constitutes a movement *toward* clarity and honesty to oneself. Marivaux is notoriously interested in states of semi-awareness, ambiguity of emotion, sentimental limbos; and *marivaudage* is a style elaborated to render these states while marking progress toward a greater clarity and distinction. In his plays, the style gives two people a way to work toward the truth of their emotional

[7] "Pensées sur différents sujets par M. de Marivaux: Sur la clarté du Discours," *Le Nouveau Mercure*, March, 1719.

interdependence without overt declaration (which would entail violation of selfhood and loss of freedom); in *Marianne, marivaudage* is a product of the author's effort to capture his heroine's self-explication, the intuitive knowing that brings her to self-consciousness: the emergence of her personal social style and its movement toward the style represented by the narrative tone and language. *Marivaudage* encompasses Marianne's youthful inexperience and her inherent knowledge, provides a coherent verbal equivalent for what is at first uncertain and unformed, without losing a sense of this fluidity and uncertainty, and incessantly marks the progress from indefinition to definition, from semi-awareness to clarity.

The limits to explication inherent in *marivaudage*—the refusal to destroy fluidity and subtlety by final hardness of outline—are reflected in the narrator's doubts about the possibility of total portraiture. In her insistence on the limits of knowing and the impossibility of expressing all that one feels about a person, the narrator calls into question the whole enterprise of the portrait. For the device rests on the assumption that there is such a thing as a coherent public personality, completely knowable, reducible to hard outline and arrest, and susceptible of categorization with other "characters." The difficulties of the act of cognition and rendering were recognized by Versac as by Mlle de Scudéry—one's penetration must be sharp, one's vocabulary must be exact—but they never questioned its possibility. Marianne's doubts are more radical. Her faith in intuitive knowledge, knowledge at a pre-logical and pre-verbal stage, her assertion that there are things she feels but cannot conceptualize and express (they are "en moi" but not "à moi"), undermine the portrait's effort to articulate each sign of individual psychology with the appropriate word in a code; her questionings abolish any clear distinction between exterior and interior, feelings and ideas, states of being and language, and apply the indeterminacy principle suggested in the "Pen-

106

sées sur la clarté du discours" to knowledge and expression of human psychology and comportment. There must be a simultaneous proffering and withholding of clarity, approach to and withdrawal from the object. Distance and intimacy, both required by the portrait, can never reach more than an uneasy equilibrium; knowledge, definition, and expression are not related in a simple progression, and may in fact interfere with one another. Marianne's recognition that she knows the people with whom she lives better than she can define them suggests that she knows them from living with them, from a day-to-day experiential apprehension which would be violated by transmutation into the static formality of the portrait. As well as calling for a style of *marivaudage*, this perception implies the necessity of a more evolving, progressive characterization of people, one more intimately involved in the narrative of the novel. The "metaphor" of the portrait must somehow be absorbed into the "metonymy" of the narrative—or give way to it, a process which tended to take place in Marivaux's moral essayism.

We will look in a moment at the most striking instance of Marivaux's response to this problem. In the case of Mme de Miran, the solution is more traditional: style, *marivaudage*, is made to bear the full burden of refining and subtilizing presentation of character, and this means that a lengthy portrait will interrupt the narrative for several pages. The portrait opens with a characteristically oblique approach, in a concessive clause:

Quoiqu'elle eût été belle femme, elle avait quelque chose de si bon et de si raisonnable dans la physionomie, que cela avait pu nuire à ses charmes, et les empêcher d'être aussi piquants qu'ils auraient dû l'être. Quand on a l'air si bon, on en paraît moins belle; un air de franchise et de bonté si dominant est tout à fait contraire à la coquetterie; il ne fait songer qu'au bon caractère d'une femme, et non pas à ses grâces; il rend la belle personne plus estimable, mais son visage plus indifférent: de sorte qu'on est plus content d'être avec elle que curieux de la regarder. (167-168)

In this first paragraph, Marianne plays with the opposition of beauty and goodness: Mme de Miran's beauty is not striking because of "quelque chose de si bon et de si raisonnable," and this abstract, imprecise "something" is given the active role of having hurt her charms—a traditional litotes for beauty. In an attempt to clarify and authenticate this observation, the narrator makes a general statement about the incompatibility of having "l'air si bon" and appearing beautiful. A dominant air—again this imponderable something—of "franchise" and "bonté" is contrary to coquetry: we have moved out to the moral person. But then, through the qualities this "air" suggests to us she returns to a phrase which captures a balance between the visual and the moral: "il rend la belle personne plus estimable, mais son visage plus indifférent." The paragraph ends with praise of being with Mme de Miran, rather than looking at her (or, presumably, making her portrait).

Throughout the portrait, the language situates the portraitist in society, suggests the reactions of Mme de Miran's associates to her—they do not find her beauty "piquant," they do not think of her as an object of coquetry. In the second and third paragraphs, we move explicitly to the social consequences of Mme de Miran's characteristics: "Aussi, m'a-t-on dit, n'avait-elle guère fait d'amants, mais beaucoup d'amis, et même d'amies." The fourth paragraph returns to the distinction of traits:

Or, à cette physionomie plus louable que séduisante, à ces yeux qui demandaient plus d'amitié que d'amour, cette chère dame joignait une taille bien faite, et qui aurait été galante, si Mme de Miran l'avait voulu, mais qui, faute de

cela, n'avait jamais que des mouvements naturels et nécessaires, et tels qu'ils pouvaient partir de l'âme du monde de
la meilleure foi. (168)

The adjectives ("louable," "séduisante," "galante") nouns
("amitié," "amour") and verbs ("demandaient," "aurait été,"
"l'avait voulu") pull together physical and moral qualities
in their social results; finally, the movements of Mme de
Miran's body have their direct point of departure in "l'âme du
monde de la meilleure foi," a remarkably *précieux* metaphor
which unites all three domains in one verbal structure.

Four paragraphs later, the narrator is playing with levels of
style, seeking the right verbal approach to Mme de Miran,
advancing toward analysis through a series of feints and
withdrawals:

Je ne vous dirai pas même que Mme de Miran eût ce qu'on
appelle de la noblesse d'âme, ce serait aussi confondre les
idées: la bonne qualité que je lui donne était quelque chose
de plus simple, de plus aimable, et de moins brillant.
. . . (169)

It is several paragraphs later (but Marivaux's paragraphs tend
to be brief and conversational) that Marianne moves with
serenity to a conclusion which formulates Mme de Miran's
attitudes toward others:

Une coquette qui voulait plaire à tous les hommes était
plus mal dans son esprit qu'une femme qui en aurait aimé
quelques-uns plus qu'il ne fallait; c'est qu'à son gré il y
avait moins de mal à s'égarer qu'à vouloir égarer les autres;
et elle aimait mieux qu'on manquât de sagesse que de caractère; qu'on eût le coeur faible, que l'esprit impertinent et
corrompu.
Mme de Miran avait plus de vertus morales que de
chrétiennes, respectait plus les exercices de sa religion qu'elle

> n'y satisfaisait, honorait fort les vrais dévots sans songer à
> devenir dévote, aimait plus Dieu qu'elle ne le craignait, et
> concevait sa justice et sa bonté un peu à sa manière, et le
> tout avec plus de simplicité que de philosophie. C'était son
> coeur, et non pas son esprit qui philosophait là-dessus. Telle
> était Mme de Miran. . . . (170-71)

These calm, olympian balancings of phrases point to the un-
ostentatious goodness and moderation of Mme de Miran's
character, and are the perfect vehicle for the expression of her
"morale mondaine" which, in its worldly and indulgent realism, reminds us of what we found, with a stronger and more
masculine tone, in Duclos and Crébillon. At the end of this
long exploration into the character of Mme de Miran, we re-
join the outer world, the social world, and the movement of
the novel.

The style of this portrait—its extra-subtle distinctions
among psychological entities, its metaphorical linkings of
moral, physical and social domains, its emphasis on its subject's ways of dealing with others—reminds us that *marivaudage* was considered by Marivaux's contemporaries to be a
"new préciosité." We have already suggested that this style is
related to Marivaux's particular attention to the optics of character portrayal. While Voltaire described him as a man who
"weighed nothings in spider webs," the terms of Marivaux's
scrutiny appear in fact to be fragmentations, modifications,
and refinements of the terms and categories employed by the
moralistes in the description of human personality. To understand Marivaux's portraiture, and in general the sense of his
fictional creation, we must look more closely at *marivaudage* as a total style.

Marivaux's conception of the proper stylistic level of the
novel—"une femme qui parle"—has its origins in a tradition
of fine conversation, specifically in the drawingrooms of Mme

de Lambert and Mme de Tencin, where he was a central figure. These salons (the latter succeeded the former upon Mme de Lambert's death) were, as we have mentioned, the first two gathering places of the eighteenth century, the centers of the fruitful exchange between *mondains* and men of letters described by the Abbé Voisenon. Products of the rebirth of Parisian social life under the Regency, they were dedicated to a cultivation and an exploration of social life, and to renovation of the language needed to pursue this exploration. Marivaux's description, in the novel, of the company assembled for dinner by Mme Dorsin (Mme de Tencin) indicates the ideal of style such a society proposed:

Ce ne fut point à force de leur trouver de l'esprit que j'appris à les distinguer pourtant. Il est certain qu'ils en avaient plus que d'autres, et que je leur entendais dire d'excellentes choses, mais ils les disaient avec si peu d'effort, ils y cherchaient si peu de façon, c'était d'un ton de conversation si aisé et si uni, qu'il ne tenait qu'à moi de croire qu'ils disaient les choses les plus communes. Ce n'était point eux qui y mettaient de la finesse, c'était de la finesse qui s'y rencontrait; ils ne sentaient pas qu'ils parlaient mieux qu'on ne parle ordinairement; c'était seulement de meilleurs esprits que d'autres, et qui par là tenaient nécessairement de meilleurs discours qu'on n'a coutume d'en tenir ailleurs, sans qu'ils eussent besoin d'y tâcher, et je dirais volontiers sans qu'il y eût de leur faute; car on accuse quelquefois les gens d'esprit de vouloir briller. Oh! il n'était pas question de cela ici; et comme je l'ai déjà dit, si je n'avais pas eu un peu de goût naturel, un peu de sentiment, j'aurais pu m'y méprendre, et je ne me serais aperçu de rien.

Mais à la fin, ce ton de conversation si excellent, si exquis, quoique si simple, me frappa.

Ils ne disaient rien que de juste et que de convenable,
rien qui ne fût d'un commerce doux, facile, et gai. (211-13)

The easy, uncontrived wit and elegance to which Marivaux
here pays tribute were in fact to a degree part of a special
language, like *préciosité*, invented in one milieu. Frédéric
Deloffre, in his intelligent and exhaustive study, *Marivaux et
le marivaudage*, to which any study of style in Marivaux must
be indebted, points out that the early eighteenth century, in
imitation of the classical period, accepted in principle three
levels of style: the low (or sometimes the simple), the middle,
and the high.[8] But the *Néologiques* or *Néo-précieux* centered
in the salons of Mme de Lambert and Mme de Tencin tended
to undermine this rigid hierarchy. M. Deloffre cites an interesting passage from Marmontel on the "style familier-noble,"
which Marmontel claims to be the style of conversation in
the best circles, where "le langage usuel doit être rempli de
finesses, d'allusions, d'expressions à double face, de tours
adroits, de traits délicats et subtils."[9] The description echoes
Marivaux's account of Mme Dorsin's drawing room, and also
defines the stylistic choice made by the narrator of *Marianne*.

Marivaux's language is basically inherited from the *moralistes*, and like them, M. Deloffre remarks, he conceives the
psyche "not as a single principle, but as composed of a certain
number of forces or tendencies, vanity, the passions, reason,
amour propre.[10] Thus an external event provokes reaction from
a specific internal force: Marianne says "ce n'était pas ma raison, c'était ma douleur qui concluait ainsi"(304). By this conception of the psyche, Marivaux refines on a common procedure of the *moralistes* to the point of imitating the *précieuses*:
distinction between two qualities that at first appear one, the

[8] Frédéric Deloffre, *Marivaux et le marivaudage: Étude de langue et
de style* (Paris, 1955), p. 38.
[9] Marmontel, *Élémens de littérature*, quoted by Deloffre, p. 207.
[10] Deloffre, p. 330.

distinction, as we saw in the portrait of Mme de Miran, illuminating essential definitions. The procedure often assumes
the grammatical form of the "synonymous antithesis," as in
the "plus de vertus morales que de chrétiennes" of the portrait
we quoted. Closely related is what M. Deloffre calls Marivaux's "substantive style," the favoring of a noun in place of
a verb wherever possible: "Je compris bien qu'il se fiait à moi
pour l'impunité de sa hardiesse"(88). This technique was
much in favor in the Hôtel de Rambouillet;[11] it allows one to
represent the substantive by a pronoun in subsequent phrases,
hence prolonging without weightiness the development of a
nuance. It also permits qualification of the substantive by an adjective which more precisely defines the nuance sought—M.
Deloffre cites a sumptuous example from one of the comedies: "Passer sa vie dans la flatteuse conviction de ses charmes."
This is like Marivaux's incessant recourse to adjectives which
qualify states of being: "c'était du noble, de l'intéressant, mais
de ce noble aisé et naturel . . ." (256).

These, and other, stylistic details belong to Marivaux's effort
to make the language of the *moralistes* a more subtle, flexible,
and dramatic tool of analysis. Just as there was a drama inherent in Crébillon's use of a certain narrative structure, there
is a drama implicit in *marivaudage*—a drama of knowing and
rendering people, of approach to and retreat from the object, of
movement and change to obtain the right perspective to
show the object to its best advantage, clear and distinct,
yet not so fixed that its life and reality are "diminished"
(to use Marivaux's term in "La clarté du discours"). And if we
return to the portrait of Mme de Miran, we find that *marivaudage* has the effect of breaking the stasis of the form, giving
it a new fluidity and indefiniteness. The sinuous sentences

---

[11] See Molière's satire of this procedure in *Les Précieuses ridicules*,
scene vii: "Gardez vous d'en salir la glace par la communication de
votre image"; quoted by Deloffre, p. 319.

which add progressive modifications of perspective, the constant redefinition of concepts and traits, the incessant verbal movement around a "character" may seem to point to greater precision and finality of outline than we find in La Bruyère, but they in fact dissolve hardness and fixity, to leave us with a greater sense of movement, flux, and indefinition: something which is, again, more like what we found in Mlle de Scudéry, before the *moralistes* had so rigidly codified the signs and language of social intercourse. At the end of the portrait of Mme de Miran, we feel less a total definition and assessment than something more particular, subtler, and more dramatic, what she is "like."

Such is surely the impression Marivaux has sought to give. In protesting, on the verge of portraying Mme de Miran, "I know the people with whom I live better than I could define them," the narrator is expressing not only the impossibility of putting into words the totality of one's knowledge about another person, but also the inevitable gap between the definition the moralist finds necessary and the way we actually come to feel about people: the eternal disjunction between portrait and subject, the static, clear, and total form, and the living, opaque person whom one apprehends gradually, in fragments, and not entirely consciously. Taken a step further, Marianne's doubts would lead to the radical position of a modern novelist like Nathalie Sarraute, who has maintained that there is no such thing as a complete "character," rounded, fixed, and coherent. This clearly is not Marivaux's position, however: nothing indicates that he believes any less than the *moralistes* in the total reality of the subject he is analyzing into its component parts. His skepticism extends rather to the knowing and rendering of others, and the portrait seems to him incompatible with the nature of worldly experience. Yet the portrait is also necessary, and this returns us to the drama of Marivaux's style: narrative alone is not sufficient to reach the "clarity of dis-

course" he seeks in his account of social life. He needs his reflections, and he needs a form that brings an arrest of movement and permits commentary and definition. Making a portrait without destroying the fluidity of life becomes a moment
of moral drama: one must not permit violation of the subject's
freedom and reality—a violation that was of course actively
sought by Versac (as by the *moralistes*) but which negates
Marivaux's *précieux* ideal of social life, an ideal embodied in
Marianne's resistance to those who would fix and dispose of
her as an ambitious orphan, who deny her freedom of self-
definition. In response to a double ideal of clarity and freedom, Marivaux's whole novelistic manner is, like *marivaudage*,
fabricated of simultaneous motions in different directions, arresting and advancing, retreating, then moving forward again.

The portrait of Mme de Miran, like that of Mme Dorsin,
naturally breaks narrative movement and detaches itself as a
complete and closed verbal structure because it is consciously
a celebratory set-piece. Marianne is summing up, casting in
a final formulation all her feelings about her benefactress (and
Marivaux, historically, is doing the same thing for his benefactress Mme de Lambert). In a case where it is important to
integrate revelation of character into the flow of narrative,
and into the evolution of Marianne's apprehension, Marivaux
manages a more fluid and (to the modern sensibility) "novelistic" solution, without, however, really abandoning the language or even the premises of the portrait.

The question of the character of M. de Climal dominates
the second and third books, and again becomes central in the
fifth. The first apprehension of M. de Climal is a simple,
rapid, visual first impression when the Père Saint-Vincent
takes Marianne to see him:

Je montai donc dans le carrosse avec ce religieux, et nous
arrivons chez la personne en question. C'était un homme de

cinquante à soixante ans, encore assez bien fait, fort riche, d'un visage doux et sérieux, où l'on voyait un air de mortification qui empêchait qu'on ne remarquât tout son embonpoint. (26-27)

Despite the wit of the narrator, there is nothing here that violates the first impression, no expression of inner states except that "air" which is immediately graspable. Climal interrogates Marianne with a mixture of hardness and religious unction ("Que les desseins de Dieu sont impénétrables!") which we, along with Marianne, take to paint the picture of a somewhat insensitive man of society who has turned to good works in an advanced age. In fact, Marianne's reaction leads us, in what will turn out to be an irrelevant train of response, to take offense at his parade of "devotion," the pompous "trappings" with which he surrounds his act of charity. The first awareness that Climal may not be what he seems comes confusedly, when Marianne is overcome with shame and resentment, as she accompanies her benefactor to Mme Dutour's:

Cependant, malgré l'anéantissement où je me sentais, j'étais étonnée des choses dont il m'entretenait; je trouvais sa conversation singulière; il me semblait que mon homme se mitigeait, qu'il était plus flatteur que zélé, plus généreux que charitable; il me paraissait tout changé. (30)

This paragraph moves along the line of Marianne's awareness, while still retaining a vocabulary of static abstractions: we go from "zealous" to "flattering," from "charitable" to "generous," from an impression which breaks through her state of semi-consciousness to the final distinct impression that he is "completely changed." A sample of his conversation is our confirmation that she is right; and when he stops to buy her gloves to protect her pretty hands, and helps her on with them, she blushes "par un instinct qui me mettait en peine de ce

que cela pouvait signifier"(31): She adds: "Toutes ces petites particularités, au reste, je vous les dis parce qu'elles ne
sont pas si bagatelles qu'elles le paraissent," a way of alerting
us that a picture of Climal is gradually being created from an
agglomeration of small details.

Climal's return, a few pages later, begins with a play on
words, as he asks for Marianne's "amitié" and she responds
with "gratitude"; he wants her to have with him "une cer-
taine liberté," to which she replies that she has too much "respect." Finally, Climal

> . . . me prit la main, qu'il baisa d'une manière fort tendre;
> façon de faire qui, au milieu de mon petit transport, me
> parut encore singulière, mais toujours de cette singularité
> qui m'étonnait sans rien m'apprendre, et que je penchais
> à regarder comme des expressions un peu extraordinaires de
> son bon coeur. (35)

By this point, the perceptive and worldly reader is aware of
Climal's designs; Marianne's sense of what is acceptable social
style and what is not has been alerted, but her astonishment
has not yet given way to a clear apprehension of what Climal
is. By the time he buys her a dress and fine linen, her awareness—that he loves her, that this is the reason for his gifts,
that she thus should return the gifts—is complete; however,

> Je consultais donc en moi-même ce que j'avais à faire; et à
> présent que j'y pense, je crois que je ne consultais que pour
> perdre du temps: j'assemblais je ne sais combien de réflex-
> ions dans mon esprit; je me taillais de la besogne, afin que,
> dans la confusion de mes pensées, j'eusse plus de peine à
> prendre mon parti, et que mon indétermination en fût plus
> excusable. Par là je reculais une rupture avec M. de Climal,
> et je gardais ce qu'il me donnait. (39)

Marianne's awareness of the situation dictates a right course of action, but in order not to be obliged to herself to follow this course, she pretends to a lack of clarity which does not really exist; she purposely attempts to jam the analytical machinery which, from the evidence, would produce a clear and distinct idea.

She has become a hypocrite with herself, so that in the following conversation with Climal, the comedy is no longer generated from verbal misunderstandings, but from her attempt to escape through a pretended failure of comprehension embodied in intentional confusion of terms:

> J'ai peur de vous aimer trop, Marianne, me disait-il; et si cela était, que feriez-vous? Je ne pourrais en être que plus reconnaissante, s'il était possible, lui répondais-je. Cependant, Marianne, je me défie de votre coeur, quand il connaîtra toute la tendresse du mien, ajouta-t-il, car vous ne la savez pas. Comment, lui dis-je, vous croyez que je ne vois pas votre amitié? Eh! ne changez point mes termes, reprit-il, je ne dis pas mon amitié, je parle de ma tendresse. Quoi! dis-je, n'est-ce pas la même chose? Non, Marianne, me répondit-il, en me regardant d'une manière à m'en prouver la différence; non, chère fille, ce n'est pas la même chose, et je voudrais bien que l'une vous parût plus douce que l'autre. (41)

Despite Marianne's excellence at choosing words which sound like those of Climal but have a very different signification in the social code, this comedy cannot last. By her next meeting with Climal, this time under the gaze of Valville, she is mentally qualifying him as a "frank hypocrite" and "my tartuffe." By the time of his declaration, she has advanced another step, for through Valville's love she has come to know how vile Climal's sentiments are:

> . . . les tendresses du neveu, jeune, aimable et galant, m'avaient appris à voir l'oncle tel qu'il était, et tel qu'il méri-

tait d'être vu: elles l'avaient flétri, et m'éclairaient sur son âge, sur ses rides, et sur toute la laideur de son caractère.[12]

But definition does not go farther than this; Climal is allowed to speak for himself in an insinuating speech reminiscent of the original Tartuffe.

When his declaration is interrupted by the arrival of Val-ville, Climal abandons Marianne, and disappears from sight for a considerable length of time. Although we now know how to evaluate Climal, and so does Marianne, there has as yet been no attempt to present a balanced estimate of him, no formal portraiture. This eventually comes—as, given his false social role, it could only have come—from Climal himself, in his deathbed confession and public reparation, before Marianne, Valville, and the Père Saint-Vincent. He begins, "Vous me croyiez un homme de bien, et vous vous trompiez, mon père, je n'étais pas digne de votre confiance"(246), and moves to this peroration:

> . . . je ne l'ai secourue, en effet, que pour tâcher de la sé-duire; je crus que son infortune lui ôterait le courage de rester vertueuse, et j'offris de lui assurer de quoi vivre, à condition qu'elle devînt méprisable. . . . j'ai été non seule-ment un homme détestable devant Dieu, mais encore un malhonnête homme suivant le monde. . . . (249)

We recognize the equilibrated phrases, the clear distinctions of actions and motives, of the portrait; Climal finds the lan-guage that corresponds to his behavior, and from a point nearly removed from life, he gives a total image of his vileness.

But this final portrait-confession arrives as the culmination

---

[12] *La vie de Marianne*, p. 108. M. Deloffre remarks in a footnote that the figurative expression *la laideur de son caractère* was excused in the original edition by italics, indicating the newness of Marivaux's quite *précieux* psychological and moral metaphor.

of a natural inductive process, of finding someone out from gesture, tone, and language, whereas the formal portrait implies a prior judgment and processing of all the facts. In the case of Climal, Marivaux has made compilation of the hard, exterior lines of the portrait follow the processes of consciousness as they operate in the world: totality and fixity come only after one has sorted out and understood fragmentary first impressions, the combination and stasis of metaphor is the end term of a metonymy, movement from one detail to another. In this sense, Marivaux seems more modern and more fully committed to the novelistic than his predecessors and contemporaries like Crébillon and Duclos; his psychological drama reminds us of Henry James or Proust. *Les Égarements du coeur et de l'esprit* dealt "realistically" with the question of first and subsequent social impressions, but there was little sense of movement toward discovery, since the narrator—and his pedagogical surrogate, Versac—continually measured the gap between what Meilcour saw and what in fact was. Marianne as narrator avoids such judgments, and the coming to consciousness of first our, then Marianne's, feelings about Climal creates a drama of consciousness, something which *Les Égarements,* a drama of evaluations and confrontations involving formal acts of consciousness and cognition, never pretended to be. And one should note, finally, that even after Climal's self-portrait, after he has laid himself bare and been left to die, a doubt and an uneasiness subsist: was he a consummate Tartuffe all his life, or was this an isolated case of lechery? Despite the precise analytical and moralistic language he applies to himself, Climal remains a somewhat shadowy figure, his suggested dimensions extending beyond what we can distinctly sum up and articulate. And this, we feel, is as it should be.

The "question of Climal" is one of the first of the social encounters that test Marianne in the novel, and some of the others demonstrate even more conclusively Marivaux's fine

novelistic sense of the drama to be found in questions of
social prerogative and rank, in the tensions of worldly behavior.
The most telling examples occur near the middle of the novel,
where it seems to me that Marivaux is at his best, his narrative
and commentary in finest balance, and his heroine at her most
interesting stage—accepted by Mme de Miran, betrothed to
Valville, and an heiress, but not yet presented to society as a
whole in these roles. Mme de Miran plans ways to prepare society for Marianne's marriage, to forestall its shock effect; as a
first step, Marianne is made to pass as the daughter of a provincial acquaintance of Mme de Miran's. In this role she becomes the friend of Mlle de Fare, and with Valville she accompanies Mlle de Fare and her mother on a country week-
end. The episode begins as a pastoral interlude, with a stroll
in the woods where the two girls and the "tender" Valville
play at flight and pursuit in a style reminiscent of Watteau.
The intrusion which is to destroy this idyll is carefully prepared for: Marianne the next morning is for the first time
dressed by a *femme de chambre*:

> Quelque inusité que fût pour moi le service qu'elle allait me
> rendre, je m'y prêtai, je pense, d'aussi bonne grâce que s'il
> m'avait été familier. Il fallait bien soutenir mon rang, et
> c'était là de ces choses que je saisissais on ne peut pas plus
> vite; j'avais un goût naturel, ou, si vous voulez, je ne sais
> quelle vanité délicate qui me les apprenait tout d'un coup,
> et ma femme de chambre ne me sentit point novice. (262)

At this moment of utter social ease, of graceful attainment to
her natural rank, Marianne is confronted with the woman to
whom she was so recently apprenticed, Mme Dutour, who has
come to sell linen at the château. The voice of Mme Dutour,
lively, vulgar, comic breaks in upon the elegant and mannered conversation to which we have been treated:

Eh! que Dieu nous soit en aide! Aurais-je la berlue? N'est-ce pas vous, Marianne? . . . Eh! pardi oui, c'est elle-même. Tenez, comme on se rencontre! . . . Comme la voilà belle et bien mise! Ah! que je suis aise de vous voir brave! que cela vous sied bien! Je pense, Dieu me pardonne, qu'elle a une femme de chambre. Eh! mais, dites-moi donc ce que cela signifie. . . . (263)

To this recognition, Marianne can make no response; her usual mechanism of reaction to the members of good society who will not recognize her aristocracy cannot operate here: "A ce discours, pas un mot de ma part; j'étais anéantie." Valville, entering at this moment, is himself reduced to silence, for he seizes instantly "toutes les fâcheuses conséquences de cette aventure"(264).

The reaction of Mlle de Fare—who is, for the reader as for Marianne, the important person to watch, the one whose judgment counts—is the instinctive response to an embarrassing social encounter: she simply denies the possibility of what Mme Dutour has asserted:

Doucement, madame Dutour, doucement, dit alors Mlle de Fare; vous vous trompez sûrement, vous ne savez pas à qui vous parlez. Mademoiselle n'est pas cette Marianne pour qui vous la prenez. (264)

And again, when Mme Dutour insists:

Mais, encore une fois, prenez garde, madame, prenez garde, car cela ne se peut pas, dit Mlle de Fare étonnée. (264)

But the angered Mme Dutour continues her rambling proof, including such damaging items as, "elle ne sait qui elle est; c'est elle qui me l'a dit aussi. . . . cette enfant, qui a été ma fille de boutique. . . . Pardi! je suis comme tout le monde, je reconnais les gens quand je les ai vus." The end of her tirade brings reaction first, significantly, from the servant, who begins to laugh behind her hand and leaves the room. Marianne dissolves in tears, Mlle de Fare lowers her eyes and says nothing.

At this point of collapse, of silence, of breakdown of the social machinery, Valville reacts with a mixture of threat and persuasion:

> Eh! madame allez-vous-en, sortez, je vous en conjure; faites-moi ce plaisir-là, vous n'y perdrez point, ma chère madame Dutour; allez, qu'on ne vous voie point davantage ici; soyez discrète, et comptez de ma part sur tous les services que je pourrai vous rendre. (265)

Mme Dutour, in her apologetic self-justifications, only makes things worse:

> Hélas! je suis bien fâchée de tout cela, mon cher monsieur; mais que voulez-vous? Devine-t-on? Mettez-vous à ma place.
>
> Eh oui, madame, lui dit-il, vous avez raison, mais partez, partez, je vous prie. . . . (265)

Mme Dutour gone, Mlle de Fare turns to Valville: "Monsieur de Valville, dit alors Mlle de Fare, qui jusqu'ici n'avait fait qu'écouter, expliquez-moi ce que cela signifie."

Her words are sharp and to the point, for it is the "signification" of the scene as a revelation about social place and social imposture that must be explained.[13] Mlle de Fare, fond as she may be of Marianne, cannot let herself be imposed upon, and one senses an edge in her voice, a perfectly polite accusation of deceit. Valville throws himself at her feet to make his

---

[13] Ironically, Mme Dutour has used the same word upon seeing Marianne with the *femme de chambre*. That a Mme Dutour can ask for an explanation from Marianne makes it of course inevitable that Mlle de Fare will demand one.

explanation, which turns on the fact that there is strong evidence that Marianne's parents, though unknown, were noble —"elle est fille de qualité, on n'en a jamais jugé autrement"; he ends by requesting that she keep the secret, and that the *femme de chambre* be won over without delay. Mlle de Fare, convinced, meets Valville's hard-headed estimation squarely: "C'est à quoi je songeais, dit Mlle de Fare, qui l'interrompit, et qui tira le cordon d'une sonnette, et je vais y remédier"(267). She and Valville then embark upon a concerted effort to rewrite the history of the past half hour; they begin with intimidation of the *femme de chambre*:

> Approchez, Favier, lui dit-elle du ton le plus imposant; vous avez de l'attachement pour moi, du moins il me le semble. Quoi qu'il en soit, vous avez vu ce qui s'est passé avec cette marchande; je vous perdrai tôt ou tard, si jamais il vous échappe un mot de ce qui s'est dit; je vous perdrai: mais aussi je vous promets votre fortune pour prix du silence que vous garderez. (267)

Her tone is a good example of what Henry James once called the "soft hardness of good society," the tone of worldly realism. Responding to the drama that Marivaux has created in the social confrontations of this scene, one wonders why critics have so exclusively concentrated on Marivaux's *sensibilité*, and why none has even talked about this episode which is so central to the action and meaning of the novel.

The consequences of this confrontation are large: although Favier promises silence, she has already talked; this becomes apparent with the entry of Mme de Fare:

> Je ne la saluai que d'une simple inclination de tête, à cause de la faiblesse que nous étions convenus que j' affecterais, et qui était assez réelle.
>
> Mme de Fare me regarda, et ne me salua pas non plus.

Est-ce qu'elle est indisposée? dit-elle à Valville d'un air indifférent et peu civil. Oui, madame, répondit-il; nous avons eu beaucoup de peine à faire revenir mademoiselle d'un évanouissement qui lui a pris. Elle est encore extrême-ment faible, ajouta Mlle de Fare, que je vis surprise du peu de façon que faisait sa mère en parlant de moi.

Mais, reprit cette dame du même ton, et sans jamais dire mademoiselle, si elle veut, on la ramènera à Paris, je lui prêterai mon carrosse. (274)

Mme de Fare's refusal to address herself directly to Marianne, her references to her daughter's guest in the third person, and without the use of *mademoiselle*, are our sure indications that the scene with Mme Dutour has not been cancelled in time. In listening to this voice, we, like the characters, divine what has happened; the drama is once again at the level of our and the characters' apprehension, from tone of voice and choice of terms, of what Mme de Fare knows and what her reaction has been.

The continuation of the scene confirms these indications that Mme de Fare has completely changed her attitude toward Marianne as a result of Mme Dutour's revelations. After her mother leaves, Mlle de Fare turns toward Valville, troubled, not yet willing to believe what has happened, and asks if it can be true that Favier has already spoken:

N'en doutez point, reprit Valville . . . mais n'importe, [Mme de Fare] sait l'interêt que ma mère prend à made-moiselle, et tout ce qu'on peut lui avoir dit ne la dispense pas des égards et des politesses qu'elle devait conserver pour elle. D'ailleurs, à propos de quoi en agit-elle si mal avec une jeune personne pour qui elle a vu que ma mère et moi avons les plus grandes attentions? (276)

Valville's argument is that the protection accorded Marianne by himself and his mother—and it is hinted that they are of a slightly better family than Mme de Fare—should have sufficed to determine Mme de Fare's behavior, and to prevent her from altering her manner with Marianne. He is willing, at this point of crisis, to use his social importance as a weapon, pushing his insistence to the very limits of the acceptable: "tâchez d'obtenir qu'elle se taise; dites-lui que ma mère le lui demande en grâce, et que, si elle y manque, c'est se déclarer notre ennemie, et m'outrager personnellement sans retour" (277).

This scene of social confrontation, where Marianne, in her first independent venture in society, is faced with the public revelation of what she socially has been before her adoption by Mme de Miran, and with the refusal of a representative member of good society to accept her new social position as the natural and rightful one, to a large extent determines the entire subsequent development of the novel. Its most immediate effect is to destroy Mme de Miran's plan for having Marianne pass as the daughter of a provincial aristocrat, and to nullify this excuse for Valville's marrying her. A new solution is needed, and that found by Mme de Miran is, from a social point of view, thoroughly realistic:

> Il ne s'agit, dans cette occurrence-ci, que de me mettre à l'abri de la censure. Il suffira que rien ne retombe sur moi. A l'égard de Valville, il est jeune; et quelque bonne opinion qu'on ait de lui, il a beaucoup d'amour; tu es la plus aimable figure du monde, et la plus capable de mener loin le coeur de l'homme le plus sage; or si mon fils t'épouse, et qu'on soit bien sûr que je n'y ai point consenti, il aura tort, et ce ne sera pas ma faute. Au surplus, je suis bonne, on me connaît assez pour telle; je ne manquerai pas d'être très irritée, mais enfin je pardonnerai tout. Tu entends bien ce que je veux dire, Marianne, ajouta-t-elle en souriant. (285)

This conception of what individual behavior must be is clearly determined by consciousness of the image projected by society. Mme de Miran plays on the system's nuances: a parent cannot permit her son to choose an ill-matched wife, but his clandestine marriage to a charming though unknown girl would not necessarily be unpardonable. Mme de Miran, in any case, given her public reputation for soft-heartedness, could be expected to pardon such a marriage and her friends would therefore eventually accept it. The measure of ruse and deception involved are the necessary sacrifice to good taste and the *bienséance* of this system, and Marianne accepts them as such. The blazon of *La Vie de Marianne* could be said to be *amor omnia vincit* only in a limited and extremely realistic sense, for love is constantly discovering its quality as an institution, its tangency with manners.

Mme de Miran's new solution, however, immediately meets an obstacle with the intervention of that foundation of the social system, the Family. Marianne is quietly abducted and brought before an assemblage of relatives gathered about the titular head of the family, who is nothing less than the Minister and who implies that, had the abduction been unsuccessful, he would not have hesitated to employ a *lettre de cachet*. The family, through the revelations of Mme de Fare, has learned what Marianne is (more pertinently, what she is not), and discovered the projected marriage with Valville; the minister proposes to her an immediate and irrevocable choice between the convent and marriage to a young *petit-bourgeois* named Villot, to whom the minister would promise rapid advancement. As Marianne waits to appear before the assembled family, there occurs a pre-arranged meeting with M. Villot. He immediately takes up the wrong tone, even in his gestures, approaching Marianne "d'un air plus révérencieux que galant." His declaration betrays his inherent unfitness as a husband for Marianne:

... si ma personne ne vous était pas désagréable, voici une rencontre qui pourrait avoir bien des suites; il ne tiendra qu'à vous que nous ayons fait connaissance ensemble pour toujours; et pour ce qui est de moi, il n'y a pas à douter que je ne le souhaite. Il n'y a rien à quoi j'aspire tant; c'est ce que la sincère inclination que je me sens pour vous m'engage à vous dire. .... Certainement je ne m'attendais pas à tant de charmes; et puisque nous sommes sur ce sujet, je prendrai la liberté de vous assurer que tout mon désir est d'être assez fortuné pour vous convenir, et pour obtenir la possession d'une aussi charmante personne que mademoiselle. (308-09)

This picture of banality comically striving for elegance, these *façons* in language, ever on the verge of falling into pure absurdity, are qualified by Marianne as "pesantes et grossières," and she has no difficulty in rejecting M. Villot. When he continues to list his advantages, declaring that "at this moment, I think only of getting ahead in life," something that Marianne, in spite of all her disadvantages, has never done, her reaction is to feel ill. The workings of her innate sense of aristocracy renders the proposal of such a suitor an object of disgust.

The effect of the scene with M. Villot, immediately preceding the encounter with the minister, is to give us a renewed sense of Marianne's force, the impetus that will not let her stop at any compromises in her movement toward her rightful place in the world. As Spitzer remarks, Marianne defines herself by saying no at the right times to proposals that would violate her freedom and arrest her flight.[14] When she says no, she is free—like Isabel Archer before her marriage to Gilbert Osmond—to continue the process of "explicitation" of what she is, and what she may become. Liberated from Villot, she

14 Spitzer, p. 106.

confronts the minister and the other important members of
the family with a free pride:

> Elle est vraiment jolie, et Valville est assez excusable, dit
> le ministre d'un air souriant, et en adressant la parole à
> une de ces dames, qui était sa femme; oui, fort jolie. Eh!
> pour une maîtresse, passe, répondit une autre dame d'un
> ton revêche.
> A ce discours, je ne fis que jeter sur elle un regard froid
> et indifférent. (317)

While this lady refuses Marianne the title of mademoiselle,
the minister is polite but imposing and inflexible:

> Vous n'avez ni père ni mère, et ne savez qui vous êtes, me
> dit-il après. Cela est vrai, monseigneur, lui répondis-je. Eh
> bien! ajouta-t-il, faites-vous donc justice, et ne songez plus
> à ce mariage-là. Je ne souffrirais pas qu'il se fît, mais je
> vous en dédommagerai; j'aurai soin de vous; voici un jeune
> homme qui vous convient, qui est un fort honnête garçon,
> que je pousserai, et qu'il faut que vous épousiez; n'y con-
> sentez-vous pas? (317)

Marianne, knowing well what is meet for her, does not consent and the scene is interrupted at this point by the melodramatic arrival of Valville and Mme de Miran, who have discovered her fate and have come to save her. Once again, however, the reader feels that the melodramatic intervention—it
is not yet a rescue, for the minister must still be persuaded to
free Marianne—is in the nature of an external confirmation, an
objective actualization of her internal moral victory, her resistance to the demands of the minister. The minister's "do your-
self justice" has, in fact, been accomplished.

Mme de Miran's plea to the minister returns to the argument that Marianne's evident nobility of style can only be the
result of high birth: "Elle ne le doit ni à l'usage du monde, ni

à l'éducation qu'elle a eue, et qui a été fort simple: il faut que cela soit dans le sang; et voilà à mon gré l'essentiel"(329). But the minister, for all his polite attention, insists on the hard aristocratic viewpoint that birth, as a question of family, is nothing without proof:

> J'avoue, reprit-il, qu'il est probable, sur tout ce que vous nous rapportez, que la jeune enfant a de la naissance: mais la catastrophe en question a jeté là-dessus une obscurité qui blesse, qu'on vous reprocherait, et dont nos usages ne veulent pas qu'on fasse si peu de compte. Je suis totalement de votre avis pourtant sur les égards que vous avez pour elle; ce ne sera pas moi qui lui refuserai le titre de mademoiselle, et je crois avec vous qu'on le doit même à la condition dont elle est; mais remarquez que nous le croyons, vous et moi, par un sentiment généreux qui ne sera peut-être avoué de personne; que, du moins, qui que ce soit n'est obligé d'avoir, et dont peu de gens seront capables. C'est comme un présent que nous lui faisons, et que les autres peuvent se dispenser de lui faire. Je dirai bien avec vous qu'ils auront tort, mais ils ne le sentiront point; ils vous répondront qu'il n'y rien d'établi en pareil cas . . .
> (331-32)

This masterly presentation of the worldly view, the attitude that society is a corporation which demands cards of identity, and may justifiably be ruthless toward those who do not have them, denies the possibility of Marianne's ever moving to a clearly-defined place in the world: the obscurity of her birth can never be dispelled by her self-definition. The minister concludes with an avowal of disbelief in the projected marriage between Marianne and Valville, and a repeated offer of M. Villot. This once more rejected, the note of irritation returns to his voice: we understand that he will not surrender to the idea of the marriage, and will continue to exercise both familial and civil authority over Mme de Miran until Marianne is safely disposed of.

This is the setting for Marianne's renunciation of love and Valville. Her speech is long, a *tirade* in all the forms, and for a moment comes precariously close to melodrama. But as she draws to a close, her sense of reality asserts itself, and we understand that she, too, is acting upon a calculation of the ways of the world:

> . . . nous ne changerons pas le monde, et il faut s'accorder à ce qu'il veut. Vous dites qu'il est injuste; ce n'est pas à moi à en dire autant, j'y gagnerais trop; je dis seulement que vous êtes bien généreuse, et que je n'abuserai jamais du mépris que vous faites pour moi des coutumes du monde. (336)

Her victory comes when the minister, exercising the supreme social prerogative, declares her liberated and the foregoing scene nonexistent: "Allez, mademoiselle, oubliez tout ce qui s'est passé ici: qu'il reste comme nul. . . ." This result, it seems, is determined by his recognition of Marianne's awareness of the limits to action in the world imposed by social usages; because of her social realism, he can no longer think of her as a romantic little adventurer.

If I have dwelt upon this scene, and upon the encounter with Mme Dutour at Mme de Fare's, it is because they are perhaps the most important scenes of social recognition in the novel. Recognition in two senses: Marianne's recognition of her own place in a certain world, with a concomitant realization of the enormous difficulties of making this view accepted; and others' recognition, either ironically, as with Mme de Fare, or straightforwardly, as with the minister, of her right to place. Both scenes render decisive moments in Marianne's experience of the world, its realities, prejudices, system, and code, and she comes out of both with an increased sense of the limitations to freedom of action within the social structure, and also a further "explicitation" of her affinity with the social upper class. Hence a working out of her relationship to the world (taken always in its limited sense, *le monde*) is at the same time an illumination of her mysterious birth and of her character, so dependent on this birth. The long involved movement toward self-awareness which we found embodied in the style called *marivaudage* depends on this exterior movement toward social definition.

This needs some clarification, for it in large measure contradicts the typical estimate of this novel, which holds, substantially, that love and a virtuous heart conquer all in a world where people mostly turn out to have good souls which can be moved by scenes of *tendresse* and *sensibilité*.[15] Such a view depends in part on the misconstrual of *sentiment* mentioned earlier: *sentiment* and *coeur* are usually equivalents of intuition in Marivaux, and the attempt to see their frequent use as an indication that "sensibility" has replaced intellectual comprehension seems to me based on the mistaken application to Marivaux of irrelevant concepts of literary history, a point our later consideration of Rousseau will give us the opportunity to clarify. There are scenes in the novel where everyone's eyes are wet with tears, but upon examination these seem to result more from an almost Cornelian "admiration" than from pathos. One must indeed understand Marivaux's *précieux* ideal: it does not valorize sentimentality, but rather cultivation

[15] For one of the fullest statements of this position, see Ruth Kirby Jamieson, *Marivaux: A Study in Sensibility* (New York, 1941). For this critic, Marianne is a parent of "the Julies and Saint-Preuxs of the next generation" (p. 35), one of those whose "quivering sensibility to impulses from within and impressions from without makes it hard for him to disguise his feelings and distasteful to restrain them" (p. 34). She finds that "Marianne, a penniless orphan of unknown parentage, presents a touching picture of virtue in distress, a fact of which she is well aware" (p. 41). Such remarks distort the novel through the adoption of a mistaken historical perspective.

of sociability, respect for the freedom of others, refinement of gesture and language. Those who have overemphasized the "feminine" side of Marivaux, the delicate analyst of the passions, the exponent of the female heart, need to be reminded that his analysis moves toward a masculine knowing, a hard-headed evaluation of others. Spitzer's comments once more seem apt here: "Je ne suis pas loin de penser que le sujet de la *Vie de Marianne* n'est pas tant le récit de telle vie de jeune fille intrépide, mais la glorification *du principe féminin dans la pensée humaine* se révélant et dans la vie et en littérature."[16] This indicates the proper balance between the romantic and feminine, and the intellectual. And Spitzer's own essay suggests that he might more accurately have said "feminine *and aristocratic* principle," capturing in one formulation the intellectual and the social forces that govern Marianne's coming to consciousness.

The traditional view of Marivaux—perhaps first fully articulated by Sainte-Beuve,[17] and unfortunately still current today—would have him a pretty and somewhat vapid miniaturist, whereas in fact, as I have tried to show, he has a strong sense of an operative milieu which is not just a backdrop for Marianne's struggle toward recognition and self-recognition, but a real antagonist and contributing dramatic agent. Social recognition and self-recognition are mutually dependent. It is in contact with the world that Marianne realizes what her principles of belief and action must be, and what her social place should be: the two, we are constantly reminded, are not separable. The scenes of social recognition—either when Marianne recognizes her affinity with good society, as in her excursion to church, or when her lack of provable gentle birth exposes her socially, as at Mme de Fare's—are also scenes of

[16] Spitzer, p. 122.
[17] See his study of 1854, reprinted in *Les Grands Écrivains français: XVIIIᵉ siècle, Romanciers et moralistes* (Paris: Garnier, 1930).

self-recognition. We follow the emergence of Marianne's sense of a correct personal style as a function of her consciousness of the image projected by society: an emergence toward a fully formed social style which is (as in *Les Égarements*) constantly held before us in the narrator's verbal style, its use of a language of polite sociability. Marivaux's theme forces him to write a novel where the image of society is of primary importance and the drama of social manners the central substance, the medium in which we see Marianne act. As a result, the reader, like the heroine, is forced to respond to the drama of manners, to the tones of voice, gestures, and mannerisms of different characters, the moral systems which these personal styles seem to imply, and how they are correctly or incorrectly related to the structures of society. The reader's consciousness and Marianne's operate in response to the same stimuli, and undergo the same initiation into a complex and difficult world.

This is not to say that Marivaux is, any more than Crébillon, a "realist" in the pictorial, representational sense of the term. There is little description or detail, and surely the attempt to make an early realist of Marivaux on the basis of the scene of the quarrel between the coachman and Mme Dutour is misguided. The contemporaries who found it "low" and "unworthy" were the heirs to those who, with Boileau, rejected Molière's farces, and the scene reminds us much more of *commedia dell'arte* than of Zola. Marivaux's *Advertissement* to the second part indicates his attitude: he suggests that readers may be interested to see "ce que c'est que l'homme dans un cocher, et ce que c'est que la femme dans une petite marchande"(56). The emphasis falls on the general and classical concept, man, and attention is directed toward a peculiar mutation thereof. As with Crébillon and Duclos, the "realism" of Marivaux is to be sought elsewhere, in language and gesture, in his worldliness, in his sense of the necessity to create an image of society as the medium in which the characters operate. The characters themselves, we have seen, conceive their own behavior to be determined by society as they imagine it; hence, society as an entity, a structure, a code, an ideological force, is bound into the texture of the novel.

Perhaps this kind of consideration about the nature of *La Vie de Marianne* is the right starting point for an investigation of a perennial question, why Marivaux abandoned his novel. The publication of *Marianne* was spread over a long period of time: Part I appeared in June 1731; Part II in February 1734; Part III in November 1735 (all of *Le Paysan parvenu* having been published between *Marianne* II and III); Part IV in March-April 1736; Part V in September 1736; Part VI in December 1736 (do we find in this unusual rapidity of composition a confirmation of the feeling that he is writing with ease, and at the top of his bent, in the fifth and sixth parts?); Part VII in February 1737; Part VIII in January 1738; Parts IX, X, and XI in March 1742. Marivaux lived another twenty-one years after completing the last installment. Perhaps, faced with a novel that took eleven years to reach the length in which we know it, we should simply conclude that Marivaux became more and more bored with the composition, finally to drop it altogether; he always found it difficult to complete his projects, and it is perhaps unreasonable to try to deduce more specific motivation from the novel itself. Yet such deduction may possibly be illuminating.

It would seem that the form of the fictional "life" in fact does not correspond to the profound subject of *Marianne*, although it usefully provides the structure of the double register so effectively exploited by Marivaux. Like Crébillon, Marivaux is really interested only in a moment of his character's life, the moment of confrontation with worldliness. This confrontation provokes Marianne's "explicitation" of self, and it is her movement into a state of lucid social consciousness and self-consciousness that forms the true subject of the novel. Marianne is not, we have said, an *arriviste*; yet she evidently has a point of departure, a state of semi-awareness, a kind of personal limbo, and a point of arrival: total clarification of what she is. In a sense, with her as with Climal, the movement goes from fragmentary discoveries of traits of character to the total portrait, clarity and hardness of outline in the knowledge and expression of self. This movement has virtually been completed after the scene at the minister's: recognition, both internal and external, cannot go much further, and there is no need to complete the "life."

Yet Marivaux was evidently unwilling to wind up his story with Marianne's marriage to whatever Count it was (we know that she will become "Madame la Comtesse de***"); the novel continues with Valville's infidelity, which permits some ironical comments on the typical novelistic hero, ever an example of perfect virtue, and also procures to Marianne another proposal, from an elderly and wise man of quality. But Marivaux cannot indulge in melodramatic complications—which would violate the ethos of his story—and things begin to languish, to the point that Marianne considers taking the veil. This provides Marivaux the opportunity for recounting the "histoire d'une religieuse" which he has been promising for some time. But the nun's story, ostensibly told to warn Marianne of the dangers of entering the convent without a sure vocation, goes on for three books (IX-XI), and when the novel breaks off, Mlle de Tervire is still an adolescent, and not visibly even about to become a nun. Clearly, she has captured Marivaux's imagination, and he has been unable to use her life's story merely as a cautionary tale. If what interested him in Marianne was a process of coming to self-awareness of a heroine whose true nature has been accidentally obscured (as Silvia's is by disguises in *Le Jeu de l'amour et du hasard*—indeed, the situation is common to most of Marivaux's heroines), then the point where that heroine is explicitly and publicly totally determined is the point where the author loses interest in her fate and turns to another character, whose destiny is as yet indeterminate.

One cannot agree with Spitzer's contention that the story of the nun would, in a finished version of the novel, have fitted into the whole like a nut in a nutshell: the sense of indeterminacy is simply too strong in these last three sections and the illustrative value of the tale too obscured. Marivaux has in fact discovered a new theme and a new style of narration along with his new heroine. Already at the outset of the sixth part, responding to the pressure of his critics. Marivaux had announced that he would moderate his "babble" and make fewer reflections, holding to a purer narrative style(273). In fact, however, Parts VI, VII, and VIII are only slightly less crammed with reflections, moral commentary on the action, than the earlier parts, and their tone is similar. Where the change does come is with the nun's story. Here we have a new narrator, and her story, so far as we know it, is not the account of an entry into the world, nor an "explicitation" of one's essential social being.

Mlle de Tervire is of noble birth; she begins with this consciousness, and is aware of the outrage done to her nobility when she is abandoned by her mother and stepfather. She becomes a virtuous and heroic orphan, the victim of paternal neglect and the evil offices of relatives and their associates. To save herself, she agrees to marriage with an unpleasant old *dévot*, only to have the marriage ruined by the scheming of the old gentleman's heirs, who contrive to have her surprised with a young abbot in her room in the middle of the night before the wedding. She resists, is rehabilitated by deathbed confessions, then is adopted by a great-aunt, whom she reconciles with her long-lost son, only to fall in love with this son's son, and to be mistreated by his mother upon the great-aunt's death.

The adventure is complicated, pathetic, and told in what is for Marivaux an extremely lean and rapid narrative style. Marcel Arland finds in this narrative the height of Marivaux's art,[18] and one can see why: it sounds more modern, more like a novel of the nineteenth century—*Jane Eyre*, perhaps. It is in these sections that one can talk validly of sentimentality: the pathetic tableau which Mlle de Tervire arranges to promote the reconciliation of Mme Dursan and her estranged son should have appealed to that lover of Greuze, Diderot. One might, I suppose, account for this change by an historical view of the evolution of taste over the last years in which Marivaux was composing his novel; but this is not necessary. The fact is that Marianne's life, the concepts and experiences it brings into play, does not call for a sentimental view of existence, whereas that of the abandoned Mlle de Tervire, the true prototype of a later day's David Copperfields and Jane Eyres, demands an exploitation of the melodrama of misfortune. Here, if anywhere, I suspect, would be the place to start an investigation of the debated subject of Marivaux's influence on Richardson. Without becoming involved in that question, and without refusing admiration to the nun's tale, one may easily find that this part of the novel is irrelevant to the story of Marianne, and distinctly less interesting.

The way in which it is less interesting can perhaps help us locate with greater precision the sources of our pleasure in the main section of *Marianne*. We remarked that the celebrated "reflections" are lacking in the nun's story, and this implies a lack of interest in the enterprise of moral commentary on social comportment. In fact, the nun's story is rather "behavioristic," in the sense of the term that we might apply to

[18] Marcel Arland, *Marivaux* (Paris: Gallimard, 1950), pp. 87-91.

Flaubert or Zola: the event, without commentary, and the emotion surrounding it, become central, the question of social relationships, gestures within a system, secondary. The view of the *moraliste*, the penetrating glance directed at the characters of society, is not absent, but its use no longer seems to be the same, for we are involved with an heroic and presumably tragic individual destiny, and this absorbs our interest. We no longer follow the process of a self-definition which is necessarily also a social definition; our interest is rather in a persecuted girl's resistance to various evils. It is perhaps true that Mlle de Tervire gains an aura of freedom from the lack of narrative commentary—and this narrator is not, after all, a mature and worldly-wise woman, but still young and sheltered in the convent—but there is a loss of the drama created by an interplay of narrative and assessment, metonymy and metaphor, in the earlier sections: the tension caused by the complex advances and retreats of *marivaudage*, the drama inherent in an attempt to find the correct point of observation for realizing "clarity of discourse." The style of the nun's tale is such that it has no place for the exciting social confrontations of *Marianne*, the scenes which to me make the book one of the first totally successful novels of manners.

This term, which we have taken to mean the dramatization of individual self-representations within a strongly-felt social context, applies only marginally, it seems to me, to Marivaux's other major novelistic effort, *Le Paysan parvenu*. This novel which M. Arland cleverly sees as a parody of *Marianne*, seems to have its source more in the tradition of Furetière and Scarron than in the worldliness of the *moralistes*.[19] This is evident not only from the subject-matter—the peasant Jacob's advancement through a semi-calculated gigoloism—but from the tone as well. The narrative voice is really an experiment:

[19] Arland, p. 73. On the sources of *Le Paysan parvenu*, see Deloffre's introduction to his edition of the novel (Paris: Garnier, 1959).

Marivaux has attempted to capture a sort of peasant frankness and directness, a sensible, good-natured, practical, unsophisticated view of the world, a compound of ingenuousness and roguery. It is difficult to maintain the unity of such a tone, and in fact we find a range of expression from classical satire to bourgeois sentimentalism. How successful Marivaux was, however, can be measured by the dismal failure of the *Suite anonyme*, where the tone becomes utterly sentimental and the reflections merely silly. Marivaux is evidently torn between genres: in a sense, the lowness of the subject excludes any manner other than the burlesque, yet he wants to treat seriously and realistically the subject of the social climber. The real achievements of the book are in its early pages, in the picture of the two *dévotes*, the demoiselles Habert, and their household. The novel becomes progressively less interesting, and breaks off after the fifth part.

Although it, too, is unfinished, *La Vie de Marianne* is in most respects a more successful book, perhaps because it is less experimental. The novel of experience in good society, the novel of worldliness as we have described it, could call upon a larger body of accepted attitudes and procedures than a serious account of a lower-class milieu, which enters most novels of the period—as, indeed, it enters *Marianne* in the episode of the coachman—only as comic incident. The novel of worldliness calls upon a certain sophisticated reader's knowledge of what people are like in society, and takes as its very theme the question, "What *are* these people like?" Typically, as we have seen, it renders the process of discovery, of enlightenment, of penetration into the truth about people, and for this exploration it uses tools first fashioned for society's auto-analysis in the literary and worldly drawing rooms. Necessarily, this theme and these tools imply what was in fact their starting point, but which has too often been neglected by critics: a conception of society as a system where certain forms of behavior are valued; where there is a code assigning specific meanings to psychological signs, gestures, and language; where man's public being is the exclusive focus of attention. It follows that this kind of novel will create an image of society as a force which patterns men's lives; more pertinently, we may say that such a novel renders an imagination of society—the image of a system and a code as it impinges upon and determines the individual ethos and style. It is in rendering this imagination that *La Vie de Marianne* is so successful: human emotions, the progress of the individual's life, personal relationships are unremittingly and profoundly examined in relation to the demands made by the imagination of society. In this novel, Marivaux holds constantly before himself the question of what people together are like, what they demand of each other, and what they do to one another.

La Vie de Marianne stands as the fullest exemplification of a theme and a novelistic manner which we have been attempting to describe and situate in these chapters. Of all the early eighteenth-century novelists who turned their attention to worldliness, Marivaux is probably the greatest. He shares with Crébillon and Duclos a perfect mastery of society and the kind of individual behavior it elicits, and he has refined their traditional tools of analysis to provide a more subtle presentation of character. Like Crébillon, he is a dramatist of social comedy; and more even than Crébillon, he is acutely aware of all the social implications of every human encounter. Despite its hesitations and its incompletion, *La Vie de Marianne* provides the fullest, richest, most complex view of the world and its manners at least until 1782 and the publication of *Les Liaisons dangereuses*. But between the masterpieces of Marivaux and Laclos the question of worldliness as ethic and literary viewpoint is singularly complicated by the challenge of Jean-Jacques Rousseau.

ALCESTE, JULIE, CLARISSA

IN 1758, Jean-Jacques Rousseau published the *Lettre à Monsieur d'Alembert sur les spectacles*. His attack on the "plot" of the Encyclopedists to establish a theater at Geneva is also a general polemic against the whole tradition of worldliness in literature as we have described it. More even than the *Discours sur les arts et les sciences,* the *Lettre à d'Alembert* embodies Rousseau's opposition to the attitudes and instruments of the *moraliste* tradition and indicates the need he felt for another kind of novel, an example of which he was to provide a few years later with *La Nouvelle Héloïse.*

Much of the *Lettre à d'Alembert* is, of course, concerned with the theater as an institution in the polis: Rousseau attempts to demonstrate that the artificial representation of the passions within the framework of a gregarious social institution is incompatible with the democratic, protestant, rural simplicity of Genevan democracy. His argument echoes the religious condemnation of the theater which had found its most eloquent spokesman in Bossuet, but he goes beyond the churchmen's emphasis on the theater as a corrupting stimulant to an audience's morals, and directs his attention to the important question of point-of-view as morality, the implied normative standards of a work of art, and these he finds, in his discussion of comedy, to be substantially those of the indulgent worldly observer, and hence condemnable.

In the main, it will be remembered, Rousseau dismisses the moral effect of tragedy—the manners it represents are too far removed from ours for it to be anything but amoral (though he later seems to contradict himself in discussions of *Zaïre* and *Bérénice*)—and turns his attention to comedy, where the manners are more nearly real and the criticism of life more direct. His foremost example is Molière, whom he admires above all other comic playwrights, but whose comedies are nonetheless "a school of vices" where goodness and simplicity are ridiculed, where the "honnêtes gens" merely discourse while the scoundrels act and are almost always triumphant. Molière's allegiance to ruse and disingenuousness, his satire of virtue, are, significantly, felt most strongly in the greatest of the *comédies de caractère, Le Misanthrope*. Molière, argues Rousseau, wished only to please the public; his theme was determined by its taste:

> Il n'a donc point prétendu former un honnête homme, mais un homme du monde; par conséquent, il n'a point voulu corriger les vices, mais les ridicules; et, comme j'ai déjà dit, il a trouvé dans le vice même un instrument très propre à y réussir. Ainsi, voulant exposer à la risée publique tous les défauts opposés aux qualités de l'homme aimable, de l'homme de Société, après avoir joué tant d'autres ridicules, il lui restait à jouer celui que le monde pardonne le moins, le ridicule de la vertu: c'est ce qu'il a fait dans le Misanthrope.[1]

For an earlier age, and for most of Rousseau's contemporaries, there was no need to distinguish between an "honnête homme" and an "homme du monde." From the middle of the seventeenth century they were by definition the same, and socially presentable manners were morally acceptable manners. Rousseau further emphasizes his distinction by turning the "homme du monde" into an "homme de Société," which suggests a more limited and frivolous role. His discrimination be-

[1] Jean-Jacques Rousseau, *Lettre à M. d'Alembert sur les spectacles,* ed. M. Fuchs (Lille and Geneva: Textes Littéraires français, 1928), p. 48.

tween "vice" and "ridicule" reminds us that in the moralists
and novelists we discussed the two were always linked, mentioned as the joint object of the *vis comica* (see, for example,
the preface to *Les Égarements*), whereas in practice, as La
Rochefoucauld and Versac informed us, the worst vice was appearing ridiculous. To Rousseau, the "vices" which Molière's
comédies de caractère claim to expose to the audience's laughter are in fact merely "ridicules," deviations from a conformist
ethic of sociability which he rejects, hence the very opposite
of vices. The comic *charge* of Molière's plays is never moral:
his ridicule (in the transitive sense) is not a weapon against
vice, but rather the arm of vice itself, since "à force de crain-
dre les ridicules, les vices n'effraient plus"(35).

Le Misanthrope is for Rousseau indeed essentially the
satire of virtue. To his mind, Alceste is basically a good,
honest, forthright, admirable man who detests the vices of his
contemporaries, whom Molière has artificially and falsely
forced into an extravagant, ridiculous social role in order to
make his moral critique of his society appear vicious and
worthy of public censure. Against Alceste Molière set Philinte:

> Ce Philinte est le Sage de la Pièce; un de ces honnêtes gens
> du grand monde, dont les maximes ressemblent beaucoup
> à celles des fripons; de ces gens si doux, si modérés, qui
> trouvent toujours que tout va bien, parce qu'ils ont interêt
> que rien n'aille mieux; qui sont toujours contens de tout
> le monde, parce qu'ils ne se soucient de personne; qui,
> autour d'une bonne table, soutiennent qu'il n'est pas vrai
> que le peuple ait faim; qui, le gousset bien garni, trouvent
> fort mauvais qu'on déclame en faveur des pauvres; qui, de
> leur maison bien fermée, verroient voler, piller, égorger,
> massacrer tout le genre humain, sans se plaindre: attendu
> que Dieu les a doués d'une douceur très méritoire à sup-
> porter les malheurs d'autrui. (51-52)

When we recall Molière's Philinte, a man who believes that "la parfaite raison fuit toute extrémité," the attack seems extravagant. We sense an increasingly violent moral fervor as Rousseau moves from Philinte's avowed ethic of easy and sophisticated indulgence for the social behavior of his contemporaries, his belief in the necessity of a "vertu traitable" for life in society, his disillusioned aphorisms (which reminded us of La Rochefoucauld), to the chain of horrible consequences which must necessarily, in Rousseau's view, derive from the worldliness of the *moraliste*. Rousseau's violence toward this thoroughly non-violent character is not the result of a misunderstanding, but a conscious attempt to make the morality of worldliness, especially reliance on observation and refusal to take a critical attitude toward society, into a sort of criminal passivity and complicity. He understood that the traditional role of the *sage*, the moral middle ground of comedy, the viewer's surrogate, was particularly significant in the case of Philinte, the proponent of attitudes that foster sociability, the representative of worldliness, because the underlying theme of *Le Misanthrope* is in fact an apology for sociability, with all that it may entail in the way of flattery, falsity, and disguise, and a censure of unsociability, however moral its derivation. In identifying himself with Alceste, Rousseau inaugurated an interpretation of the play which gained favor with the Romantics and is not dead yet; but unlike most Romantics and some modern critics, Rousseau is quite aware that this interpretation is not in accord with Molière's intentions. Alceste's final retreat to the country (which, however fertile, was generically labelled by his generation *le désert*)[2] cannot be assimilated to Romantic pastoral; for Molière it is an extravagant, unimaginable withdrawal from civilized society. Rousseau knows that his rehabilitation of Al-

[2] Cf. a stage direction to *Le Malade imaginaire* in the 1682 edition of Molière's works: "un lieu champêtre, et néanmoins fort agréable."

ceste and condemnation of Philinte contradict Molière's point of view; his aim is to expose the falsity of that point of view, the viciousness of prescriptive, totalitarian worldliness, the literary stance and techniques it had engendered—he indeed very explicitly rejects Philinte's maxims and Célimène's portraits.

The question of *Le Misanthrope* of course partakes in a wider debate in the eighteenth century, largely if not completely begun by Rousseau, on the value of civilized sociability. Diderot, in a letter that aligned him unpardonably with the "coterie holbachique," perorated, "Adieu le citoyen! C'est pourtant un citoyen bien singulier qu'un Ermite," and Voltaire, after perusing the *Discours sur les origines de l'inégalité*, wrote to its author, "J'ai reçu, Monsieur, votre nouveau livre contre le genre humain. . . ."[3] To the Encyclopedists, and the *Philosophes* in general, rejection of citizenship in society meant rejection of all that had civilized man and made the progress of enlightening possible—all, in fact, that made life worth living. Voltaire's defense of luxury in "Le Mondain" is a facetious version of this same commitment to life in organized, refined society—life in *le monde* as it was understood by moralists and novelists of worldliness; and Diderot's *La Religieuse* demonstrates the horrible effects of separation from the civilizing effects of sociability. Rousseau, who cites with approval Alceste's thunderous reaction to Célimène's portrait-making, rejected all manifestations of worldliness in literature as well as life, and the time at which he was breaking from society to retreat to the Ermitage, developing his theory of conspiracy on the part of the *Philosophes*, was also the time when he was beginning the daydream that was to result in his novel of anti-worldliness.

[3] Denis Diderot, *Correspondance*, ed. Georges Roth (Paris, 1955), I, 233; Voltaire, *Correspondance*, ed. Theodore Besterman (Geneva, 1957), XXVII, 230.

The *Lettre à d'Alembert* is directed to the question of the theater, but its arguments by implication extend to the novel and indicate clearly both why Rousseau rejects the novel of worldliness and why he must apply his lesson of morality to his time in a form of the novel. Both the institutional, sociable aspect of the theater, and its esthetic of distance made it an impossible vehicle for his purposes; theatrical morality, the morality of make-believe, is, he argues, like the behavior of the comedian necessarily false, answerable only to the audience's desire for pleasure. And those modern plays, *tragédie bourgeoise et domestique* or *comédie larmoyante*, which tended to destroy the esthetic of distance and substitute for it a more direct moral action, a closer and more sentimental relation to the viewer (the esthetic advocated by Diderot in the *Entretiens sur le Fils Naturel*) violated the nature of the theater and succeeded merely in boring the spectator. Clearly, Rousseau's message of individualism, of private, anti-worldly morality, could only come in the form of the novel, a new kind of novel. To a degree, the model for this new kind of novel had already been given by Richardson. We will return to his contribution after having looked at Rousseau's example in *La Nouvelle Héloïse.*

Perhaps the best way to approach this novel would be to try, by an act of historical empathy, to imagine what it must have been like, in 1761, to open a novel and immediately be exposed to two voices chanting at a high pitch of emotion:

> Quelquefois nos yeux se rencontrent; quelques soupirs nous échappent en même temps; quelques larmes furtives . . . ô Julie! si cet accord venait de plus loin . . . si le ciel nous avait destinés . . . toute la force humaine. . . .[4]

[4] *Julie, ou la Nouvelle Héloïse,* ed. René Pomeau (Paris: Garnier, 1960), pp. 6-7.

Il faut donc l'avouer enfin, ce fatal secret trop mal déguisé! Combien de fois j'ai juré qu'il ne sortirait de mon coeur qu'avec la vie! (12)

Puissances du ciel! j'avais une âme pour la douleur, donnez-m'en une pour la félicité. (15)

Apart from the slenderest indications in Saint-Preux's first letter, there is no identification, no indication of situation or background; even full names are missing. We are plunged into the middle of the "letters of two lovers in a small town at the foot of the Alps," and our usual means of perception —the penetrating glance, the knowing voice of the narrator, the references to name and family, *le monde* and *la société* —are absent. Instead, there are simply two tones of voice. Before we know these lovers by any external perception, we are made to listen to them, to hear their spontaneous expression of their emotions, to live with them. We are, after a few pages, close to them, involved in their emotional situation; we feel a proximity, a warmth—and these are our knowledge of them. It is totally different from our distanced knowing of characters in Mme de Lafayette, Crébillon, Duclos, or Marivaux. As Rousseau points out in the "Préface de Julie," there is no "epistolary style" here, for his lovers "make known only themselves."

Our knowing of Julie and Saint-Preux is hence immediate and intimate. Rousseau's conception of *les belles âmes* depends on the reader's entry into the interior beings of the characters before he can, or wants to, judge them from the exterior. Instead of the distanced portrait, attempting to resolve all human characteristics into the hard outlines of a categorical moral and psychological vocabulary, we have an effort to abolish the hard exterior, to render the interior transparent. In the *Confessions*, where his entire effort is to render a total, direct, interior knowledge of himself, a knowledge not limited to the

148

social appearance, Rousseau makes the claim, "On a vu dans tout le cours de ma vie que mon coeur transparent comme le cristal n'a jamais su cacher pendant une minute entière un sentiment un peu vif qui s'y fut réfugié."[5]

An identical impression is sought in *La Nouvelle Héloïse*, for the uniqueness of Rousseau's two principal characters disqualifies the generalizing, public language of the classical moralists; Julie and Saint-Preux simply cannot be known except through a direct impression and intuition, a total transparency in relation to the reader. The first two books, especially, establish this condition: take, for example, a passage from the letter Saint-Preux writes after his possession of Julie, the letter which begins "Mourons ô ma douce amie":

Si je ne t'aime plus? Quel doute! Ai-je donc cessé d'exister? et ma vie n'est-elle pas plus dans ton coeur que dans le mien? Je sens, je sens que tu m'es mille fois plus chère que jamais et j'ai trouvé dans mon abattement de nouvelles forces pour te chérir plus tendrement encore. J'ai pris pour toi des sentiments plus paisibles, il est vrai, mais plus affectueux et de plus de différentes espèces; sans s'affaiblir, ils se sont multipliés: les douceurs de l'amitié tempérèrent les emportements de l'amour, et j'imagine à peine quelque sorte d'attachement qui ne m'unisse pas à toi. O ma charmante maîtresse! ô mon épouse, ma soeur, ma douce amie! que j'aurai peu dit pour ce que je sens, après avoir épuisé tous les noms les plus chers au coeur de l'homme! (124)

Someone who expresses himself in this manner can have no secrets from us. To a remarkable extent, the passage breaks

---

[5] *Les Confessions, Autres Textes autobiographiques,* ed. Bernard Gagnebin et Marcel Raymond (Paris: Bibliothèque de la Pléiade, 1962), p. 446. The question of "transparency," central to Rousseau's esthetics and ethics, has been brilliantly studied by Jean Starobinski in *Jean-Jacques Rousseau: la transparence et l'obstacle* (Paris, 1957).

with all the amorous rhetoric of the eighteenth century. If
one were to compare it with the most impassioned letters of
La Marquise de M***, in the novel of Crébillon, or the outbursts of Manon and Des Grieux, one would find that, while
the vocabulary here is substantially that of all eighteenth-
century novelists—abstract, scarcely metaphorical, categorical,
not free from traditional epithets—a new use of sentence
rhythms, a new musical pitch, completely transforms the
impression made. Psychology no longer appears as a codified
complex of signs translatable into language; hardness and
clarity of line have been destroyed. The gentle flux and re-
flux, the movement from the alternate exclamations and in-
terrogations of the start, the sentence that takes its rhythm
from a repeated "Je sens, je sens," through to the outbreak
of the naming of Julie, all make this a new rhetoric of
the emotions, one which, if we give it our imaginative sympathy, leads us to the very rhythms of Saint-Preux's soul.
The effect of this rhetoric, in the first two books, is to make
us consent to the unstated proposition that people who
talk and feel like this—and the feeling and speaking are one,
the passage from sensibility to word immediate—can do no
wrong. What they are, in our apprehension of them, pre-
cludes wrong. Yet, of course, this acceptation is not society's,
and Rousseau must establish both the invalidity of society's
epistemology and ethics, and the rightness of his protagonists'
moral emotionalism.

In his fifth letter, Saint-Preux exclaims:

> Nous sommes jeunes tous deux, il est vrai; nous aimons
> pour la première et l'unique fois de la vie, et n'avons nulle
> expérience des passions: mais l'honneur qui nous conduit
> est-il un guide trompeur? a-t-il besoin d'une expérience sus-
> pecte qu'on n'acquiert qu'à force de vices? (16)

This mistrust of experience reminds us of its exclusive valorization by the *moralistes*, by Crébillon and Duclos, to whom learning about society was both a means and an end. Julie, complaining to Claire about the ministrations of a former governess, also displays a dislike of experience, of initiation in the ways of men, be it merely vicarious:

> . . . pour nous garantir des pièges des hommes, si elle ne nous apprenait pas à leur en tendre, elle nous instruisait au moins de mille choses que des jeunes filles se passeraient bien de savoir. (17)

This refusal to learn by experience and precept is seconded by a rejection of moralist literature in Saint-Preux's highly selective program of study for his pupil:

> N'allons donc pas chercher dans les livres des principes et des règles que nous trouvons plus sûrement au dedans de nous. Laissons là toutes ces vaines disputes des philosophes sur le bonheur et sur la vertu; employons à nous rendre bons et heureux le temps qu'ils perdent à chercher comment on doit l'être, et proposons-nous de grands exemples à imi- ter, plutôt que de vains systèmes à suivre. (32)

In her lengthy letter to Milord Edouard on the education of her children, in the fifth part, Julie proposes a plan of "error- less learning," whereby education would obviate the necessity of "lost illusions" in experience: "Je voudrais bien sauver à mon fils cette seconde et mortifiante éducation, en lui donnant par la première une plus juste opinion des choses"(557).

This devalorization of experience extends to the experience of what others are like: the ideal of penetration, of finding someone out, is inimical to both Julie and Saint-Preux. As Claire explains to Julie,

> . . . les âmes d'une certaine trempe . . . transforment, pour ainsi dire, les autres en elles-mêmes; elles ont une sphère

d'activité dans laquelle rien ne leur résiste: on ne peut les connaître sans les vouloir imiter, et de leur sublime éléva- tion elles attirent à elles tout ce qui les environne. C'est pour cela, ma chère, que ni toi ni ton ami ne connaîtrez peut- être jamais les hommes. . . . (180)

Once again, emphasis falls on the radiance of the two lov- ers' transparency: since they are limpid to themselves, they tend to endow everyone else with their nimbus; they never encounter the hard exterior and the mask. Hence we are not surprised when we find Julie objecting to the group of letters which Saint-Preux has sent her from Paris, describing in what is for him an unusually public, witty, and perceptive style, life in society:

Je ne vous ai point caché combien j'étais peu contente de vos relations: vous avez continué sur le même ton, et mon déplaisir n'a fait qu'augmenter. En vérité, l'on prendrait ces lettres pour les sarcasmes d'un petit-maître plutôt que pour les relations d'un philosophe, et l'on a peine à les croire de la même main que celles que vous m'écriviez autrefois. Quoi! vous pensez étudier les hommes dans les petites manières de quelques coteries de précieuses ou de gens désoeuvrés; et ce vernis extérieur et changeant, qui devait à peine frapper vos yeux, fait le fond de toutes vos remarques! (277)

Saint-Preux's sin has been attempting to talk like a *mondain,* to make portraits of the types he has encountered, to render a social exterior which, to Julie, is irrelevant. His remarks on Parisian men of society do implicitly refer us to the tradi- tion of La Bruyère:

Quiconque aime à se répandre et fréquente plusieurs so- ciétés doit être plus flexible qu'Alcibiade, changer de prin- cipes comme d'assemblées, modifier son esprit pour ainsi dire à chaque pas, et mesurer ses maximes à la toise. . . . (210)

This kind of public cognition and evaluation has nothing to do with *les belles âmes,* who must know instinctively, must intuitively appreciate one another through faculties other than the penetrating eye. Rousseau, when he finds Julie indulging in a maxim of La Rochefoucauld's, is categorically, disapproving: "Never," he comments in a footnote, will La Rochefoucauld's "sad book be liked by good people"(352). Like portraits, aphorisms belong to the Philintes.

In the "Préface de Julie," Rousseau's imaginary interlocutor complains of the novel, "Pas un portrait vigoureusement peint, pas un caractère assez bien marqué, nulle observation solide, aucune connaissance du monde" (740). The criticism evidently is accepted as praise by the author, for such techniques and such goals belong to a tradition of worldliness which his novel specifically repudiates. To penetration, summation, distance, judgment, universality, and hardness of outline, Rousseau opposes transparency, particularity, closeness, empathy, individuality, and a rhythmic, lyrical immediacy. The ideal society of Clarens toward which the novel moves is a place where people know one another perfectly, where transparency and immediacy are translated into a way of life, communal, self-subsistent, frugal, yet celebratory of itself. During their *matinée à l'anglaise,* Julie, Saint-Preux, and Wolmar move beyond the need for words, to a state of enraptured meditation where they understand one another in a medium of silent ecstasy.[6] The condition of emotional being envisioned by Saint-Preux in the mountains—so contrary to the sharp, exciting stimulus sought by most eighteenth-century protagonists—is finally attained:

. . . tous les désirs trop vifs s'émoussent, ils perdent cette pointe aiguë qui les rend douloureux; ils ne laissent au fond du coeur qu'une émotion légère et douce. (52)

[6] See the fine analysis of this scene by Ronald Grimsley in *Jean-Jacques Rousseau: A Study in Self-Awareness* (Cardiff, 1961), pp. 144-46.

At the symbolic center of the Clarens community is the Elysée garden: shaded, watered, asymmetrical, impenetrable to the spying eye.

Yet this paradise is organized and directed by a man who reminds us of some of the worldly-wise characters animated by Crébillon or Duclos, the sage Wolmar. Wolmar has penetrated the former love of Saint-Preux and Julie; and he claims to be constantly aware, even when they are themselves unaware, of the progress of their "cure." A sort of paternal analyst, he undertakes to further the cure by such therapy as having the two lovers return with him to the scene of their first kiss, thereby profaning a sacred locale. This prompts Julie to exclaim in a letter to Claire, "Tu ne veux pas me croire, cousine, mais je te jure qu'il a quelque don surnaturel pour lire au fond des coeurs . . ." (480). There is no need to believe the gift supernatural; Wolmar is simply a *philosophe* and a *moraliste*, a penetrating observer of men's ways. As such, his paternal influence is useful in making possible the polis of the *belles âmes*. His role is not untouched by sadism, however. In explaining his "system" to Claire, he declares that it will not surprise her to learn that Julie and Saint-Preux are more in love than ever, nor even to learn that they are nearly "cured"; but, he continues,

> Mais que ces deux opposés soient vrais en même temps; qu'ils brûlent plus ardemment que jamais l'un pour l'autre, et qu'il ne règne plus entre eux qu'un honnête attachement; qu'ils soient toujours amants et ne soient plus qu'amis; c'est, je pense, à quoi vous vous attendez moins, ce que vous aurez plus de peine à comprendre, et ce qui est pourtant selon l'exacte vérité. (491-92)

Wolmar evidently enjoys his knowledge of Julie and Saint-Preux's past, and quite revels in the spectacle of their temptations, combats, and sublimations. There is something rather

sinister about Wolmar, despite his honorable aims: it is as
if Rousseau could not prevent himself from constantly suggesting the underlying inhumanity of this seer through the
deeds of men. The author's punishment for this character—
and even Wolmar feels it as such—is his atheism, or rather,
for these are the terms in which it is put, his inability
to believe.

To his lack of faith, his dependence on the penetrating assessment of men, Julie responds more and more with an inner
light, a sense of the right intuitive communication between
people:

> C'est dans cette délicatesse qui survit toujours au véritable
> amour, plutôt que dans les subtiles distinctions de M. de
> Wolmar, qu'il faut chercher la raison de cette élévation
> d'âme et de cette force intérieure que nous éprouvons l'un
> près de l'autre, et que je crois sentir comme vous. (676)

Rejecting Wolmar's distinctions, his fragmentations of being,
Julie reaches a point where her being seems to become limit-
less, expanding to embrace all around her:

> ... je ne vois rien qui n'étende mon être, et rien qui le di-
> vise; il est dans tout ce qui m'environne, il n'en reste aucune
> portion loin de moi.... (677)

The closedness, the hardness, the carefully composed exte-
riority of the social animal considered by the moralist are replaced by an embracing, inclusive warmth, a self which embraces other selves. Even this immensity, however, is not
enough, and Julie prepares a final moment in the itinerary of
her soul:

> Ne trouvant donc rien ici-bas qui lui suffise, mon âme
> avide cherche ailleurs de quoi la remplir: en s'élevant à la
> source du sentiment et de l'être, elle y perd sa sécheresse et

sa langueur; elle y renaît, elle s'y ranime, elle y trouve un nouveau ressort, elle y puise une nouvelle vie. . . . (683)

Hence even the society of Clarens is left behind as Julie moves beyond men, to a realm in which love and virtue can be truly reconciled.

This reconciliation of love and virtue, and their attempted fusion into a society of perfect friendship, is the overt subject of the book. Like so many of his attitudes, Rousseau's view of female "virtue" is consciously perverse: traditionally, in the eighteenth-century novel, a young woman's "virtue" and her "honor" were a question of technical virginity; part of Rousseau's effort is to reverse this proposition, to make Julie virtuous despite her technical fault, to suggest that it is better to have once fallen as a maid, and then to have become a faultless wife, than to have preserved virginity until marriage, subsequently to lead a libertine's life. Clarissa Harlowe, for whom sexual violation seems to have set off an inevitable movement toward death, could not achieve this liberation from her century.

The real fault of Julie and Saint-Preux, what they must expiate and repair at Clarens, is having been unfaithful to themselves, having lost a way of life: "Infortunés, que sommes-nous devenus? Comment avons-nous cessé d'être ce que nous fûmes? Où est cet enchantement de bonheur suprême?" (315), exclaims Saint-Preux near the middle of the novel. A measure of their loss is the fact that Julie could propose adultery as a solution to their predicament and that Saint-Preux could accept it with arguments based on the ways of the world:

Pourquoi voudrions-nous être plus sages nous seuls que tout le reste des hommes, et suivre avec une simplicité d'enfants de chimériques vertus dont tout le monde parle et que personne ne pratique? Quoi! serons-nous meilleurs moralistes que ces foules de savants dont Londres et Paris sont peuplés, qui tous se raillent de la fidélité conjugale, et regardent l'adultère comme un jeu? (316)

But we who have been trained to listen to the voice of *les belles âmes* know that this is not the true Saint-Preux, and that another state of being must be found, for as Julie says, "L'innocence et l'amour m'étaient également nécessaires"(323). The reconquest of innocence-in-love, the state of emotional and moral transparency, under the watchful eye of Wolmar at Clarens, is the story of most of the rest of the book. It is not an easy conquest, for the present is constantly threatened by the past; remembrance asserts its reality and its claim to consideration, perhaps most strikingly in the lake voyage to La Meillerie, where Saint-Preux can use the rocks he had engraved with Julie's initial as an objective correlative to evoke his past love: "O Julie, éternel charme de mon coeur! Voici les lieux où soupira jadis pour toi le plus fidèle amant du monde" (502). The attainment of virtue comes, to the extent that it does come, by making the past remain past and totally separate from the present.

And here we realize one of Rousseau's triumphs in the book: his rendering of a sense of time, of duration. In announcing Saint-Preux's cure, Wolmar asserts, "Il l'aime dans le temps passé: voilà le vrai mot de l'énigme. Otez-lui la mémoire, il n'aura plus d'amour"(492). The judgment is not completely accurate, but it is nonetheless true that people do age in this novel: they undergo the process of time and are aware of having been changed by it. In the "Préface de Julie," Rousseau's critic complains that the end of the book makes its beginning all the more reprehensible; that the two parts will be read by different people, that one should not have to go through youthful errors to arrive at mature virtue; to which Rousseau replies:

Mes jeunes gens sont aimables; mais pour les aimer à trente
ans, il faut les avoir connus à vingt. Il faut avoir vécu longtemps avec eux pour s'y plaire; et ce n'est qu'après avoir
déploré leurs fautes qu'on vient à goûter leurs vertus. . . .
C'est une longue romance, dont les couplets pris à part
n'ont rien qui touche, mais dont la suite produit à la fin
son effet. (744)

Rousseau here defines his novel as a complex of temporal-
ly interrelated particulars, and locates it toward Jakobson's
"metonymic" pole. Crébillon, Duclos, and Mme de Lafayette
shared an essentially classical conception of time, posited on
the effect gained by concentration and unity; even Marivaux
conceived duration basically as a causal chain of motives and
events. Just as he abolishes the hard clarity of outline of portraiture, Rousseau breaks the "metaphoric," summary stasis of
these novelists' representations, and makes us feel time as
a process: an element that will be central to most of the best
nineteenth-century novels.

One should not attempt to turn Rousseau into a Realist,
yet his stand against the novel of worldliness, and some of
the new ideals he suggests, move toward the next century's
realism and coincide with Richardson's reorientation of the
novel. For one thing, as Erich Auerbach observed,[7] his "political" pastoral, his emphasis on an ideal society constituted as a criticism of real society, directed critical scrutiny
to the established order, inaugurating a point of view which
will inform much nineteenth-century fiction, where analysis
and description of society is a product of the outsider's stance,
the critical, hostile, and ambitious eye which details what it
must assault, overcome, or acquire—the stance of Rastignac,
or Vautrin, and one of the reasons Balzac's novels are socially so much more revolutionary than he believed them to

7 *Mimesis*, p. 411.

be. Further, Rousseau's devalorization of worldly experience, of man's social representations and public acts of
knowing; his insistence on the unique, the direct, the ex-
pansive, and the transparent; his use of letters written as
direct expressions of his characters' inner beings, prepare
us for another moral relation between author and reader.
Julie suggests this new relation in defending Pope's *Essay
on Man*:

> M. de Crouzas vient de nous donner une réfutation des
> épîtres de Pope, que j'ai lue avec ennui. Je ne sais pas au
> vrai lequel des deux auteurs a raison; mais je sais bien que
> le livre de M. de Crouzas ne fera jamais faire une bonne
> action, et qu'il n'y a rien de bon qu'on ne soit tenté de
> faire en quittant celui de Pope. Je n'ai point, pour moi,
> d'autre manière de juger de mes lectures que de sonder les
> dispositions où elles laissent mon âme, et j'imagine à peine
> quelle sorte de bonté peut avoir un livre qui ne porte point
> ses lecteurs au bien. (239)

To which Rousseau appends a footnote: "Si le lecteur ap-
prouve cette règle, et qu'il s'en serve pour juger ce recueil,
l'éditeur n'appellera pas de son jugement." In other words,
in the judgment of literature the criterion of truth is to be
replaced by that of moral efficacy, the way literature acts
on the reader's soul, the way it changes life.

This permits us to understand why Rousseau's great lesson of morality to his century had to find expression in a novel.
As he announces in the Preface,

> Il faut des spectacles dans les grandes villes, et des romans
> aux peuples corrompus. J'ai vu les moeurs de mon temps
> et j'ai publié ces lettres. Que n'ai-je vécu dans un siècle où
> je dusse les jeter au feu! (3)

His hero echoes him: "Les romans sont peut-être la dernière

instruction qu'il reste à donner à un peuple assez corrompu pour que tout autre lui soit inutile"(255). The novel of worldliness, like Molière's comedy of character and manners, was a hard-headed appraisal of men, an assessment of the way things are; it must be rejected on the grounds set forth in the *Lettre à d'Alembert*. But fiction can be something else: the novel envisioned by Jean-Jacques will not stop at the question of how men are, but will show them how they might be. And here the closeness, immediacy, and emotional involvement permitted by the genre are of vital importance, both esthetically and morally—since esthetics and ethics are finally one for Rousseau. Only in a novel could we be put into such an intimate, participative relationship with the *belles âmes* and be changed by our frequentation of them.

This intimacy and emotional involvement on the part of the reader depend to an important degree on the appeal to the reader's imaginative participation created by the reproduction of everyday realities. The critic of the "Préface de Julie" complains that the novel is too simple, that nothing remarkable happens: "Est-ce la peine de tenir registre de ce que chacun peut voir tous les jours dans sa maison ou dans celle de son voisin?" he asks(739). Such simplicity is evidently of moral value to Rousseau: by his critic's system, he claims, one will find in literature only the image of men as they wish to appear. His two young Vaudois lack epistolary stylishness, but they are direct, simple, truthful. And the rendering of this natural, truthful simplicity demands a greater attention to daily domestic realities: we must learn details of agriculture at Clarens, witness peasant dances, be told of children's games and family feasts. Sainte-Beuve once remarked (discussing the *Confessions*) that Rousseau has a proletarian sense of the real: he never forgets to tell us what he had to eat and drink.[8] What in fact makes this detailing of the real necessary is Rousseau's opposition to worldliness. Since he is setting up an anti-world—even a non-world, since it falls outside the limits of the enclosure which ordinarily defined what could be expressed in language—an image opposed to the ethos in which his reader habitually shares, he is obliged to win the reader's imaginative participation through patient description of the particular. And this same obligation will be felt, as we have already mentioned, by all the nineteenth-century novelists, who are presenting one particular, specialized fragment or image of the world.

Most obviously, and perhaps most importantly, Rousseau's sense of the real includes the setting. He reproached Richardson with failing to provide a locale to which a remembrance of his characters remained attached, and undoubtedly in *La Nouvelle Héloïse* the role of memory, rendered, as at La Meillerie, in concrete images, had much to do with Rousseau's creation of the seen and felt life of Clarens and its surroundings. His choice of setting was in fact determined by a memory image which possessed the solidity and reality he needed to anchor his characters:

> . . . mon imagination fatiguée à inventer vouloit quelque lieu réel qui put lui servir de point d'appui, et me faire illusion sur la réalité des habitans que j'y voulois mettre. Je songeai longtems aux iles Borromée dont l'aspect délicieux m'avoit transporté, mais j'y trouvai trop d'ornement et d'art pour mes personnages. Il me falloit cependant un lac, et je finis par choisir celui autour duquel mon coeur n'a jamais cessé d'errer.[9]

[8] Sainte-Beuve, "Les Confessions de Jean-Jacques Rousseau," *Causeries du Lundi* (Paris: Garnier, 1851), III, 72.
[9] *Confessions*, pp. 430-431.

From this emotional discovery of a landscape, Rousseau went on to realize the physical world in a manner inconceivable in any earlier novel. His willed rejection of the social ethos and system found in the earlier novel of worldliness evidently entailed the loss of *le monde* as stage and medium for his novel, and the loss of the code of signs, gestures, and words which constituted reality for Crébillon, Duclos, and Marivaux. These losses made necessary a search for another kind of reality which could furnish the terms of his conception and representation of life, a reality found both in his emotional moralism and in the solid presence of the physical world, in nature, landscape, place. Although his landscape is rural and to a degree idealized, it is a major source of the minutely described cities of Balzac, Dickens, Flaubert, or Zola: they too —from the exigencies of their historical situation if not from choice—had to rediscover reality for themselves, and like Rousseau, and to an even greater extent, they sought it in the irreducible solidity and presence of objects.

La Nouvelle Héloïse was one of the great popular successes of all times, and there is evidence that it did indeed exercise direct moral influence, and changed the lives of its readers.[10] From Rousseau's account in the *Confessions*, from letters and other contemporary reactions, we know that there were hundreds of people prepared to respond to the appeal of Saint-Preux and, especially, Julie. That numbers of readers refused to believe the lovers of Vevey fictional characters is testimony to the power of illusion and intimacy that their creator succeeded in evoking. Although every eighteenth-century novel as memoir or collection of letters claimed authenticity in a prefatory editorial note, one cannot imagine a reader taking the works of Crébillon, Duclos, or Marivaux as "literal-

---

[10] See the "Grand Écrivains de la France" edition of *La Nouvelle Héloïse*, ed. Daniel Mornet (Paris, 1924), Vol. I, *passim*; also Philippe Van Tieghem, *La Nouvelle Héloïse de Jean-Jacques Rousseau* (Paris, 1929).

ly" real and true; they do not operate in the medium of illusion and the literal. *La Nouvelle Héloïse*, on the other hand, by eliciting the reader's close participation in its concretely detailed and immediate fictional life, helped to orient the novel toward the illusionistic realism of the nineteenth century.

La Nouvelle Héloïse was consciously an act of defiance to Rousseau's century, a novel of anti-manners, of anti-worldliness that it would be impossible for future novelists to ignore. But its influence on the novel is never wholly separable from that of Richardson's fictions, especially *Clarissa*. Rousseau's work in fact coincides with an evolution in the esthetic of fiction initiated by Richardson. Contemporary readers were immediately cognizant of the close affinities between the two authors; the *Journal Étranger* even published in 1761 a *Parallèle,* translated from the English *Critical Review*.[11] And it seems probable that one of the motivations of Diderot's *Éloge de Richardson*, published in January of 1762, was to establish clearly that, in anything worth claiming, Richardson had preceded and surpassed the hermit of Montmorency.

The esthetic of the *Éloge de Richardson* is a natural extension of the argument that Diderot had pursued earlier in his espousals of a new drama, the *Entretiens sur le Fils Naturel*

[11] See Mornet edition of *La Nouvelle Héloïse,* Vol. 1, pp. 268-69. Despite their similarities—the similarities of position in relation to the tradition of worldliness and the future evolution of the novel, upon which I am insisting in this chapter—there are, of course, very important differences between Rousseau and Richardson in their practice of the novel. One should note especially that Rousseau inevitably inherits much from the esthetic of French classicism, including a sense of the value of a simple, linear plot involving few characters; he indeed accused Richardson of being too close to "les plus insipides romanciers qui suppléent à la stérilité de leurs idées à force de personnages et d'avantures" (*Confessions*, pp. 546-47). One might add that while Rousseau is sometimes proletarian, he is not, like Richardson, petty bourgeois.

(1757) and *De la Poésie dramatique* (1758), and it is strikingly close to the esthetic found in the *Lettre à d'Alembert* and *La Nouvelle Héloïse*. From the outset of the *Éloge de Richardson*, Diderot contrasts Richardson with the *moralistes* and, presumably, those novelists who wrote under their influence: "Tout ce que Montaigne, Charron, La Rochefoucauld et Nicole ont mis en maximes, Richardson l'a mis en action." He goes on to explain:

> Une maxime est une règle abstraite et générale de conduite dont on nous laisse l'application à faire. Elle n'imprime par elle-même aucune image sensible dans notre esprit: mais celui qui agit, on le voit, on se met à sa place ou à ses côtés, on se passionne pour ou contre lui; on s'unit à son rôle, s'il est vertueux; on s'en écarte avec indignation, s'il est injuste et vicieux.[12]

Once again, we sense that we are faced with an important attack on the classical esthetic of distance, embodied in the narrative voice—its distance from the actions of the protagonist—the tone and language of the earlier form of novel. Diderot's elaborations point to a total destruction of such a doctrine, and the substitution for it of an almost physical involvement with the action of the novel:

> O Richardson! on prend . . . un rôle dans tes ouvrages, on se mêle à la conversation, on approuve, on blâme, on admire, on s'irrite, on s'indigne. Combien de fois ne me suis-je pas surpris, comme il est arrivé à des enfants qu'on avait mené au spectacle pour la première fois, criant: *Ne le croyez pas, il vous trompe . . . Si vous allez là, vous êtes perdu.* Mon âme était tenue dans une agitation perpétuelle. Combien j'étais bon! combien j'étais juste! que j'étais satisfait de

[12] Denis Diderot, *Éloge de Richardson*, in *Oeuvres esthétiques*, ed. Paul Vernière (Paris: Garnier, 1959), pp. 29-30.

moi! J'étais, au sortir de ta lecture, ce qu'est un homme à la fin d'une journée qu'il a employée à faire le bien. (30)

This rapture reminds us that Richardson was perhaps the first novelist successfully to exploit certain elements which we as a matter of course expect to find in every best seller: suspense, excitement, vicarious enjoyment. Although some earlier novelists may hold our attention through the power of their fabulation, it is with Richardson that the reader is made a full participant in the danger—and the titillation—of the characters. As Richardson himself pointed out in the Preface to *Clarissa*, his characters' letters are composed while the writers are wholly engaged with their subjects, "so that they abound not only with critical situations, but with what may be called *instantaneous* descriptions and reflections."[13] For Diderot, this immediacy and participation are of moral value: in reading Richardson, he has often thought he would "willingly give his life" to resemble Clarissa, and would "rather be dead" than be like Lovelace. Such a reaction is utterly different from that provoked by the distanced, witty, evaluative tone of the novel of worldliness; and it should be noted that the eroticism of Crébillon and his contemporaries—a product of the masculine drive to expose, know, conquer and control —bears no resemblance to the participative titillation which *Clarissa* and *Pamela* undoubtedly procured to their female readership.

After delivering the conventional attack on the adventure novel and the romance, Diderot praises Richardson's realism:

Le monde où nous vivons est le lieu de la scène; le fond de son drame est vrai; ses personnages ont toute la réalité possible; ses caractères sont pris du milieu de la société; ses in-

---

[13] Samuel Richardson, *Clarissa Harlowe*, ed. Ethel M. M. McKenna (London, 1902), I, xi.

cidents sont dans les moeurs de toutes les nations policées. . . . (30-31)

"Toute la réalité possible" seems ambiguous, until we realize that Diderot intends it simply as a superlative:[14] it is impossible for one to give a greater sense of the real than does Richardson. He defines more precisely what he means when, in refuting those who object to Richardson's *longueurs* and his multiplication of vulgar detail, he argues, "Sachez que c'est à cette multitude de petites choses que tient l'illusion" (35). Illusion is a product of attention to the particular, and this kind of illusion is necessary, we have seen, to capture the reader's imaginative and emotional participation in a world and a drama which must be made close and immediate to him if the novel is to attain the moral effect which Richardson, like Rousseau, seeks. Refashioning the convention of a bundle of letters which the novelist has simply edited, Diderot would in fact persuade us that *Clarissa* and *Pamela* possess the absolute, diffuse authenticity of the real; that they literally belong to life rather than art:

> Une idée qui m'est venue quelquefois en rêvant aux ouvrages de Richardson, c'est que j'avais acheté un vieux château; qu'en visitant un jour ses appartements, j'avais aperçu dans un angle une armoire qu'on n'avait pas ouverte depuis longtemps, et que, l'ayant enfoncée, j'y avais trouvé pêle-mêle les lettres de Clarisse et de Paméla. Après en avoir lu quelques-unes, avec quel empressement ne les aurais-je

[14] Harry Levin, in *The Gates of Horn* (New York, 1963), p. 65, suggests that Diderot's phrase refers rather to the dynamics of realism: Richardson achieved all the realism possible at a given historical moment, a break-through which would be followed by further progress, more audacious realisms. This is an important interpretation of the connotations of Diderot's remark from within an historical perspective; it does not seem to me, however, that the historical perspective is Diderot's own: to him, *Clarissa* was the ultimate in realism.

pas rangées par ordre de dates! Quel chagrin n'aurais-je
pas ressenti, s'il y avait eu quelque lacune entre elles! Croit-
on que j'eusse souffert qu'une main téméraire (j'ai presque
dit sacrilège) en eût supprimé une ligne? (36)

Illusion could not be more voluntarily complete; participation could not be more total. One is reminded of Richardson's own report, in the Postscript to *Clarissa*, that during
the publication of the novel he received numerous pleas from
young ladies that the novel might have a "fortunate ending."[15] These readers had fallen in love with his heroine,
a state of affairs not encouraged by the novel of worldliness,
where commerce is essentially between narrator and reader.
Here is indeed one of the essential revolutions worked by
Richardson and Rousseau: the triangular relationship that
must always exist, in a novel, among author, protagonist,
and reader, is modified by them to put almost exclusive emphasis on the close commerce of reader and protagonist, the
empathetical relationship which Diderot felt so strongly. While
this is partly a consequence of the epistolary form, so well
adapted to producing the immediacy both Richardson and
Rousseau sought, the novel of letters need not give such an
impression of familiar commerce with the characters. *Les
Liaisons dangereuses* where, as the "Publisher" warns us, "almost all the emotions are feigned or dissimulated," is an
example to the contrary, as is Crébillon's *Lettres de la Marquise de M****, where one feels the authorial arrangement of
experience to provide an ironic and detached view, utterly
different from Richardson's. Nor need one write an epistolary novel to achieve the closeness of Richardson and Rousseau: the novels of Balzac or Dickens, and the standard best-
seller of the nineteenth and twentieth centuries, in varying

[15] *Clarissa Harlowe*, IX, 307.

degrees solicit the reader's emotional participation and identification with the hero.

The kind of "heroism" displayed in Richardson's novels is also significantly new. The full title of *Clarissa* bears quotation here, for it gives an accurate picture of the heroine's concerns:

> Clarissa, or, the History of a Young Lady: Comprehending the Most Important Concerns of Private Life. And particularly shewing, the Distresses that may attend the Misconduct both of Parents and Children in Relation to Marriage.

The emphasis on "private life," and on the bourgeois institutionalization of private life, marriage, is striking. Crébillon, too, we noted, considered "la vie privée" as the domain of the novel, but his coupling of the term with "des travers et des retours d'un homme de condition" immediately suggested the inevitability of the public side of his novel, its enactment within a public system of manners. Richardson's "scenes from private life" do involve public conflict, but in a different way and from a different viewpoint. His point of view, like Rousseau's, is individualistic; both Pamela and Clarissa are forced to encounter society and to struggle with it. Whether they be eventually victorious, like Pamela, or whether, like Clarissa, they succumb, the emphasis falls on an individual destiny, worked out in interplay with other individuals, more than on society as a public system of characters and values. The protagonist is a hero who must struggle to assert the rights of an individual interpretation of life against the interests of others—and sometimes even the interests of "society" as a whole. Significantly, this hero is very often a heroine, that is of the more socially deprived sex, the one whose freedom of action is more limited.

The values at stake in *Clarissa*—questions of feminine virtue and marriage—are private, individualistic, bourgeois, and (one is tempted to apply the remark to Rousseau as well as Richardson) protestant. Ian Watt sees Richardson, like George Eliot and Henry James, as preoccupied with the "tragedy of feminine individualism" within the "Puritan tradition,"[16] and one could, generalizing, see an important source of the modern novel in this preoccupation and within a religious tradition dedicated to questions of personal ethics. This is not to attempt to make a protestant of Balzac, who is in many ways a very direct descendant of Richardson; perhaps, however, the individualistic ethic of Romanticism operated as his puritanism, for the upheaval of society brought by the French Revolution, and the destruction of literary absolutism worked by Romanticism, redirected attention to the question of the individual and his moral destiny—as also to Rousseau and to the eighteenth-century English novel.

Both Richardson and Rousseau redefine the kind of response a reader is supposed to make to a novel: from the detached, intellectual, evaluative, we move to the involved, emotional, sympathetic. With the novel of worldliness, the reader's participation was on the levels of epistemology (finding people out) and social ideology (judging the extravagant or mistaken); the measure of realism demanded by such a novel was that of the classically *vraisemblable*, the morally and psychologically accurate and appropriate; narrative development was subordinated to scenic representations of manners, and the arrest necessary to present a total "metaphoric" summary and evaluation of character and motive. *Clarissa* and *La Nouvelle Héloïse* define the experience of reading as vicarious emotion, and therefore posit new esthetic criteria. Of primary importance now is the tangibility of the atmosphere each

16 *The Rise of the Novel*, p. 225.

novel creates, the physical reality of its fictional world which fosters and authenticates identification. This attention to the tangible particular entails, as Jakobson demonstrates, a greater attention to narrative, to development of the hero's life in time, in movement from one contiguous particular to another—a "metonymic" organization of reality.

Together, Rousseau and Richardson (the latter abetted by French propagandists like Prévost and, most intelligently, Diderot) reorient the novel first toward the sentimental melodrama, so popular in the second half of the eighteenth century, then toward the mode most familiar to us, bourgeois realism. Their kind of novel defines itself for the historical critic—and in the case of Rousseau defined itself for the author as well—in deliberate opposition to the tradition of worldliness, and it can help us to situate and understand the unique strengths and the particular field of validity and excellence of the novel of worldliness, as well as its historical precedence and chronological limits. From the 1760's on, the novel of worldliness can no longer be considered a dominant literary "kind"; for no perceptive novelist is it possible to write without an awareness of Richardson and Rousseau. Yet there are repeated instances of a basic allegiance to the enterprise of the novel of worldliness.

There are relatively few French novelists of note between Rousseau and the first generation of the nineteenth century—Laclos, Sade, and Restif de la Bretonne come first to mind—and they tend to define themselves very much in terms of their adherence to the Richardsonian or Rousseauian novel (this is certainly the case of the last two names) or in opposition to it (see the preface of the aging Crébillon to his *Lettres de la Duchesse de****). The case of Laclos is particularly interesting, for he wrote what must at first glance seem the most obvious novel of worldliness, the *summa* of the

tradition, yet he wrote with a strong awareness of the con-
tributions of Rousseau and Richardson. Our discussion of
Laclos will center on his adherence to the ethic and style of
the novel of worldliness, and his parallel questioning of this
ethic and its techniques.

LES LIAISONS DANGEREUSES

Les Liaisons dangereuses begins with a game, played by a fictive Publisher and an equally fictive Editor. The "Préface du Rédacteur" seems the usual *trompe l'oeil* of the eighteenth-century novel; the Editor insists that the material he has "collected" is authentic and apologizes for the lack of polish of some of the letters, pointing to the "realism" of the book, where each correspondent has his personal style and tone. But, in more original fashion, this statement has already been undercut by a liminary "Avertissement de l'Éditeur," where the Publisher warns us that what we are about to read is in fact only a novel. The author, it seems, destroyed any pretense to verisimilitude by setting his drama of wickedness in modern times:

> En effet, plusieurs des personnages qu'il met en scène ont de si mauvaises moeurs, qu'il est impossible de supposer qu'ils aient vécu dans notre siècle; dans ce siècle de philosophie, où les lumières, répandues de toutes parts, ont rendu, comme chacun sait, tous les hommes si honnêtes et toutes les femmes si modestes et si réservées.[1]

By the end of his statement, the Publisher has maliciously directed his irony against his audience: what proves the novel unrealistic is that "nous ne voyons point aujourd'hui de

[1] Pierre-Ambroise-François Choderlos de Laclos, *Les Liaisons dangereuses* in *Oeuvres complètes*, ed. Maurice Allem (Paris: Bibliothèque de la Pléiade, 1959), p. 5. To facilitate reference to different editions, I will give in parentheses after each quotation the number of the letter from which it is taken.

Demoiselle, avec soixante mille livres de rente, se faire Religieuse, ni de Présidente, jeune et jolie, mourir de chagrin." This irony succeeds admirably in putting us on our guard, preparing us for a reading of these "Lettres recueillies dans une Société, et publiées pour l'instruction de quelques autres," in which, the Editor warns us, almost all the emotions expressed are "feigned or dissimulated." We are prepared to enter a world where play, witty and dangerous, is reality; where dissimulation and feigning are method and subject of an epistolary exchange.

The opening of the novel establishes a contrast between the spontaneous and the artfully controlled. The first letter, from Cécile Volanges to Sophie Carnay, abounds, for someone rereading the novel, with ironies of innocence: "Tu vois, ma bonne amie, que je tiens parole, et que les bonnets et les pompons ne prennent pas tout mon temps. . . ." Cécile's victimization in particular, and the theme of victimization in general, is immediately constituted when one adds the second letter to the first. Madame de Merteuil's persiflage to the Vicomte de Valmont—"vous abusez de mes bontés, même depuis que vous n'en usez plus"; her portrait of Cécile—"cela n'a que quinze ans, c'est le bouton de rose; gauche, à la vérité, comme on ne l'est point, et nullement maniérée"; and her plan for seduction of Cécile in order to avenge herself on the Comte de Gercourt, all spoken in the witty, cool, intelligent voice we come to know so well, indicate the dangers of ignorance and naturalness and the inevitable superiority of intelligent falsity.

The difference in tones points to a trait of *Les Liaisons dangereuses* which has continually impressed critics: in contrast to *La Nouvelle Héloïse,* and much more than in *Clarissa,* the letters of the principal characters are active. Only the ignorant, like Cécile, recount naively what has happened; the others, and especially Valmont and Mme de Merteuil, use letters to specific ends and are unfailingly conscious of their audience. As the Marquise admonishes a more experienced, but no less naive Cécile, letters are not a spontaneous expression of one's own soul, but an instrument to work on another's:

> . . . vous dites tout ce que vous pensez, et rien de ce que vous ne pensez pas. Cela peut passer ainsi de vous à moi, qui devons n'avoir rien de caché l'une pour l'autre: mais avec tout le monde! avec votre Amant surtout! vous auriez toujours l'air d'une petite sotte. Vous voyez bien que, quand vous écrivez à quelqu'un, c'est pour lui, et non pas pour vous: vous devez donc moins chercher à lui dire ce que vous pensez, que ce qui lui plaît davantage. (CV)

Each letter from the Marquise and Valmont, to the Présidente, to Mme de Volanges, to Cécile, to Danceny, is written not only with the recipient in mind, but to produce a precise effect on the recipient. Never has the epistolary form been so completely motivated as it is here: not only is the art of the letter a central question, the letter itself, in a physical sense—Valmont's problems in delivering his epistles to Cécile and the Présidente, for example—becomes a subject of correspondence, a theme as well as a form.

While there is a pact between Valmont and Mme de Merteuil to reveal everything to one another, and to aid one another's schemes, the Valmont-Merteuil and Merteuil-Valmont correspondence is perhaps the most feigning of all, in that they are continually posing for one another. They are accomplices, and their complicity of course reveals to us selves different from those they present to the world. But this complicity is based on emulation and rivalry, on the desire of each to present himself as the more masterfully successful schemer. Whereas in the novels of Crébillon, Duclos, and Marivaux—as in the writings of the *moralistes*—we were guided by the distanced evaluations, the "penetrations" and "fixations" of the narrator, here, in this epistolary drama, the characters alone use these techniques on others: ways of knowing and of rendering are weapons for their personal combats and no narrator or reader's surrogate intervenes to arrest the battle and suggest final judgments. Hence the novel, as more than one critic has pointed out, resembles a vast game of mirrors, where it is dangerous to accept any one view of reality as true or objective. Almost all the characters have an interest in make believe—making someone else, or society as a whole, accept a certain image of themselves, and often even in making themselves believe in a certain conception of self. The texture of the novel effectively imitates its subject: we, as readers, are involved in an essentially epistemological problem—how to know, how, from fragmentary and slanted accounts of characters and events, to put together a total and objective view.

Whatever eventual evaluations we come to, our enlistment in this game is originally with the *meneurs du jeu*, Valmont and the Marquise de Merteuil. Laclos' use of the epistolary form makes this inevitable; the letters of the active, intelligent beings are the most exciting to read, and we are caught up in the complicity of two people who would make each other believe that they control the world through their intelligence. Sharing their conquests, exchanging their victims' letters, perpetually witty and good-humored, they seduce us into a sense of possessing their attractiveness and power. As Jean-Luc Seylaz accurately observes, "Laclos a créé avec une puissance rarement égalée *l'illusion* de ce monde où l'homme pénétrerait véritablement au coeur des êtres et où savoir serait vraiment pouvoir. 'Connaître les êtres pour agir sur eux. . . .' "[2]

[2] *Les Liaisons dangereuses et la création romanesque chez Laclos*, p. 129. (This is by far the best book written on Laclos, and I am much indebted to it, although I often disagree with M. Seylaz' emphases.) Laurent Versini, *Laclos et la Tradition* (Paris: Klincksieck, 1968) came to my attention too late for me to be able to make use of its rich documentation on the sources of Laclos' novel.

Stendhal's phrase from an unidentified Idéologue has its fullest range of application here. The Marquise and Valmont participate in a mythology of intelligence and voluntarism; they have consciously put their highest faculties in service to an ideological conception of self as a completely systematic being. They have elaborated a personal system of knowledge and control, and the question of the uses and misuses of the system is in fact the profound subject of the novel. They control people through knowing them because, they understand, knowledge of another enables one to deprive him of his freedom—by playing on his psychological composition to elicit certain tropisms, by manipulating him into unenviable social roles, by blackmail—to fix and limit him, while the knower preserves, indeed increases his own freedom of movement. The Marquise and Valmont continually remind us of the place of this system in their lives: Valmont speaks of his "principles" of seduction, the "purity" of his method, the absoluteness of his self-control; the Marquise counters with the refinement of her acting, the secrecy of her movements, the inviolability of her reputation. As we follow their complicity and witness the flawless evolution of their schemes, we become aware of the degree to which the system and code of an earlier novel of worldliness has been purified and refined into a perfect mechanism which they perfectly understand and govern.

As with Crébillon and Duclos, so here the erotic is an important element in the system, and a central expression of its mechanization. André Malraux found in the novel an "eroticisation of the will,"[3] but the definition could also be turned around ("the voluntarization of the erotic"), so closely interdependent are the pleasure principle and the will to power. The erotic is in fact the domain in which the drive

[3] "Laclos," *Tableau de la littérature française, XVIIe-XVIIIe siècles, de Corneille à Chenier* (Paris: Gallimard, 1939), p. 427.

to dominance, power, and freedom operates most flawlessly. To place someone in an erotic situation is to hold him within the closest possible limits, to allow him no room for evasion or cheating in an encounter that must lead to mastery on the one hand and enslavement on the other. To regard someone as a purely erotic object is to reduce his psychology to the most mechanical and simplified elements, to make an already rigid code of psychological signs still more mechanistic. Indeed, to reduce social relations to erotic relations, human behavior to erotic comportment, as Valmont and the Marquise continually try to do, is to operate an important mechanization of social laws and human existence. Like Versac or Duclos' Comte de***, but with heightened self-consciousness and absolutism, Valmont and the Marquise have based their systematic mastery on reduction; like La Rochefoucauld, they find meaning by imposing limits. *Les Liaisons dangereuses* is profoundly a novel about system, processes of systematization, man as a creature of system (and also, a point we will come to, as a being irreducible to system).

Once again, as in the earlier novel of worldliness, use of system, control of life, are seen as the use of a language which shows, or at least gives the illusion, that the two central characters are masters of other beings. They pride themselves on their power to transmute experience into aphorism: see, for example, the Marquise's lapidary "l'amour que l'on nous vante comme la cause de nos plaisirs, n'en est au plus que le prétexte"(LXXXI), or Valmont's "la seule volupté a le droit de détacher le bandeau de l'amour"(VI). Valmont, and especially the Marquise, excel at portraiture; they use its language of classification and judgment to "dispose" of others, to destroy their freedom, to reduce them to little more than a metaphor for a type of being. To Valmont, Mme de Tourvel is "la belle prude," Danceny "ce beau héros de roman"; to Mme de Merteuil, Cécile is "cela" and "l'espèce."

When Valmont describes his seduction of Cécile to Mme de Merteuil, his language indicates perfect control through careful decoding of the girl's psychological signs, and precise encoding in the right language: "Elle avait pourtant à combattre l'amour, et l'amour soutenu par la pudeur ou la honte, et fortifié surtout par l'humeur que j'avais donnée, et dont on avait beaucoup pris" (XCVI). Such clarity and accuracy of perception in the midst of seduction proves mastery of one's victim and oneself. The situation, Valmont makes us believe, is simply another term in the same old story, ultimately justifiable for the way it can be made into aphoristic wit: "Enfin, de faiblesse en reproche, et de reproche en faiblesse, nous ne nous sommes séparés que satisfaits l'un de l'autre, et également d'accord pour le rendez-vous de ce soir."

Mme de Merteuil's reply to this letter indicates both her participation in the same system and her rivalry with Valmont for control of Cécile. It is she who has initiated and pursued—with overtones of a refined Lesbianism as well as voyeurism—the seduction of Cécile, using Valmont as her instrument. But Cécile falls to simple force (which is, Roger Laufer has pointed out, Valmont's way of asserting masculine independence from the Marquise's control of the project),[4] and her confession to the Marquise indicates that seduction has wrought no basic changes; she will never be capable of playing the supporting role in intrigues, as the Marquise had hoped:

> . . . de sorte que, tandis que nous nous occuperions à former cette petite fille pour l'intrigue, nous n'en ferions qu'une femme facile. Or, je ne connais rien de si plat que cette facilité de bêtise, qui se rend sans savoir ni comment ni pourquoi, uniquement parce qu'on l'attaque et qu'elle

[4] "Les Liaisons dangereuses," Style Rococo, Style des "Lumières" (Paris: José Corti, 1963), p. 143.

ne sait pas résister. Ces sortes de femmes ne sont absolument que des machines à plaisir. (CVI)

The portrait rapidly and contemptuously transforms Cécile from a living virtuality into a type and an object: "femme facile" is further defined by "cette facilité de bêtise"; she then becomes one of "ces sortes de femmes," fixed and dehumanized as a "machine à plaisir": such machines, the Marquise tells us a moment later, are easily worked by anyone, since their mechanisms are purely erotic. Cécile's entire psychological organization is in fact revealed to be mechanical: the Marquise goes on to lay bare the conventionality of her platitudinous and second-hand analyses of experience, the mechanism of her bad faith.

The two world masters repeatedly reanalyze other characters' self-analyses as the self-deceptions of automatons, thereby enhancing our sense of their analytical preëminence and vital freedom. Laclos, as M. Seylaz well expresses it, creates an "intériorité à deux degrés" whereby the psychological penetration of the *meneurs du jeu* is made to appear particularly profound.[5] Whereas in Crébillon, Duclos, or Marivaux the use of the analytical tools fashioned by the *moralistes* to give an account of man in society, the vocabulary of clear perception, estimate and summary, pointed to the narrator's control and distance from his subject, here the use of these tools and this language are persuasive indications of two characters' control of other characters, their role as novelists of the experience of others, their distanced, Olympian mastery of reality.

What system means in terms of the individual's public style is, for Valmont, perfectly familiar from earlier conquerors like Versac. His domination depends on achieving an extreme, sensationalistic form of publicity. Mme de Volanges captures the essential terms when she says, "Je ne m'arrête pas

[5] Seylaz, p. 76.

à compter celles qu'il a séduites: mais combien n'en a-t-il pas perdues?"(IX). But for the woman who would establish mastery of society, the style demanded is more complex; her outward reputation must be one of "severe virtue," while she in private manipulates and controls men for her pleasure, and disarms them so they cannot publicize their exploits. She must be two people, but the private and public selves are useless when taken separately, for the same woman must be able to taste "la gloire de la défense et le plaisir de la défaite"(X). Her personal system, like that of the famous Ninon de Lenclos, is elaborated to undermine an established order of male domination: as she epigrammaticizes in a line of verse, "Ces Tyrans détrônés devenus mes esclaves" (LXXXI).

Hence she is justified in boasting to Valmont, "Et qu'avez-vous donc fait, que je n'aie surpassé mille fois?"(LXXXI). The fullest expression of the systematization of worldliness and the voluntarization of self is the letter—significantly placed at the exact center of the novel—in which she recounts her self-education to Valmont. Since she is working to reverse the results of a given system while operating within it, accepting its code and values, dissimulation is the initial term of her formation. As a young girl permitted neither to act nor speak, she became an observer and learned to hide the objects of her attention; she studied to give the semblance of emotions opposite to those she felt and employed self-inflicted pain to assure perfect self-control. Passing to a more active social participation, no longer content to escape "penetration" by others, she learned to show herself under different forms, to accord gesture and word to circumstance, to reveal only so much of herself as was useful. And from this effort upon herself, this exploration of the prestige of disguise, she learned to know others: "Ce travail sur moi-même avait fixé mon attention sur l'expression des figures et le caractère des physionomies; et j'y gagnai ce coup d'oeil pénétrant. . . ." On the verge of marriage, she tells us in a phrase which could stand as emblem for the erotic will to knowledge and power, "Je ne désirais pas de jouir, je voulais savoir."

Knowing, after the death of M. de Merteuil, involved experimentation with young rustics and also reading: of novels to know what one could do, of philosophers to know what one should think, of moralists to know how one must appear. After completion of these studies, she turned to winning the suffrage of the "party of the Prudes," the old women who make the reputation of the young in society. Then she was prepared to perform on the public stage: "Alors je commençai à déployer sur le grand Théâtre, les talents que je m'étais donnés." This performance is always brilliantly determined by the hypersensitive consciousness of society she has formed in herself: an example is her management of the difficult moment at the start of a liaison:

> Vous savez combien je me décide vite: c'est pour avoir observé que ce sont presque toujours les soins antérieurs qui livrent le secret des femmes. Quoi qu'on puisse faire, le ton n'est jamais le même, avant ou après le succès. Cette différence n'échappe point à l'observateur attentif et j'ai trouvé moins dangereux de me tromper dans le choix, que de me laisser pénétrer. Je gagne encore par là d'ôter les vraisemblances, sur lesquelles seules on peut nous juger.

The Marquise sees all her acts as played under the surveillance of a social observer as attentive to every nuance of tone as she is herself, and the object of her system of comportment is to destroy "les vraisemblances," any pattern that would permit a presumption against her, that would give anyone else a hold on her. Her precautions have guaranteed her the heroic freedom of Corneille's protagonists: the high point of her career, she announces in Cornelian language, was her choice to encounter Valmont: "il me semblait que vous manquiez à ma gloire; je brûlais de vous combattre corps à corps."

At the center of this letter is the Marquise's statement, "Je puis dire que je suis mon ouvrage." What she is she has become through an intelligent and voluntary application of system, of self-control directed to the control of others. The mastery of others is a direct result of her total self-knowledge; she has delved into her heart, not to discover, like Rousseau, her own transparency, but rather the essential duplicity about which every man is organized:

> Descendue dans mon coeur, j'y ai étudié celui des autres. J'y ai vu qu'il n'est personne qui n'y conserve un secret qu'il lui importe qui ne soit point dévoilé: vérité que l'antiquité paraît avoir mieux connue que nous, et dont l'histoire de Samson pourrait n'être qu'un ingénieux emblème.

Delilah is the answer to Don Juan, the way to arrest, fix, and silence a Valmont. If Mme de Merteuil holds the secrets of many modern Samsons, she also possesses a *femme de chambre* who is a literal slave, since the Marquise preserves a certain paper that could send the girl to prison. In this servant we see the final term of her control of life through the reduction of others to mechanism; while she retains the freedom of a Homeric God, manipulating the affairs of petty men: "Me voilà comme la Divinité; recevant les voeux opposés des aveugles mortels, et ne changeant rien à mes décrets immuables"(LXIII).

The most remarkable display of the Marquise's use of penetration, wit, disguise, and control comes in her love scene with the Chevalier de Belleroche. She prefaces the encounter with readings from Crébillon's *Le Sopha*, the tales of La Fontaine, and *La Nouvelle Héloïse*, to rehearse the different tones she wishes to take. The tones become veritable metamorphoses:

Je ne crois pas avoir jamais mis tant de soin à plaire, ni avoir jamais été aussi contente de moi. Après le souper, tour à tour enfant et raisonnable, folâtre et sensible, quelquefois même libertine, je me plaisais à le considérer comme un Sultan au milieu de son Serail, dont j'étais tour à tour les Favorites différentes. En effet, ses hommages réitérés, quoique toujours reçus par la même femme, le furent toujours par une Maîtresse nouvelle. (X)

These protean transformations into different mistresses allow her to remain ungraspable, unfixed, free, while the essential self, the woman, receives pleasure—which is in fact dependent on her being both herself and another. The metamorphoses point to a desire to be at the same time master and slave—to achieve mastery from within seeming enslavement—an ideal which, in its psychological subtlety, goes beyond anything imagined by Valmont (he accuses the Marquise of humiliating herself by expending so much energy on the Chevalier's pleasures) and will be an indirect cause of their falling out.

The complicity and rivalry of Valmont and the Marquise serve to hold constantly before us an image of the society which elicited their personal systems; as confidents, counsellors, and competitors, they continually remind one another of what society expects of them. The Marquise feels obliged to warn Valmont that his pursuit of the Présidente has lasted too long, and has begun to expose him to ridicule in society:

Je crois devoir vous prévenir, Vicomte, qu'on commence à s'occuper de vous à Paris; qu'on y remarque votre absence, et que déjà on en devine la cause. J'etais hier à un souper fort nombreux; il y fut dit positivement que vous étiez retenu au Village par un amour romanesque et malheureux: aussitôt la joie se peignit sur le visage de tous les envieux de vos succès et de toutes les femmes que vous avez négligées. Si vous m'en croyez, vous ne laisserez pas

183

prendre consistance à ces bruits dangereux, et vous viendrez
sur-le-champ les détruire par votre présence.

Songez que si une fois vous laissez perdre l'idée qu'on ne
vous résiste pas, vous éprouverez bientôt qu'on vous résistera en effet plus facilement. . . . (CXIII)

Like the Comte's remarks on the choice of a new mistress, in
Duclos' novel, this warning captures perfectly the circular
process of conquest, reputation, and liberty of action in a society where what matters is maintaining a self-representation which forces others to conceive their roles in relation to
it. When Valmont details his comic nocturnal adventure
with the Vicomtesse de M. . . , the Marquise immediately sees
how it may be put to use: "Je serai bien aise d'avoir un prétexte pour rompre avec elle: or, il n'en est pas de plus commode, que d'avoir à dire: On ne peut plus voir cette femme-
là" (LXXIV). The story of Prévan and the Three Inseparables, then his adventure with Mme de Merteuil, offer objective confirmation of this process, telling illustrations of
the disaster of discovery and bad publicity in a world that
matches attention to maneuver with love of *médisance*. Of
Prévan's three victims, one is in a convent, while the other
two languish exiled in their country estates, and Prévan himself, after his scene with the Marquise, is dismissed from his
regiment and banished from "good company."

Prévan first becomes important in the novel when, at a
dinner party where Valmont is of the company, he makes a
satirical portrait of Mme de Merteuil, designed to prove that
her virtue is merely a product of flighty inconsequence,
étourderie. He succeeds in making his audience accept this
image, and further undertakes to prove that the chaste Marquise can be seduced. Valmont insists, in his account to the
Marquise, on Prévan's potential danger. Valmont has long
managed to undervalue Prévan through his credit with

"some thirty of our most fashionable women," thus preventing him from appearing on "what we call le grand théâtre." But the "éclat" of his triple success has "fixed all eyes on him," given him the confidence he lacked previously, and made him truly redoubtable: "C'est enfin aujourd'hui le seul homme, peut-être, que je craindrais de rencontrer sur mon chemin . . . et j'ai l'espoir qu'à mon retour, ce sera un homme noyé" (LXX). After receiving this challenge—a challenge both to reaffirm her public image and prove her superiority to the fearful Valmont—the Marquise naturally seeks combat with Prévan: as she vaunts, using Valmont's customary language, "Il faut vaincre ou périr. Quant à Prévan, je veux l'avoir et je l'aurai; il veut le dire, et il ne le dira pas: en deux mots, voilà notre Roman. Adieu"(LXXXI).

Her technique with Prévan is a splendid illustration of her knowledge of the rules of the game, and her ability to manipulate them, her capacity to preserve public alibis while tacitly assuring Prévan that resistance will be purely formal. The process of seduction is an exquisitely mannered comedy—as Prévan's handling of the Three Inseparables was itself an intricate ballet—where the forms of society are tokens in the two characters' moves, a conventional language in which they can understand each other from the slenderest indications:

> Je déclarai que je ne jouerais point; en effet, il trouva, de son côté, mille prétextes pour ne pas jouer; et mon premier triomphe fut sur le lansquenet. (LXXXV)

The Marquise manipulates selection of the tone which she finds most suitable to the development of their relationship and the protection of her public image:

> Prévan s'étant bientôt rendu maître de la conversation, prit tour à tour différents tons, pour essayer celui qui pourrait me plaire. Je refusai celui du sentiment, comme n'y croyant pas;

j'arrêtai par mon sérieux, sa gaieté qui me parut trop légère pour un début; il se rabattit sur la délicate amitié; et ce fut sous ce drapeau banal que nous commençames notre attaque réciproque.

It is irrelevant to object that such a reciprocal attack is founded on a psychology which, M. Seylaz observes, appears to us schematic "dans sa façon de déchiffrer les soupirs, la langueur, de s'en servir comme de signes irréfutables":[6] as we have repeatedly seen, the whole society is an agreement on the significance of these signs, their value as code, and voluntarily accepts the psychological systematization they imply; the game of society would come to a halt without such mechanism. With the Marquise and Prévan, movement toward a rendezvous requested and reluctantly accorded proceeds without interruption: as the Marquise remarks, "Qu'il est commode d'avoir affaire à vous autres *gens à principes*! . . . votre marche reglée se devine si facilement!" The final act of the comedy turns on a convention of clothing, which permits Mme de Merteuil to make good her boast that she would both have Prévan and keep him from talking. Released from his hiding place in the Marquise's wardrobe, he promptly "subjugates" her; but when he wishes to remove his clothes for a more elaborate second attack, she rings for the servants—and he is found in her bedroom at an indecent hour fully clothed, proof that she had not coöperated with his schemes.

Prévan is ruined because he has failed to secure public proof of Mme de Merteuil's assent, and she is hence able to make his presence in her bedroom appear a brutal violation of the forms of which it was in fact a result. The Marquise is able to write Mme de Volanges an "official" version of the incident, recounting in pompous moral platitudes the appearance she has so brilliantly maintained. This letter is a final manipulation of

[6] Seylaz, p. 76.

the social forms she so well understands; it perfectly closes an incident which is a decisive illustration of three elliptical and penetrating propositions on *Les Liaisons dangereuses* by Baudelaire:

> Livre essentiellement français.
> Livre de sociabilité, terrible, mais sous le badin et
>   le convenable
> Livre de sociabilité.[7]

The love of society and its forms—on the part of Laclos as well as his characters—the enactment of human destinies entirely within the frame of society and in terms of its conventions, the epistolary form itself, make "sociability" tone and subject of the novel. Like the novels of Crébillon and Marivaux, which, in their social view of the world are also "essentially French," *Les Liaisons dangereuses* is a brilliant comedy of manners. Yet the good manners, as Prévan's end, like the whole novel, illustrates, conceal the *terrible* which not only lies beneath but is built into them.

The sociability of *Les Liaisons dangereuses* is "terrible" because the society is so closed, the image it projects so coercive, human relationships systematized with such rigorous logic and purity. That is why the book seems so "classic," so reminiscent of Racine, Mme de Lafayette, and the original tradition of worldliness. Like the palace of Racinian tragedy, or the court of *La Princesse de Clèves*, this is a world where one cannot escape those one flees, and where meetings with those one seeks take place under the eyes of others. That personal relationships have come to be seen so exclusively in erotic terms reflects this enclosure and rigorous systematization. The erotic relationship might appear an irreducible, solid reality amidst the factitiousness of social forms; yet it is in fact the most self-conscious, self-reflexive of relationships.

[7] Charles Baudelaire, *"Les Liaisons dangereuses," Oeuvres complètes* (Paris: Bibliothèque de la Pléiade, 1958), p. 998.

Hence, as for Crébillon, for Laclos the erotic is perhaps essentially the most exacerbated form of social relations. Eroticism in this novel implies not only a conception of self —the point most modern critics have insisted upon—but also a conception of the group, a society which has given exclusive value to games of domination and control, pursuit and enslavement, which can, in human logic, find their outcome only in the erotic relationship. Hence the social confrontations of Laclos' novel necessarily have an erotic dénouement —indeed, the book is structured on a series of erotic encounters which measure the strength of the contestants.

In these contests, our allegiance is a product of our complicity, and the language used by Valmont and the Marquise to fix and dehumanize any potentially competitive forces— Prévan, Gercourt, Danceny, Mme de Volanges—enlists our total consent. Yet use of a language and a form may not always convince: when the Marquise turns her abilities as a portraitist to the Présidente, we sense a nuance of jealousy that suggests the control is more hoped-for than real:

> Qu'est-ce donc que cette femme? des traits réguliers si vous voulez, mais nulle expression: passablement faite, mais sans grâces: toujours mise à faire rire! avec ses paquets de fichus sur la gorge, et son corps qui remonte au menton! Je vous le dis en amie, il ne vous faudrait pas deux femmes comme celle-là, pour vous faire perdre toute votre considération. . . . Allons, Vicomte, rougissez vous-même, et revenez à vous. Je vous promets le secret. (V)

The portrait expresses the terms to which Mme de Merteuil would like to reduce the Présidente, the kind of dismissal she would like to achieve, and the letter is admirably designed to shame Valmont out of any further attention to the Présidente. But the fact that the Marquise feels a need to attempt to disengage Valmont in this manner, joined to the

fact of Valmont's increasing preoccupation with Mme de
Tourvel, and, finally, the dignified, impressive tone of her
own letters, suggest that this character can perhaps not so
easily be circumscribed and fixed within the system.

The question of the Présidente's relation to the system depends on our understanding of Valmont's pursuit, his use of
system in tracking his prey. His public image is that of a
totally calculating being; as Mme de Volanges describes it,
"Encore plus faux et dangereux qu'il n'est aimable et
séduisant, jamais, depuis sa plus grande jeunesse, il n'a fait un
pas ou dit une parole sans avoir un projet . . ."(IX). He has
eliminated chance from human affairs and established himself as an irresistible destiny to his designated victims. Like the
Marquise, he often conceives his mastery of others as mastery of different social representations, roles or masques, and
a protean command of metamorphoses which guarantees his
freedom from fixation and limitation. We are made aware
of this conception of self in Valmont's first statements of intent and project, in his first letter, to the Marquise:

Mais de plus grands interêts nous appellent; conquérir est
notre destin; il faut le suivre. . . .

Voilà ce que j'attaque; voilà l'ennemi digne de moi; voilà
le but où je prétends atteindre. . . . (IV)

And, in his next letter:

J'aurai cette femme; je l'enlèverai au mari qui la profane:
j'oserai la ravir au Dieu même qu'elle adore.

Qu'elle croie à la vertu, mais qu'elle me la sacrifie; que ses
fautes l'épouvantent sans pouvoir l'arrêter; et qu'agitée de
mille terreurs, elle ne puisse les oublier, les vaincre que dans
mes bras. Qu'alors j'y consens, elle me dise: "Je t'adore"; elle

seule, entre toutes les femmes, sera digne de prononcer ce
mot. Je serai vraiment le Dieu qu'elle aura préféré.

Pour que je sois vraiment heureux, il faut qu'elle se donne;
et ce n'est pas une petite affaire. (VI)

Valmont's verbal style is a continual parody: of the Cornelian
heroic ideal; of military language (a letter will be a "bulle-
tin," he is to be judged like Turenne); of Rousseau and the
union of *les belles âmes*, turning his victim into a predestined mate; of religious concepts, substituting himself, as Baudelaire perceived, for Satan, rival of God, even, if we extend
the sense of his mythology, killing God to take his place as
creator and manipulator of the creatures who exist only in
his own image.

These travesties respond to a sadistic need to degrade. Valmont's mode of seduction takes us back to the root meaning
of the word: a leading away from the right path, *dévoiement*, as Georges Blin has characterized it[8]—debasement, per-
version of normal human relationships and social forms. He
makes Danceny persuade his beloved Cécile to yield the key
that will give him, Valmont, access to her bedroom; and
later, when he takes charge of Cécile's correspondence, he can
boast, "Que n'aurai-je pas fait pour ce Danceny? J'aurai été à
la fois son ami, son confident, son rival et sa maîtresse!"
(CXV). He uses the language of religious unction to gain
the Présidente's hearing, stages a scene of charitable works,
undergoes a false conversion and arranges the meeting which
finishes in the Présidente's bed through the intercession of a
priest. Substituting himself for the Présidente's husband, he
postmarks a letter from "Dijon." He is fond of the equivocal,
enjoys telling the truth when he is sure his correspondent

[8] In a course professed at the Sorbonne, 1962-63. M. Blin developed a
critique of Valmont which has influenced my view of the novel, but, if
I remember correctly, he largely overstated his case in trying to make
of Valmont an essentially ridiculous—even stock-comic—figure.

will not grasp its literal meaning, and writes the Présidente a letter which is one extended *double-entendre* on the bare back of a prostitute.

These perversions of the beliefs and characteristic expressive systems of others are again intended to prove Valmont's perfect control of social and psychological realities. But the perpetual recourse to travesty, and the tone of some of the quotations given above, may suggest the question, to what extent is Valmont taken in by his posing, to what degree is he prisoner of the roles he sees for himself? At what point does his mock-heroic take on for him the dimensions of the heroic? The exaggeration and violence of his language, the extravagance of his metamorphoses, suggest a lack of distance from his acting that would seem to contradict his image of self and system. His love of *dévoiement* leads to damaging involvement. An example is the scene of charitable works, where, parodying a taste of the times well represented by the paintings of Greuze, he arranges a pathetic tableau from his rescue of a bankrupt family, in order to impress the Présidente's spy. When the patriarch of the family sinks to his knees exclaiming "Tombons tous aux pieds de cette image de Dieu," Valmont admits, "J'avouerai ma faiblesse; mes yeux se sont mouillés de larmes, et j'ai senti en moi un mouvement involontaire, mais délicieux"(XXI). In the next sentence, the sentiment is mocked by being offered as the ulterior motivation of all charity. Yet the admission to an involuntary emotion is an important indication of the extent to which parody can become emotional reality for Valmont.

As we progress in the novel, we receive more important confirmation of the suspicion that Valmont is not perfectly in control of his roles. As the Présidente continues to resist his control, his tone becomes ever more violent, until he expresses his vision of her still future capitulation in these terms:

Si pourtant on aime mieux le genre héroïque, je montrerai la Présidente, ce modèle cité de toutes les vertus! respectée
même de nos plus libertins! telle enfin qu'on avait perdu
jusqu'à l'idée l'attaquer! je la montrerai, dis-je, oubliant ses
devoirs et sa vertu, sacrifiant sa réputation et deux ans de
sagesse, pour courir après le bonheur de me plaire, pour
s'enivrer de celui de m'aimer, se trouvant suffisamment dé-
dommagée de tant de sacrifices, par un mot, par un regard
qu'encore elle n'obtiendra pas toujours. Je ferai plus, je la
quitterai; et je ne connais pas cette femme, ou je n'aurai
point de successeur. Elle résistera au besoin de consolation,
à l'habitude du plaisir, au désir même de la vengeance. Enfin,
elle n'aura existé que pour moi et que sa carrière soit plus
ou moins longue, j'en aurai seul ouvert et fermé la barrière.
Une fois parvenu à ce triomphe, je dirai a mes rivaux:
"Voyez mon ouvrage, et cherchez-en dans le siècle un second exemple!" (CXV)

Since this letter is written to the Marquise, who has ridiculed Valmont for the slow pace of his campaign against the
Présidente, some of its bragging, its insistence on absolute
and divine control of his victim, who will have existed only
insofar as she was his creature, can be explained by his need
to preserve and further his image with his accomplice. Yet
the excessive rodomontade suggests even more a need to confirm his image to himself. The frenetic, exclamatory tone
suggests the weakness of emotional involvement; the exaggerated insistence on his future mastery of the Présidente points
to his own present dependence on her, his lack of psychological liberty and freedom of movement.

"The era of the Byrons was coming," said Baudelaire
apropos of Valmont,[9] and indeed this rhetoric suggests Byronic posturing. Valmont's repeated insistence on the

[9] Baudelaire, p. 997.

grandiose significance of his coming victory over the Présidente, his detailing of diversionary tactics—the night with the Vicomtesse de M. . . , the seduction of Cécile—are designed to direct the Marquise's and his own attention away from the question of his relations with the Présidente. As early as his first letter, he admitted, "J'ai bien besoin d'avoir cette femme, pour me sauver du ridicule d'en être amoureux"(IV). The statement is ambiguous, however, since "love" has here only a conventional public meaning, referring to a kind of appearance Valmont must avoid. The nature of his sentiments toward Mme de Tourvel is, at this point in the novel, obscure, and must remain so, for the only accounts we receive are those designed for the Marquise. What exactly transpires at Mme de Rosemonde's château can never be known, for all Valmont would communicate is that which appears most successfully calculated and executed according to system. The extent to which his behavior is really governed by calculation is uncertain. When he refuses to profit by the Présidente's nervous attack, he insists that his abstention proves allegiance to his method. As he has repeatedly insisted, the Présidente must give herself for his victory to be real; simply taking her is not enough. To this, the Marquise replies that even a woman who gives herself must be taken, and she accuses Valmont of refraining because of motives of timidity and emotional involvement—in short, because of his love for the Présidente.

It is almost impossible to determine whether such an act constitutes fidelity or infidelity to the system, but it is certain that the letter in which Valmont describes Mme de Tourvel's nervous seizure reveals a real loss of control on his part, pity, and a depth of emotional sympathy which suggest that he regards her as more than the usual erotic object. His "satanism" indeed seems to be in conflict with a real need to worship and be worshipped. And his next letter, announcing Mme de Tourvel's treacherous departure, lays bare his dependence on the object of his pursuit. From its opening line —"je suis joué, trahi, perdu; je suis au désespoir"—a frantic tone reigns. Self-questioning—"Non, je ne conçois rien à ce départ; il faut renoncer à connaître les femmes"—alternates with rage: "Quel plaisir j'aurai à me venger! je la retrouverai, cette femme perfide; je reprendrai mon empire sur elle." He moves from wounded vanity at not having known, and hence not having controlled, the psychological motions of the Présidente, to a self-examination which, despite or perhaps because of its bravado, comes close to sincerity:

> Mais quelle fatalité m'attache à cette femme? cent autres ne désirent-elles pas mes soins? ne s'empresseront-elles pas d'y répondre? quand même aucune ne vaudrait celle-ci, l'attrait de la variété, le charme des nouvelles conquêtes, l'éclat de leur nombre, n'offrent-ils pas des plaisirs assez doux? Pourquoi courir après celui qui nous fuit, et négliger ceux qui se présentent? Ah! pourquoi? . . . Je l'ignore, mais je l'éprouve fortement.
>
> Il n'est plus pour moi de bonheur, de repos, que par la possession de cette femme que je hais et que j'aime avec une égale fureur. (C)

This passage, in a sinuous rhetoric of self-questioning inherited from Racine, marks to a degree the crumbling of a system. "Fatality" in Valmont's previous letters is ironic and satanic: he would be fatality, God and Satan, to Mme de Tourvel. Here, however, he applies the word to his own psychology. The rhetorical questions that follow are all intended to reassure Valmont, as well as the Marquise, of his irresistibility, as if the barrier presented by the Présidente had thrown everything into question. When he admits, "Je l'ignore, mais je l'éprouve fortement," he is committing a major infidelity to his system of lucidity, intelligence, and power. His *odi et amo* admits to a strength of emotion that both he and the Marquise have continually denied to be possible; in this last line, in fact, he sounds like the Présidente herself, wounded and tortured by love. Perhaps we should finally say that the violent, frenetic tone of the passage is its truth.

If Valmont is falling in love with the Présidente, and as a consequence is unconsciously attesting to the undermining of his system, his hatred of the Présidente's resistance to his control permits him still to maneuver. Even these maneuvers, however, may be more an illusion reflected from Valmont's letters than an absolute reality. In Letter XLIV Valmont reports his discovery that Mme de Tourvel not only has preserved all his letters, but has even pieced together the one she tore up, and bathed it in her tears, and, further, has recopied in a trembling hand the first letter Valmont sent her. For the reader, the consequences of this discovery are subtle and important. It establishes, first, that the Présidente has been in love with Valmont from the outset, and his maneuvers have been necessary, and will be necessary, only in bringing her to the point of declaration and submission. This in turn proves that Valmont's psychological estimate of the Présidente and his judgment of his own progress have been substantially correct, and that the Marquise's refusal to believe in his accomplishment marks a lack of penetration on her part, or a blindness motivated by jealousy, or perhaps a dissimulation of what she has perceived out of motives of rivalry and jealousy. Unquestionably, Valmont's moves after Mme de Tourvel's departure—the feigned conversion, the use of Père Anselme to gain access to her house—will produce the desired results. Yet we must finally recognize that all these maneuvers depend for their effect on a love (on the part of the Présidente) which really has nothing to do with Valmont's system, and which in fact will rapidly transcend and defeat the system.

In recounting his scene of triumph, Valmont again impresses us with the force of his psychological penetration, the extent to which he controls Mme de Tourvel's mechanisms: "Le maintien mal assuré, la respiration haute, la contraction de tous les muscles, les bras tremblants, et à demi élevés, tout me prouvait assez que l'effet était tel que j'avais voulu le produire"(CXXV). But the accompanying insistence on fidelity to principles, operation by system, seems excessive:

> Jusque-là, ma belle amie, vous me trouverez, je crois, une pureté de méthode qui vous fera plaisir; et vous verrez que je ne me suis écarté en rien des vrais principes de cette guerre, que nous avons remarqué souvent être si semblable à l'autre. Jugez-moi donc comme Turenne ou Frédéric.

In reality, Valmont has needed only to demonstrate to the Présidente that sacrifice of herself would assure his happiness, that his sole alternative is suicide; her love has done the rest.

In fact, the exultation with which the letter begins:

> La voilà donc vaincue, cette femme superbe qui avait osé croire qu'elle pourrait me résister! Oui, mon amie, elle est à moi, entièrement à moi; et depuis hier, elle n'a plus rien à m'accorder.

raises the question of who has triumphed over whom. For Valmont continues, "Je suis encore trop plein de mon bonheur, pour pouvoir l'apprécier, mais je m'étonne du charme inconnu que j'ai ressenti." His language is strong: *étonner,* in its classical sense, suggests a reaction of shock, while *charme inconnu,* to someone who has indicated that he had experienced all sensations, calls attention to itself. His return to the significance of his seduction as systematic conquest seems a way of protecting himself from something new and unknown:

Ce n'est donc pas, comme dans mes autres aventures, une simple capitulation plus ou moins avantageuse, et dont il est plus facile de profiter que de s'enorgueillir; c'est une victoire complète, achetée par une campagne pénible, et décidée par de savantes manoeuvres. Il n'est donc pas surprenant que ce succès, dû à moi seul, m'en devienne plus précieux; et le surcroit de plaisir que j'ai éprouvé dans mon triomphe, et que je ressens encore, n'est que la douce impression du sentiment de la gloire. Je chéris cette façon de voir, qui me sauve l'humiliation de penser que je puisse dépendre on quelque manière de l'esclave même que je me serais asservie; que je n'aie pas en moi seul la plénitude de mon bonheur; et que la faculté de m'en faire jouir dans toute son énergie soit réservée à telle ou telle femme, exclusivement à toute autre.

Clearly, Valmont senses that what has happened to him is in some way unique, and he can only explain this sensation —to himself as much as to the Marquise—by transforming it into the effect of a glorious victory won by knowing maneuvers. His elaborate detailing of reasons not to be ashamed of his sensation is directed toward refusal of the idea that he might in any way be dependent on Mme de Tourvel, that his happiness might owe anything to a particular erotic object—Mme de Merteuil has mocked those who confuse love with the lover—and toward assertion that he is the self-sufficient master of his happiness. Yet his very insistence undermines the sense of freedom that he would convey: "love" has clearly become a problem for Valmont because he has discovered its quality as dependency, the negation of his whole system.

Most revealing, perhaps, of Valmont's actual experience is his remark,

L'ivresse fut complète et réciproque; et, pour la première fois, la mienne survécut au plaisir. Je ne sortis de ses bras que pour tomber à ses genoux, pour lui jurer un amour éternel; et, il faut tout avouer, je pensais ce que je disais.

This permits us to say at least that he has experienced a completely new sensation, and has achieved something that was reputed impossible in the libertine literature of the time, an intoxication which outlasts the culmination of erotic enjoyment. And this, it seems to me, is a source of the jealousy the Marquise undoubtedly displays in her succeeding letters. She is, as Baudelaire and other critics have maintained, jealous of the Présidente, for she feels herself humiliated by a somehow superior woman; but also, and perhaps more importantly, she is jealous of Valmont himself for having achieved the union and the self-abandonment that she judged virtually impossible. In an earlier letter, when she described the metamorphoses she performed for the Chevalier de Belleroche, we saw her love of control and freedom of movement, but also her desire to be subjugated. And this suggests that under her will for lucidity and mastery, for making things move according to her dramatic prearrangement, there is a contrary desire to lose herself. Her playfulness, her elaborate part-acting, point to a certain lack, perhaps desperation at the impossibility of losing conscious control. For, to Valmont, in criticizing the Présidente's potential for pleasure, she holds forth another ideal:

Cet entier abandon de soi-même, ce délire de la volupté où le plaisir s'épure par son excès, ces biens de l'amour. ... (V)

Whereas, she adds, "dans le tête-à-tête conjugal le plus tendre, on reste toujours deux." Do her jealousy of Valmont, then her sudden turn to Danceny, suggest an unrewarded search for perfect union, for the situation where her independent personality might be totally absorbed and subjugated to "reciprocal intoxication"?

Valmont with the Présidente has moved beyond the erotic and emotional scheme avowed by the Marquise, and she perceives this from the language he uses to describe his new experience. From this point on, Mme de Merteuil's letters to Valmont are a continual sarcasm, mocking the terms in which he has recounted his adventure and his sentiments; they display a remarkably ill-concealed bitterness of tone, joined to a teasing invitation to renew their old liaison, which culminates in her statement of "terms":

> J'exigerais donc, voyez la cruauté! que cette rare, cette étonnante Madame de Tourvel ne fût plus pour vous qu'une femme ordinaire, une femme telle qu'elle est seulement: car il ne faut pas s'y tromper; ce charme qu'on croit trouver dans les autres, c'est en nous qu'il existe; et c'est l'amour seul qui embellit tant l'objet aimé. (CXXXIV)

Such is the avowed credo of both Valmont and the Marquise, and it is necessary to her conception of self that she maintain it, and force him to maintain it. Early in the novel, we saw, she fixed Mme de Tourvel in a portrait as an awkward, unfashionable, cold, and rather ridiculous prude; to permit her to exceed the frame of that portrait, and show herself other, would be to accept defeat. Further, her conception of eroticism, and of human relations in general, is founded upon individual self-control and self-containment, the voluntary inclusion of all emotional reality within the self, and denies the possibility of complementation from another being. Finally, she may sense that Mme de Tourvel enslaved has achieved a domination which exceeds any exercised by the Marquise, for Valmont is in fact enslaved to Mme de Tourvel's enslavement to him—a situation of which he is partially aware, and which he combats by a passing infidelity with the *courtisane* Émilie, a gesture of libertinage to assure himself of his freedom. The Marquise, metamorphosing herself into a harem for Belleroche, showed an understanding of the power of servitude, and now instinctively perceives that final dominion is exercised by the victim.

For these compound reasons—the Marquise never reveals which motives are decisive in her conduct—the Présidente, and more precisely Valmont's experience with the Présidente, constitute a threat. The Marquise maneuvers to destroy it; she sends Valmont a model letter of rupture organized around the refrain, *ce n'est pas ma faute*:

> On s'ennuie de tout, mon Ange, c'est une Loi de la Nature; ce n'est pas ma faute.
>
> Si donc je m'ennuie aujourd'hui d'une aventure qui m'a occupé entièrement depuis quatre mortels mois, ce n'est pas ma faute.
>
> Si, par exemple, j'ai eu juste autant d'amour que toi de vertu, et c'est sûrement beaucoup dire, il n'est pas étonnant que l'un ait fini en même temps que l'autre. Ce n'est pas ma faute.
>
> Il suit de là, que depuis quelque temps je t'ai trompée: mais aussi ton impitoyable tendresse m'y forçait en quelque sorte! Ce n'est pas ma faute.
>
> Aujourd'hui, une femme que j'aime éperdument exige que je te sacrifie. Ce n'est pas ma faute.
>
> Je sens bien que voilà une belle occasion de crier au parjure: mais si la Nature n'a accordé aux hommes que la constance, tandis qu'elle donnait aux femmes l'obstination, ce n'est pas ma faute.
>
> Crois-moi, choisis un autre Amant, comme j'ai fait une autre Maîtresse. Ce conseil est bon, très bon; si tu le trouves mauvais, ce n'est pas ma faute.

Adieu, mon Ange, je t'ai prise avec plaisir, je te quitte sans regret: je te reviendrai peut-être. Ainsi va le monde. Ce n'est pas ma faute. (CXLI)

This letter, which has lost none of its shock value in close to two centuries, is well-calculated for effect on Mme de Tourvel: as the Marquise later vaunts, "Croyez-moi, Vicomte, quand une femme frappe dans le coeur d'une autre, elle manque rarement de trouver l'endroit sensible, et la blessure est incurable" (CXLV). What makes it such an utterly effective weapon against the Présidente is its tone of cheap, cynical worldliness. While Mme de Tourvel, like Julie, has seen her fall in some measure redeemed and sanctified by the total investment of self that she and Valmont have consciously and willingly made to realize a union of *belles âmes*, the letter insists upon the ordinariness and falsity of the affair, termed a mere "adventure," and on the partners' lack of moral responsibility. As she gradually gave herself over to passion and to Valmont, Mme de Tourvel moved closer and closer to the sublimity of Julie:

> O vous, dont l'âme toujours sensible, même au milieu de ses erreurs, est restée amie de la vertu, vous aurez égard à ma situation douloureuse, vous ne rejetterez pas ma prière! Un intérêt plus doux, mais non moins tendre, succédera à ces agitations violentes: alors, respirant par vos bienfaits, je chérirai mon existence, et je dirai dans la joie de mon coeur: Ce calme que je ressens, je le dois à mon ami. (XC)

This is the musical chant of Rousseauian passion, and it seems to elicit a response in Valmont. In a letter to Mme de Rosemonde, after her fall, the Présidente shows herself convinced—and may convince us—of the rare quality of his love:

> Je l'avouerai, je lui trouvais auparavant un air de réflexion,

de réserve, qui l'abandonnait rarement et qui souvent me ramenait, malgré moi, aux fausses et cruelles impressions qu'on m'avait données de lui. Mais depuis qu'il peut se livrer sans contrainte aux mouvements de son coeur, il semble deviner tous les désirs du mien. Qui sait si nous n'étions pas nés l'un pour l'autre! . . . (CXXXII)

The last sentence echoes Saint-Preux; the image it evokes is utterly destroyed by the letter announcing boredom and infidelity, qualifying fidelity as "obstination" and describing tenderness as "pitiless," equating four months of love with four months of virtue (which the Présidente has left far behind in her assumption into passion), and disavowing any kind of responsibility to a person, rather than a conception. The letter, the Présidente must feel, could not have been written by the Valmont she knew—and I think she is right—and the split between the two images of reality seems fully sufficient cause for her subsequent delirium, announced by a dignified and moving farewell to society in which she has recourse to an almost Biblical image: "Le voile est déchiré, Madame, sur lequel était peinte l'illusion de mon bonheur" (CXLIII).

If Mme de Merteuil's letter is perfectly designed to destroy the Présidente, it is also composed to entrap Valmont through his vanity: it is almost a parody of his worldliness, and Valmont, who has to a degree been taken in by his own travesties, does not possess a sufficiently sure sense of style to distinguish parody from the real thing. As the Marquise tells him,

Oui, Vicomte, vous aimiez beaucoup Madame de Tourvel, et même vous l'aimez encore; vous l'aimez comme un fou: mais parce que je m'amusais à vous en faire honte, vous l'avez bravement sacrifiée. Vous en auriez sacrifié mille, plutôt que de souffrir une plaisanterie. Où nous conduit pourtant la vanité! (CXLV)

Mme de Merteuil has operated in confidence that fear of ridicule, as the *moralistes* assured us, is a tyrant who governs worldly behavior. To be more precise, we can say that Valmont's loyalty to the conception of self and the system he has so insisted upon in his letters forces him to this act: as the Marquise pertinently argues, "Après tout, une femme n'en vaut-elle pas une autre? ce sont vos principes" (CLII). He has been trapped by the Marquise's superior knowledge of him, her ability to manipulate his extreme self-consciousness. Her acrid tone of triumph is our confirmation of her jealousy of Valmont, her desire to reassert her limiting control over him:

> J'avoue de bonne foi que ce triomphe me flatte plus que tous ceux que j'ai pu obtenir jusqu'à présent. Vous allez trouver peut-être que j'évalue bien haut cette femme, que naguère j'appréciais si peu; point du tout: mais c'est que ce n'est pas sur elle que j'ai remporté cet avantage; c'est sur vous: voilà le plaisant et ce qui est vraiment délicieux. (CXLV)

And, despite his boasts about the ease of his rupture, despite his insistence on the lustre it will add to his reputation, Valmont himself recognizes, even before receiving this letter, that he has in fact been trapped: he commits the decisive and revealing step of attempting to make his way to the Présidente to renew their liaison. He has failed to realize, however, or failed to admit to himself, that the blow was indeed mortal; and letter CXLIV reveals a torturing anxiety as the suspicion grows that the Présidente may indeed be lost for good.

For the Présidente once again has escaped the limitations within which the Marquise and Valmont attempted to confine her. She has collapsed, and will die of a broken heart as, the worldly "Publisher" assured us, no one in reality ever does. But she represents another order of reality. One of the extraordinary successes of the novel is its preservation of the Présidente's autonomy. Modern critics, seduced by the attractiveness and satanic dimensions of the Marquise and Valmont, have tended to ignore Mme de Tourvel, or to find her insipid;[10] such views show an inattention to her letters and their progression of tone. Composed at first to impose on Valmont an image of severe virtue and frigidity, then to implore her persecutor to desist from pursuit of his quarry, these letters are progressively more permeated by warmth and passion; her surrender of self is accompanied by dignified and intelligent self-analysis. She is unsparingly lucid in analyzing her own bad faith: when, just before her surrender, she believes herself abandoned by a Valmont who has turned to God, she forces herself to recognize that a conversion which should make her happy in fact makes her miserable. Her first letter after her fall, written in reply to a note from Mme de Rosemonde applauding her continued resistance, shows a perfect estimate and acceptance of her new dependency:

Je n'ai reçu qu'hier, Madame, votre tardive réponse. Elle m'aurait tuée sur-le-champ, si j'avais eu encore mon existence en moi: mais un autre en est possesseur: et cet autre est M. de Valmont. Vous voyez que je ne vous cache rien. Si vous devez ne me plus trouver digne de votre amitié, je crains moins encore de la perdre que de la surprendre.

---

[10] Such was M. Blin's view. M. Seylaz, however, devotes a few excellent pages to the tone and significance of this character; and M. Laufer accurately remarks that the whole novel can be read as "the discovery of the Présidente" (*Style rococo*, p. 146). Contemporary readers seem to have appreciated the Présidente: see, for example, the Comte de Tilly's judgment: "Le portrait de Madame de Tourvel est adorable, et a fait verser bien des larmes à la jeunesse des deux sexes. . . . Voilà un hommage à la vertu. . . . C'est encore un tribut au véritable amour!" *Mémoires du Comte Alexandre de Tilly pour servir à l'histoire de la fin du dix-huitième siècle*, in Laclos, *Oeuvres complètes*, Appendices, p. 709.

Tout ce que je puis vous dire, c'est que, placée par M. de
Valmont entre sa mort ou son bonheur, je me suis décidée
pour ce dernier parti. Je ne m'en vante, ni ne m'en accuse:
je dis simplement ce qui est. (CXXVIII)

The worldly masters show no greater powers of self-analysis. If she does not penetrate the motives of others, Mme de
Tourvel, like Julie, delves within to know herself.

The story of the Présidente demonstrates one of the advantages of the epistolary form in Laclos' expert hands. We are
closer to the Présidente than are any of the other characters in the novel; unhampered by strict allegiance to any system, without ulterior motive, we listen to her letters, her self-
betrayals and analyses, and we understand her instinctively
and sympathetically, as we do the Julie to whom her conception owes so much. Her voice alone, its spontaneity, musical-
ity, and instinctive morality, confirms her independence from
the system in which the other characters live. From her
point of view, her experience is Rousseauian, and nothing
in the novel infirms this view. Far from having existed only
by and for Valmont, as he predicted in Letter CXV—that is,
having existed only in terms of his public use of her in *le
monde*—she posits her own sphere of being. Laclos has been
careful not to permit Mme de Tourvel to fit the Marquise's
portrait of her; she goes far beyond it, following a curve
of passion which is incomprehensible to Valmont and the
Marquise, but which nonetheless both of them glimpse obscurely, and which makes Mme de Merteuil afraid. Hence
the Marquise demands and arranges the sacrifice, by insisting that there are not, that there cannot be, more things in
heaven and earth than are dreamt of in Valmont's philosophy.

The existence of the Présidente brings dissension and
combat between Valmont and the Marquise—a combat
which appears as an episode in a debate about the limits of

man. It is essential to the Marquise, and she makes Valmont feel it is essential to him, that the limits they have dedicated themselves to establishing, proving, and commenting, be maintained. The Marquise cannot admit that a Mme de Tourvel, such as she seems to be, and a relationship like that which seems to obtain between her and Valmont, have any reality; to do so would be to declare her own system, her life's work—and the effort it involved is insisted upon in the letter describing her self-education—misdirected and worthless. She finds meaning in the world by stating its limits, as did La Rochefoucauld, or Versac, or anyone who relied on the distanced, abstract, categorical evaluative vocabulary of the *moralistes*. The use of that language, we saw, inevitably implies a refusal to allow man's dimensions and potentialities beyond certain close confines; but with the Marquise we reach a final term in the voluntary, active, calculated imposition of limits upon other beings, and upon the whole of reality.

That Valmont accepts these limits on himself is part of his personal tragedy. Earlier, in the midst of his pursuit of the Présidente, he foresaw the ordinary dénouement of his seductions: "Ah! le temps ne viendra que trop tôt, où, dégradée par sa chute, elle ne sera plus pour moi qu'une femme ordinaire"(XCVI). When he does not feel this degradation—when he finds instead a psychological liberation in his dependence on his victim—he is not allowed, through enforced allegiance to what he was, to profit from his sense of newness and enlargement: instead, he is trapped by the Marquise's piece of cheap and limiting worldliness. The system and the style that were to guarantee his freedom and his dominion among men ironically become the instruments of his entrapment.

One must understand his sense of loss, of tragedy—comprehended by him only obscurely—to understand the end of the novel and the ferocity of the war between the two collaborators. Having made his sacrifice, Valmont feels it is imperative at least to reap the benefit that ought to be his for having aligned himself with the Marquise and her philosophy: the return of the Marquise as a mistress. For her, however, victory would be incomplete, her great act of manipulation annulled, were Valmont to be rewarded: loyalty to the idea of free mastery demands that she refuse herself to him and work instead upon Cécile's Danceny. Therefore, there is challenge and response: "Hé bien! la guerre"(CLIII). We have these four words where before there were lengthy and artful letters: the polite social forms of combat have broken down. With this falling out of the two master plotters, the two self-styled representatives of the forces of intelligence and domination, we realize that the elegant, flawless system of intelligence, knowing and controlling, has reached a point of collapse, and that the passions have reasserted their claim. The final catastrophe, the revelation to the public, in the form of these letters, of the secrets of seduction and domination, is the work of uncontrollable pride, jealousy, and resentment.

We witness, in following Valmont's end, a progressive obscuration of the hero. We know that, with the declaration of war between himself and the Marquise, he writes a desperate letter to Mme de Volanges—his chief enemy, as he is well aware—asking her to intervene on his behalf with the Présidente. We do not see that letter, nor the one he sends with it to the Présidente, and which Mme de Volanges keeps from its designated recipient. All we have is her remark, "Mais que direz-vous de ce désespoir de M. de Valmont? D'abord faut-il y croire, ou veut-il seulement tromper tout le monde, et jusqu'à la fin?" (CLIV). The "Editor" cleverly puts himself on the same ground: "C'est parce qu'on n'a rien trouvé dans la suite de cette Correspondance qui pût résoudre ce doute, qu'on a pris le parti de supprimer la Lettre de M. de Valmont." From this point on, we have only one epistle from Valmont—a sarcasm directed to the Marquise—and then the rest is silence, except for his posthumous message in the form of the "Compte ouvert entre la Marquise de Merteuil et le Vicomte de Valmont." While we can be more conclusive than Mme de Volanges and the Editor—we surely have sufficient evidence that Valmont's despair at loss of the Présidente is far from feigned—the artistic advantage gained by suppressing the letter is evident. For who could write such a letter? What would an unfeigning Valmont sound like? Where could he find the terms, the vocabulary, the code to express himself?[11]

The obscurity, then, subsists, and the hero disappears. But it is undeniable that we feel, at the end, as throughout the novel, that we understand Valmont; we feel a closeness to him, a comprehension of his ideals and weaknesses that enable us to see his story as essentially tragic. Tragic, because other possibilities, potentialities for a widening and a deepening of the self, have been glimpsed—obscurely by him, more clearly by the reader. The same cannot be said for the Marquise, and while she is the character whose will most determines the course of action in the novel, she is not heroic in the same sense as Valmont, and she is not a tragic figure. She remains faithful to her system, and this means that she must ever remain distant from us: there is no self-betrayal nor, until the end, any weakness, and even this is a function of her last desperate attempt to preserve system. She is, in terms of her own system, perfect, and it is surely significant that it takes the *deus ex machina* of smallpox to lay her low. Our final vision of her, disfigured, one-eyed, fleeing with her

---

[11] A draft of the letter to Mme de Volanges—crossed out by Laclos—does exist, and can be found in *Oeuvres complètes*, pp. 830-831. The letter to Mme de Tourvel, never opened, of course remains a total mystery.

jewels to Holland where she will lead a life of "sinister adventures," is totally appropriate.

This ending, inevitably, has bothered critics, from the publication of the novel to the present. As La Harpe sententiously announced, "Le vice ne trouve donc pas ici sa punition en lui-même, et ce dénouement sans moralité ne vaut pas mieux que le reste."[12] To be sure, but how could vice find punishment in itself? For punishment, like reward, is dependent on people, on the community; and what Laclos has brilliantly done in the last pages of his novel, with the brusque obscuration of his protagonists, is to redirect our critical attention to the society in which they lived. The question has of course been implicit throughout. In the first letter, Cécile tells us "il ne tiendrait qu'à moi d'être toujours à rien faire," and we are constantly reminded that members of this society are at their wits' end for ways to pass the time. One senses, from his maneuvers as well as his choice of images, that Valmont could easily, with a *carrière ouverte aux talents*, have been a Talleyrand. But for the most part aristocrats were condemned to make the bedroom their Europe. As Denis de Rougemont remarks, in a statement aptly quoted by M. Seylaz, "De la Régence à Louis XVI, Don Juan a régné sur le rêve d'une aristocratie déchue de l'héroisme féodal."[13] The protagonists' Cornelian language suggests this transferral of heroic mastery from one realm to another, and underlines the narrowing and even atrophy of being it has entailed. Further, Cécile's first letter, and indeed her entire story, pose the question of education. The Marquise and Valmont propose to take advantage of Gercourt's "ridiculous prejudices" in favor of "cloistered educations" (II), and when Cécile becomes Valmont's "pupil," he

___

[12] *Correspondance littéraire*, Letter CLIII; in Laclos, *Oeuvres complètes*, Appendices, p. 704.
[13] *L'Amour et l'Occident* (Paris, 1939), p. 203; quoted by Seylaz, p. 107.

delights in instructing her to use a technical vocabulary that will astound Gercourt after their marriage. The two plan, as they say, to "form" Cécile, and her whole story reads as a sort of anti-Émile. Most ironically, and damningly, the tone and attitude of the "pupil's" letters demonstrate no noticeable change as she passes from a state of innocence to corruption. Valmont's account of his own education, though written to gain the Présidente's sympathies, sounds objective enough, since it is nearly a condensation of *Les Égarements du coeur et de l'esprit*:

> Entré dans le monde, jeune et sans expérience; passé, pour ainsi dire, de mains en mains, par une foule de femmes, qui toutes se hâtent de prévenir par leur facilité une ré-flexion qu'elles sentent devoir leur être défavorable. . . . (LII)

More important is the novel's "terrible sociability," its constant reference to the rules that govern the interplay of social beings. From Mme de Volanges' first warning to the Présidente, with its balancing of "séduites" and "perdues," we are aware of the coercive publicity and imposed hypocrisy of this world, and the way they determine the systematic personal style of those who have an intelligent consciousness of society's image. Society has arranged its rules and relations to valorize a kind of behavior that finds ultimate expression in the erotic, then publicly decreed that such behavior is immoral. As is indicated by the Marquise's joy at finding Vicomtesse de M. . . in such a position that she can say of her, "It is impossible to frequent that woman," society has elaborated both publicity and hypocrisy to the point that it feels it must overreact to scandal. The case of Prévan is a perfect example, and his rehabilitation at the end of the novel, when an admiring crowd surrounds him and shuns the Marquise, is equally absurd as his earlier disgrace.

As the Marquise has told us, it is the old women, the "party of the prudes," who make the reputation of the young, and are the moral authority of society. The one older woman whom we come to know well is Mme de Volanges, and her characterization is strikingly indicative of this society's weaknesses. Her dealings with her daughter are inept—ignorant and complacent—from the outset, and her warnings to the Présidente display a love of sensationalism which tends to discredit them: "Écoutez, si vous voulez, la voix du malheureux qu'il a secouru; mais qu'elle ne vous empêche pas d'entendre les cris de cent victimes qu'il a immolées"(XXXII). Yet she admits that she, like the rest of society, continues to receive Valmont. She is used by Mme de Merteuil as a mouthpiece of justification after the scene with Prévan; throughout the novel it is she who piously recites the Marquise's virtues. When Danceny's collection of letters starts to make the rounds of Paris, however, she immediately purveys their contents: "Il se répand ici, ma chère et digne amie, sur le compte de Madame de Merteuil, des bruits bien étonnants et bien fâcheux" (CLXVIII). While protesting her friendship for the Marquise and her disbelief in the rumors, she repeats the damaging evidence in detail.

Toward the end of the novel, the majority of letters are from Mme de Volanges, and it is she who recounts the fates of all the characters except Valmont. This alone would entitle us to see in her the representative of the public view. In fact, however, these gossipy letters explicitly include reëntry of the supporting cast, different representatives of society who voice their reactions. The last public action of the novel is performed at one of the central institutions of its sociability, the Comédie Italienne, and it is Mme de Volanges who narrates, with evident pleasure, this "cruel scene," where all the women present indignantly rise and leave the bench where the Marquise has seated herself: "Ce mouvement marqué d'indignation générale fut applaudi de tous les hommes, et fit redoubler les murmures, qui, dit-on, allèrent jusqu'aux huées"(CLXXIII). We must take an ironic view of this moral indignation—and these bad manners—on the part of "good company," for the novel has indicated that most of these women differ from the Marquise only in the lesser success and daring of their exploits; their present advantage comes only from their being luckier in their disguises, and their love is not of morality but of *médisance*, which they can now direct toward the previously inviolate Mme de Merteuil. Mme de Volanges' final letter reports the *mot* of the Marquis de*** about Mme de Merteuil, "que la maladie l'avait retournée, et qu'à présent son âme était sur sa figure. Malheureusement tout le monde trouva que l'expression était juste"(CLXXV). This witty sarcasm referring to the destruction of a disguise, the ruin of a face as an appearance, is the final moral judgment of this society, and it is utterly appropriate to the society.

By painting such a picture of hypocrisy and self-righteous moralism in Mme de Volanges, who has the last word, and in the society for which she speaks, Laclos may renew our allegiance to the amoral intelligence of Valmont and the Marquise. Their egotistical manipulation of others seems the only adequate response to the bad faith of their contemporaries. But their mythic dimension in the reader's mind is already assured in any case, and I think Laclos is doing something more important with his last pages, directing our attention to the total structures of the world behind the system of the *meneurs du jeu*, to the sociological foundations of the personal styles the novel has dramatized. "J'ai vu les moeurs de mon temps et j'ai publié ces lettres." By this epigraph, Rousseau meant to suggest that his novel constituted a lesson to his contemporaries; Laclos uses it to imply that his novel is an exemplum of contemporary behavior. *Les Liaisons dan-*

gereuses had an immediate *succès de scandale* and, if we accept the report of the notoriously unreliable Comte de Tilly, this was one of its author's intentions: "Je résolus de faire un ouvrage qui sortît de la route ordinaire, qui fît du bruit, *et qui retentît encore sur la terre quand j'y aurai passé,*" he quotes Laclos as having said.[14] Ever the sensationalist, Tilly saw the book, from his post-Revolutionary perspective, as "un de ces météores désastreux qui ont apparu sous un ciel enflammé, à la fin du XVIIIᵉ siècle."

We need not accept so flamboyant a judgment, nor need we wholly agree with Roger Vailland's contention (based, I think, on the picture of Laclos painted in Émile Dard's biography) that Laclos is the "class enemy of the Valmonts,"[15] to see in the novel a critique of a certain society and its characteristic philosophy, ethic, and way of dealing with people. The critique of society comes to us essentially through a critique of the personal styles it has elicited, the stance, techniques, and instruments of worldliness as they are elaborated and deployed by Valmont and the Marquise. Laclos patently admires the two characters into whom he invests his great intelligence, and is attracted to the medium of sociability in which they operate; but by letting the instruments of worldliness develop their ultimate possible application at the service of a systematic and destructive will to power, he dramatizes the weaknesses and limits inherent in the outlook and practice of worldliness. Despite his original enlistment with the forces of seduction and mastery, by the end of the novel the reader is compelled to see their limitations in the limits they attempt to impose on others. These limits are such, finally, that elements of life escape their estimation and their control; hence their system is made to seem limited, and the society that dic-

[14] In Laclos, *Oeuvres complètes*, p. 708.
[15] *Laclos par lui-même* (Paris, 1953), p. 8; see Émile Dard, *Le Général Choderlos de Laclos* (Paris, 1905).

tated the system is itself made to appear less than the whole of reality.

In contact with the "other reality" of the Présidente, the operation of systematic worldliness becomes self-defeating. Through the breakdown of the system and through the story of Valmont's experience with the Présidente, Laclos suggests that there are things on earth undreamt of in the philosophy of worldliness. The mark of Rousseau is evident here: his critique of the system upon which the literature of worldliness reposed—a closed order of social conformity, coercion, and manipulation—and his exaltation of the autonomy and inherent morality of real passion, total union with another being, have influenced both Laclos' view of society and his conception of love. In his essays on the education of women, Laclos establishes his allegiance to Rousseau when he contrasts the natural state of woman to what she has become in society—a slave of man, powerless before a social system built to institutionalize her slavery.[16] Mme de Merteuil's feminine libertinage is one answer to this situation, a conscious attempt to redress the balance within the system, to make of men "Ces Tyrans détrônés devenus mes esclaves." Mme de Tourvel does not revolt; she rather takes a stance without the system, and Laclos, like Rousseau, preserves the autonomy of the passion which needs no social context. Mme de Tourvel's emotions and her destiny, from her point of view, have nothing to do with system; she maintains throughout a dignity, a resistance to the reductive force applied by the Marquise and Valmont, which allow her finally to escape from their system, and to imply a larger view of the world than that inherent in worldliness. What started as a parody of *les belles âmes* becomes, perhaps, their eulogy. If Mme de Tourvel is a victim, she is nevertheless probably

[16] See "Des Femmes et de leur éducation" and "Essai sur l'éducation des femmes," in *Oeuvres complètes*.

happier, and freer, than her torturers—and this too implies an alternative conception of life, for those who can comprehend it.

But this last remark must return us once more to Laclos' hard realism, his refusal to conclude. The world of the novel is evidently not yet ready to accept its Mme de Tourvels; the picture of society rendered in the novel indicates that it is not Valmont alone who is incapable of committing himself to this kind of sensibility, and there is no allusion to worlds elsewhere. Perhaps emphasis falls, finally, on the limits of action in the world. "Livre de moraliste aussi haut que les plus élevés, aussi profond que les plus profonds," said Baudelaire,[17] and what makes us feel this to be so is Laclos' ability both to sum up, to exemplify a tradition, social and novelistic, in an expression which exercises a powerful seductive appeal (Valmont and the Marquise have become almost mythic figures to many moderns), and at the same time to suggest a critique of the system which is more nuanced and subtle than Rousseau's, but just as telling.

The subtlety of Laclos' viewpoint is, of course, partly a result of his choice of the epistolary form, and largely the product of his manipulation of that form. As in *Clarissa* or *La Nouvelle Héloïse*, so here we inevitably feel a closeness to the letter writer, and in *Les Liaisons dangereuses* we feel closest to those who most entertain us—the Marquise and Valmont —and to the one who, at the end, most moves us, the Présidente. Yet we are warned at the outset that most of what we are going to read is feigned—calculated, twisted, oblique—and this even applies to the Présidente's letters, since she cannot admit to Valmont, or to herself, what her real feelings are. Hence, from the closeness we feel in *Clarissa* or *La Nouvelle Héloïse*, we are forced back into an ironic,

[17] Baudelaire, p. 997.

distanced, evaluative worldly standpoint. Any naive, or naively moralistic, or even naively cynical attitudes on the reader's part cannot long subsist, and perhaps more than any other novel—certainly more than any other novel of its century—the book demands an alert and emotionally tough reader, or its effect could be corrosive indeed. Correctly read, as Baudelaire remarked, if this book burns, it is in the manner of ice.

One may ask, finally, if the many varying interpretations elicited by the book, the strong disagreements about its ethic and even about its profound subject, may not indicate the precariousness of its equilibrium. That is, given the form, our untrusting relationship with the characters, and Laclos' commitment to a realism of presentation, authorial attitude can only be suggested in the most subtle, ambiguous, indirect ways: the perceptual and evaluative clarity of worldliness are necessarily gone, since the ethic and instruments of worldliness are given over to the characters exclusively, submerged in the drama. Such indirection, such a refusal to intervene and conclude, are part of the greatness of the book. But one should note that for a later writer, Stendhal, whose attitudes toward society were equally and more self-consciously ambivalent, the form of the novel of letters, so dependent on society, so committed to sociability, and the version of the author-reader-protagonist triangle this novel allows, would not suffice; things would have to be reoriented to permit the author to reassert his voice and his presence, to allow a more direct play of sympathy and judgment on the protagonist, and on the ethic of worldliness.

In the last chapter, we looked at a major revolt against the tradition of worldliness as ethic, way of life, and novelistic stance in the critical statements and novel of Rousseau, and compared this reaction to the new orientation given to the novel by Richardson; in this chapter we considered a novel which, published twenty years after *La Nouvelle Héloïse,* is written both to sum up the viewpoint and practice of worldliness, and to suggest their limitations. I have tried to emphasize the interdependence of the reaction against the tradition of worldliness as social attitude and as novelistic technique. Under the influence of Richardson and Rousseau, the novel was being oriented toward the realism of the bourgeois epic, with its demand for the reader's close sympathetic participation with a protagonist in an exploration of his emotions amidst the detailed realities of quotidian existence in society—this now understood to mean the entire polis, although each given novel would "specialize" and represent only a fragment of this whole. At the publication of *Les Liaisons dangereuses*—with the Revolution only seven years away—some critics claimed that the manners described by Laclos were those of a minority, and that there were worlds elsewhere, something that the novel of worldliness does not, cannot consider.[18] These others worlds, in France, were not, despite the example of Rousseau, notably exploited (Restif, some of Diderot, possibly Bernardin de Saint-Pierre could be considered exceptions), but the novelists who came of age under the Empire and the Restoration quickly made up for this lack. The novel of worldliness, dependent as it was on the sociability of a certain class, the artificial, rigid, and meaningful manners of a closed system, where a move at lansquenet or tric-trac had, along with each word and gesture, a precise meaning within a code, could not survive the Revolution, and must have seemed, in its attitudes and techniques, already limiting to a society that devoured the novels of Rous-

---

[18] Almost all contemporary commentators seem to have agreed that Laclos had accurately represented the manners of a certain society, but some claimed that this society was only a fraction of *le monde.* See the documents assembled in the *Oeuvres complètes,* Appendices.

seau and Richardson. The confidence of the *moralistes* that they could know and say all about man, an essentially social animal, is directly challenged by Rousseau, and implicitly criticized by Laclos.

Yet, as I hope these discussions of Crébillon, Duclos, Marivaux, and Laclos have indicated, in many ways the assumptions of eighteenth-century society provided the novelist of manners with his golden age. The image projected by society possessed such absolute force that every personal style could be related to it through the mediate term of the individual's consciousness of society as a system of values and gestures. Author and reader, both members of this system, shared a commerce such that, by the narrator's turn of phrase, by a character's gesture, all the important moral and social issues could be dramatized. Since the World was one, not an agglomeration of fragmentary sub-worlds, there was no need for descriptive realism, for positioning man among the things that, in later novels, will be our clue to his place, ethic, and manner of being. In turning to Stendhal, we will be examining a writer who was acutely conscious of what was lost, for the writer, with the disappearance of the Old Régime. Educated by a man of eighteenth-century culture, he was instinctively loyal to all the writers we have discussed, and hoped in his work to perpetuate their kind of novel while remaining cognizant of the new demands of the new social order and the Romantic sensibility. Worldliness as we have defined it was an ideal and a temptation for Stendhal, and our discussion of him will focus on how he sought means in his fiction to use and dramatize ethic and viewpoint, while always maintaining a critical distance from them, creating other possibilities and worlds for his characters.

STENDHAL AND THE STYLES
OF WORLDLINESS

STENDHAL's earliest ambition, it appears, was "to write comedies like Molière and live with an actress."[1] The second half of this program was fulfilled by the age of twenty-two, but Stendhal was forced more and more to an awareness that the first part could never be: first in the *Racine et Shakespeare* of 1817, then in some notes jotted in the margin of his copy of *Le Rouge et le noir*, and finally in a preface to the *Lettres sur l'Italie* of the Président de Brosses, Stendhal formulated his discovery that "comedy is impossible in 1836." The French Revolution, he argues, produced a schism in the public that makes theatrical comedy impossible in the nineteenth century: at a performance of Molière's *Bourgeois Gentilhomme* in 1836, half the audience would find the well-bred young hero, Dorante, ridiculous, while the other half laughed at the bourgeois M. Jourdain. Under the Old Régime, the comic dramatist had the enviable advantage of writing for a public forced to spend hours together every day in conversation at Versailles or in Parisian drawing rooms—a public whose sensibility was formed by a common experience of sociability, and hence brought to the same "triggering point" for the comic ("au même point de *détente pour le comique*").[2] In the post-Revolutionary era, the public is frag-

[1] *La Vie de Henry Brulard*, ed. Henri Martineau (Paris: Garnier, 1961), p. 12.
[2] Stendhal, "La Comédie est impossible en 1836," in *Mélanges de*

mented, factionalized, split into classes and interest groups with different backgrounds and different ideals, hence different reactions to the manners dramatized on the stage. With the loss of a unified public, the dramatist loses any close, constituted relationship with his whole audience; he loses what Stendhal calls the "admirable effects of reciprocal sympathy"[3] that result when each gesture and inflection of voice is immediately understood by the audience in the sense that the dramatist gave it. *Ridicule*, the basis of Molière's comedy, satire of deviations from a social norm, is no longer a viable method for no clear norm, no clear, undisputed image of society governs the public's consciousness. To write for the theater in the nineteenth century, one had to turn toward something more direct and cruder than comedy of manners— toward farce or melodrama.

Stendhal's recognition that the comedy of Molière was no longer possible in the nineteenth century marked the final liquidation of the dream actively pursued since adolescence, when he had resolved to be the world's greatest comic poet. It was in an effort to realize this dream that he had multiplied commentaries on Molière and other dramatists, written a treatise on the comic, studied elocution with a retired actor, and haunted the orchestra and the dressing-rooms of Parisian theaters.[4] Born in 1783, educated by an eighteenth-century man of taste and letters, his grandfather Dr. Gagnon,

---

littérature, ed. Henri Martineau (Paris: Le Divan, 1933), III, 431. My view of the place of this essay in Stendhal's thought owes much to Harry Levin's excellent summary of Stendhal's intellectual development in *The Gates of Horn* (New York: Oxford University Press, 1963). See especially the chapter entitled "The Comedy of the Nineteenth Century," pp. 98-113.

[3] "La Comédie est impossible," *Mélanges*, III, 433.

[4] See especially the pieces collected in *Molière, Shakespeare, la comédie et le rire*, ed. Henri Martineau (Paris: Le Divan, 1930); also the *Journal* and the *Pensées*.

Stendhal had inevitably first conceived his literary career in the theater, in the form that more than any other possessed its letters of nobility. This was the appropriate vehicle for expressing one's intelligent and satirical appreciation of social foibles, and it was gilded by an aura of Parisian sociability that intoxicated the young Stendhal. When he recognized that the social system on which the comedy of Molière and his eighteenth-century successors had rested was now defunct, he drew the important conclusion, "Je regarde le roman comme la comédie au XIXe siècle."[5]

Yet this marked only a partial solution, for it is evident that the kind of novel he might write would be affected by his discovery of the schism in the public's social consciousness. Theatrical comedy, the most public, institutional, sociable of literary forms, obviously suffers most from a social revolution, but the destruction of *le monde* in its Old Régime connotation also entails the impossibility of a certain subject and narrative manner in the novel. Compared to the theater, the novel has the advantage of addressing itself to one reader at a time, and it may also—*Clarissa* is the prototype—be "private" in subject and manner, directed to an exploration of the private and individual sensibility, and appealing to a reader's sympathetic identification with the inner life of a hero or heroine. But if one's concern is still essentially comedy of manners, the drama to be found in the forms of man's public social behavior, the question of audience is vital to the novelist as well. There must be a system of comportment—values, words, tones, gestures—shared by author and reader, who must identify their viewpoints with the outlook of the system, rather than with the opposing vision of an outsider, an individual struggling to assert a personal interpretation of life. In the fragmented post-Revolutionary world, the novelist is

---

[5] "La Comédie est impossible: Notes du *Rouge*," *Mélanges*, III, 417.

deprived of any preassumed system in which he and his reader participates; he can no longer exploit Society as the medium of his novelistic world in confidence that this medium embraces and contains author and reader and gives them their terms of reference and standards of judgment. He can no longer use the witty and urbane voice of the novel of worldliness and be sure it will be understood.

His discoveries about the situation of the modern writer indeed threatened to invalidate all the literature Stendhal most admired, the literature that had composed his education and formed his world view. From his grandfather, he had learned that the goal of all human inquiry was *"la connaissance du coeur humain,"*[6] knowledge of human psychology, which of course to the eighteenth century was not separable from what we would call sociology: knowledge of men's motives and acts within the social context. This confident, neo-classical enterprise of knowing man was pursued by the young Henri Beyle almost exclusively in books: in the classical *moralistes*, especially La Bruyère and La Rochefoucauld; in the moralists, memorialists and historians of the eighteenth century, Duclos, Besenval, Marmontel, Chamfort, and Saint-Simon, many of whom were being published for the first time in the years following the Revolution; in the Idéologues; in the novels of Laclos, Crébillon, Rousseau, Marivaux, Duclos, Nerciat, and Cervantes.

We know that Stendhal accorded nearly unlimited faith to the eighteenth-century's observers of worldly behavior. When he arrived in Paris in 1799, he tells us, his imagination of society was formed exclusively from the *Mémoires secrets* of Duclos, the *Mémoires* of Saint-Simon, and the eighteenth-century novelists.[7] *La Vie de Marianne* seemed to him "an excellent book to read before going into society"; Saint-Simon

[6] *La Vie de Henry Brulard*, p. 218.
[7] *La Vie de Henry Brulard*, p. 353.

was "the greatest French historian I have read"; Duclos was an observer with a mind perfectly analogous to his own; Marmontel was useful in teaching him dispassionate, non-romantic judgment.[8] If all of Stendhal's writings are filled with references to the authors we have discussed—if, for example, *De l'amour* constantly cites and paraphrases Crébillon, Duclos, and Laclos—it is because Stendhal found in them an intoxicating image of man become master of his social environment through knowledge of the psychological mechanisms of others and the laws of the social system, man as a voluntarily systematized and stylized controller of reality. To this image corresponded the style—precise, witty, elegant and unpretentious—which his grandfather had early taught him to prize,[9] and which he throughout his life held up as a model of good taste and right manner of being against the flowery pomposities of Chateaubriand and other "bombastic" Romantics, whose style always seemed to him a vehicle of hypocrisy, an effort to blur and disguise rather than define and articulate the truth. Social success, women, pleasure, literary greatness seemed within one's grasp if one cultivated the ethos, techniques, and style of worldliness, a stance toward life which derived from the classical *moralistes*, and had been finally systematized in *Idéologie* and Stendhal's own mechanistic psychology and philosophy, *Beylisme*.

Stendhal's first ambitions as a writer, whether in the theater or the novel, were to imitate this stance, to assume this tone, to reflect this image of man in a work which explored behavior within a medium of polite sociability. But stance,

[8] *Pensées*, ed. Henri Martineau (Paris: Le Divan, 1931), II, 99-100; *Pensées*, II, 273; *Journal*, ed. Henri Martineau (Paris: Le Divan, 1937), V, 217; *Journal*, I, 253-54.

[9] See his description in *La Vie de Henry Brulard* (pp. 254-55) of how his grandfather mocked him whenever he failed to find "la tournure la plus simple et le mot propre," and fell into either the pretentious or the vulgar.

tone, image, and medium depended for their literary exploitation on the existence of the unified and coercive social system, with its universal linguistic and psychological code, which is now defunct; "la connaissance du coeur humain" in the sense Dr. Gagnon and Stendhal attached to it depended on an experience of le monde, which has been shattered. To write about the kind of human relationships that interested him, in the tone and manner he had been trained to believe in, Stendhal would have to find, or fabricate, a world which would furnish the modern equivalent of le monde and bring his reader into some close relation with it. He would have to establish a milieu that was enough a public stage to permit a dramatization of manners, yet also corresponded to a reality. He would have to locate and represent some contemporary system of manners which would allow him to consider experience as more than fragmentary experiences of politics, or love, or social place, or morality—an experience of the total ethos and way of life I have called worldliness. The worldliness of the Old Régime was one, a system embracing and relating all fragments of experience; now, on the contrary, in a world that is really an uneasy amalgam of discrete, specialized societies, worldliness has become only a single possible stance which has no necessary basis in the totality of experience and reality. If worldliness is to be dealt with at all, it cannot be taken for granted; it must be isolated, molded, formed from the exploded mass of realities which make up the modern world. One is led to wonder if the novel of manners is essentially any less impossible than theatrical comedy in the nineteenth century.

If Stendhal's historical perspective on society destroys his ambition to be a dramatist and renders problematical his stance as a novelist, his attitudes are further complicated by his ethical relativism. For he regards as a liberation the loss of a common social ethic in terms of which one judges the individual. The subjects of Louis XIV all strove to imitate a certain social model; when this imitation was imperfect, the failure was met with a bitter, mocking kind of laughter.[10] Working from Hobbes' definition that laughter is generated from our sudden and unexpected perception of superiority to someone else, Stendhal discovered that classical comedy is founded on an authoritarian social ideal, that Molière ridiculed deviations from a coercive social norm. He found in Saint-Lambert the accusation that Molière had attacked all traits opposed to "l'esprit de société," then went on to read the *Lettre à d'Alembert* and approved Rousseau's attack on the ethic of worldliness.[11] An intellectual and political liberal like Stendhal, a man deeply involved in the enthusiasms of the early years of the Napoleonic epic, could not accept the implications of social absolutism. While he admired, even idolized, the mastery of life demonstrated by a character like Valmont, and regretted loss of the system which made this mastery possible, he also instinctively rejected the system's closure and its claims to absolute authority. His denunciation of the "despotism of ridicule,"[12] his admiration for the personal qualities he called "energy" and "the unexpected," point to a desire to go beyond the limits of the worldly sensibility. Similarly, the Romanticism he championed is essentially a relativistic and evolutionary view of taste, a rejection of the moral and esthetic absolutism on which classicism is based.

Stendhal then both regrets the loss of *le monde*, a public system of values and rules, gestures and codes, and sees a liberation in the demise of an enclosed, monolithic, ethically conformist social order. It follows that "worldliness," from a natural and inevitable stance in life and literature, becomes

---

[10] *Racine et Shakespeare*, ed. Henri Martineau (Paris: Le Divan, 1928), p. 50.
[11] *Molière* . . . , p. 289; *Pensées*, I, 165-66; *Pensées*, II, 230.
[12] *Racine et Shakespeare*, p. 322.

one among many viewpoints, one conceivable attitude in the world, one possible style in what Stendhal, in a very eighteenth-century definition, liked to call the pursuit of happiness, "la chasse du bonheur."[13] Worldliness becomes a problem and an issue for Stendhal and for those of his characters who take as their ideal the easy mastery of life demonstrated by Versac or Valmont: if it is no longer *the* style of life, it becomes a problem *in* style. In his own existence, Stendhal tended to respond with the pose of the dandy, the stylized social being who insists that life meet him on his own terms, who creates his own history and his own milieu by his personal style—a figure that was to have a large importance throughout the nineteenth century as more and more writers sought to set the imaginative creation against life and history, and to affirm the autonomy and superiority of the artifact. In Stendhal's fiction, the attitudes and techniques of worldliness become a dramatized problem, no longer an assumed point of view, but one that is created, celebrated, put into question, and forced to demonstrate the range of its validity. It is Stendhal's ways of dramatizing attitude and techniques and of defining worldliness and his characters' and readers' relationship to it, that I want to explore in the novels.

In his first novel, *Armance*, Stendhal's attitudes toward worldliness appear as an ill-resolved ambivalence, a tension which undermines more than it enriches. Stendhal originally conceived of doing "a nineteenth-century La Bruyère,"[14] and the milieu he chose is the closest thing to the *monde* of the eighteenth century that he could find. With the circles of the Restoration aristocracy, the life of country

---

[13] See, for example, his definition of character: "J'appelle *caractère* d'un homme sa manière habituelle d'aller à chasse du bonheur, en termes plus clairs mais moins significatifs: *l'ensemble de ses habitudes morales.*" *La Vie de Henry Brulard*, pp. 330-31.

[14] *Mélanges intimes et marginalia*, ed. Henri Martineau (Paris: Le Divan, 1936), II, 76.

houses and Parisian drawing rooms, he has evidently attempted to revive and recreate the lighted public stage. But his historical perspective complicates this reconstruction:[15] since this society is not really *le monde*—a phenomenon at the same time real, psychological, and moral which the eighteenth-century novelist was not forced to situate and describe—Stendhal must define and limit his world in time and space, a process which brings into sharp relief what we feel to be his instinctive reaction, that Restoration society, though glamorous, is mostly a rather ludicrous fake. Stendhal's tone shows no dependence on this world, no intimacy with that of his characters, and it is also unclear what position he takes outside the society, what "worlds elsewhere" he suggests. *Armance* lacks the vibrance and intimacy of tone we know from the later novels, and shows rather a narrator hesitating among roles.

The nature of Stendhal's hero contributes to this hesitation: Octave de Malivert, rich and an aristocrat, is at the same time within this society and estranged from it because of his impotence and the shame he derives from it. While the narrator's dissertations on Restoration manners are detached, witty, often comically brilliant, Octave's spleen and fierce antisocial outbursts put us into the presence of a deeper emotional reality. Like *La Princesse de Clèves*, to which Stendhal was fond of comparing his novel, *Armance* dramatizes a struggle between secret and social personalities, and it turns on the difficulty of a confession[16]—which in Stendhal's book becomes a metaphor for the impossibility of bringing a deep personal emotion into the social theater. The social comedy

[15] On the importance of Stendhal's historical perspective in his novelistic presentation of society, see the classic discussion by Erich Auerbach, *Mimesis*, pp. 400-10.

[16] On this and other parallels, in situation and language, between the two novels, see Georges Blin's fine "Étude sur *Armance*" in his edition of the novel (Paris: Éditions de la revue Fontaine, 1946).

and the misanthropic individualism go off in different directions, and are never fused into a necessary relationship. Octave's suicide at the end wrenches the book from any possible total equilibrium. It is a Byronic ending, and in fact the whole book shows the same kind of imbalance, the pendulum swings from the satiric to the posturing, that we find in the Byron of *Childe Harold*, before he reached the masterful double vision of *Don Juan*.

While its second part is played out in the same Restoration drawing rooms, and Julien Sorel does make his "entrée dans le monde," *Le Rouge et le noir* is not centrally concerned with the experience of worldliness. Julien is a parvenu, a transplanted provincial, and insofar as the novel adopts his angle of vision, it views good society from the outside. Moreover, he is a parvenu who attaches little *social* value to making his way in society; his ambition is to prove his personal worth to himself. He is quite unlike Balzac's Rastignac, for example: society is not something to be appropriated, but rather the antagonist and the obstacle, the hard stone against which to strike the flint of his character. Julien does admire the manners of good society, the taste and tact of Mme de Rênal and the Marquis de la Mole; yet his class reaction constantly cuts through any comedy of manners to something more basic, an economic, social, and emotional reality irreducible to manners, and not susceptible of representation within the frame of the novel of manners. There is a point at which he nearly becomes part of the world of manners: when, after following Korasoff's precepts for worldly success, he has adopted the style of his century, paid court to the Maréchale de Fervaques in the language of Chateaubriand, brought Mathilde to her knees, and become M. le Chevalier Julien Sorel de la Vernaye. But when the moment of crisis arrives, he has recourse to an act which shatters the worldly ethos, and at his trial reverts once more to the class reaction, the identification of self as a peasant in revolt. At the last, in the face of death, he seeks a personal style that has nothing to do with manners or society, or even the human community.

The narrator of the novel, while he can of course be ironically detached from Julien, shows little sympathy for Restoration society. Most of its members are fixed as representative grotesques. The people he admires are pure vestiges of the Old Régime, perfect but charming anachronisms like the Bishop of Besançon and the Marquis de la Mole—just as he admires Mathilde for her allegiance to the heroic code of her Renaissance ancestors. The narrator's tone, despite its good humor, is, as Stendhal was to qualify it a few years later, too "Roman"[17]—by which I think he means too militant and too hard—for the novel to be truly worldly. And there is no attempt to create a figure of worldly wisdom and mastery, as there will be in the later novels.

In the later novels, the question of "how to be," of what role to play in good society, will assume central importance, and the problems of heroism will be intimately involved with an individual's behavior within a structured, mannered society whose image governs the private consciousness. This is patently the case in *Une Position sociale*, the first fictional work of any importance undertaken by Stendhal after *Le Rouge et le noir*, and at one time the projected third part of *Lucien Leuwen*. *Une Position sociale* is an apprenticeship for a novel of worldliness. It exploits a closed social milieu—that of diplomats to the Vatican—with identifiable social "characters." The narrator plays the role of witty portraitist (in his marginal notes he questions whether he is not being "too La Bruyère"[18]) and tries to recreate the texture of social intercourse through conversations. He asks himself in the mar-

---

[17] In a marginal note to *Une Position sociale, Mélanges de littérature*, I, 143. A similar remark is found in the marginalia to *Lucien Leuwen*.
[18] *Mélanges de littérature*, I, 138n; I, 146n.

gin what tone he should adopt toward this society, and wonders whether the familiarity and indulgent, humorous urbanity of Fielding (he was in the process of rereading *Tom
Jones*) is not the best model. When we reach *Lucien Leuwen*,
we find that the problem of tone is solved, the chosen world
is impressively embracing as well as fully structured and
mannered, that social comedy is brilliantly enacted, and the
question of worldliness has been made the dramatic center.
Despite the fact that Stendhal never finished the novel, and
never published it, *Lucien Leuwen* is a masterful and coherent
commentary on the modalities of worldly experience in the
nineteenth century.

The source of *Lucien Leuwen* was completely fortuitous,
and the way Stendhal responded to it is instructive. His
friend Mme Jules Gaulthier sent him a manuscript entitled
Le Lieutenant for his criticism. In recording his impressions for her, Stendhal tried to define what should be the
tone and manner of fictional "comedies of society" (referring
her especially to *La Vie de Marianne*);[19] then he began to try
his hand at rewriting the manuscript, and soon was launched
on a novel of his own. His *donnée*—presumably from Mme
Gaulthier's manuscript, though this has been lost—is a rich
young uppermiddle class Parisian in the France of the July
Monarchy, who has been fired from the École Polytechnique
for demonstrating against the Government, and is caught in
a life of frivolity and inertia which makes him term himself
only a "brilliant perhaps."[20] The phrase is important, for Lucien (like his author, who at this point had not even a sketch
for the rest of the novel) does not know what he will become.

The early chapters of the book are in fact a debate on

[19] Letter of May 4, 1834, *Correspondance*, ed. Henri Martineau (Paris:
Le Divan, 1933-34), VIII, 270-72.
[20] *Lucien Leuwen*, in *Romans et Nouvelles*, ed. Henri Martineau
(Paris: Bibliothèque de la Pléiade, 1952), I, 1077.

the virtualities of this hero. On the first page, Lucien's father proposes an epitaph for him:

> Savez-vous, lui disait-il un jour, ce qu'on mettrait sur votre tombe de marbre, au Père-Lachaise, si nous avions le malheur de vous perdre? *"Siste viator*! Ici repose Lucien Leuwen, républicain, qui pendant deux années fit une guerre soutenue aux cigares et aux bottes neuves."(768)

This indeed suggests lackadaisical and unprepossessing heroism. As his cousin Ernest Dévelroy complains, Lucien, whose father is a millionaire and whose dismissal from Polytechnique was politically motivated, has squandered an enviable social position; he has not yet developed that "consistency" which would make him someone in society. What Lucien needs is a role; Dévelroy himself has chosen to court admission to the Académie des Sciences Morales, which will assure him institutional sponsorship, but Lucien might very well succeed by assuming a sombre Byronic air, suited to his good looks and much in vogue. But to Lucien's father, who fears above all that his son's air of serious good sense will lay him open to the *ridicule* of being thought a Saint-Simonian socialist, another form of life is imperative: he orders Lucien to occupy his box at the Opéra, where he will find three or four young dancers:

> Tu les conduiras au *Rocher de Cancale*, où tu dépenseras au moins deux cents francs, sinon je te répudie; je te déclare *saint-simonien*, et je te défends de me voir pendant six mois. Quel supplice pour un fils aussi tendre! (777)

Yet for Lucien, this style of life, however agreeable, does not appear an answer to his worldly nothingness: he chooses instead a commission as lieutenant in the 27th Regiment of Lancers. If, however, the army provides him with a role perfectly acceptable for a rich young bourgeois of good family, its drawbacks become apparent with Lucien's first visit to his new master, Lieutenant Colonel Filloteau, who resembles less a hero of the Grand Army than a clerk from lower Normandy. His style, his bombast and pious mouthings of fidelity to the government ("la nécessité de réprimer les factieux"), disgusts Lucien, and gives him a vision of the ignoble warfare that the nineteenth century will demand, "la guerre aux tronçons de choux, contre de sales ouvriers mourant de faim" (774). Yet his sense of the emptiness and frivolity of any other style forces him to accept this role, and he departs with Filloteau for his first garrison, at Nancy.

These first two chapters of the novel are cast almost entirely in a witty conversational debate. Stendhal has transformed what was apparently Mme Gaulthier's lengthy and rather pompous prose exposition of her hero's situation into a play of different voices and conversational styles. This transformation is significant, because the total style of the novel, its texture, is hence at once intimately involved with its profound subject—the question of what role to play in the world, what style of life to adopt. Stendhal has in fact posed Lucien's dilemma as a problem in style, in its full range from conversational mannerism to total style of life: Lucien is placed amidst different voices which point to different personal styles, and forced to choose his own from among them. The subject of the novel and its presentation are absorbed into one another; the novel is a play of styles around a central question of style. Stendhal will exploit a conversational method throughout, and the issue of style will furnish the terms in which he poses his hero's problems and choices. At the outset, reflecting on the faults of Mme Gaulthier's manuscript and working his own transformation, Stendhal has begun to find a solution to the problem of making experience of the world into the experience of worldliness.

Lucien's initiation into the worlds of Nancy is primarily

a series of exercises in style. Rejecting the vulgarities of his co-
officers and various forms of bourgeois, from the exalted but
boring idealism of the republicans through the bureaucratic
platitudes of government officials to the posturings of the local
middle-class beauty whose verbal style and gestures are evidently conceived to remind one of her 20,000 franc dowry,
Lucien turns toward the more glamorous Legitimist aristocracy, which is proud and disdainful of anything that suggests
the Citizen King or the newly-enfranchised middle classes.
Its closure indeed creates its glamour. Lucien is forced to play
a complicated and diverting game of social hypocrisy—sub-
scribing to the *ultra* newspaper, going to church, buying an
enormous carriage to supplement his tilbury, decking out five
lackeys in livery ordered from Paris, and learning to speak a
fair imitation of Faubourg Saint-Germain style—in order to
penetrate within the circles of *mondanité*. When he succeeds
in making himself accepted, he is captivated by what seems to
be the polite, attentive formality of style of the aristocrats,
their apparent freedom from the vulgarities of the present
age, their masterful disdain and *sans-gêne* which contrast with
the deadness of the bourgeois and seem to strike the true note
of the Old Régime. Yet it soon becomes evident that they are
not the real thing any more than the bourgeois, and Lucien
finally laments:

> Mon sort est-il donc de passer ma vie entre des légitimistes
> fous, égoïstes et polis, adorant le passé, et des républicains
> fous, généreux, et ennuyeux adorant l'avenir? Maintenant,
> je comprends mon père, quand il s'écrie: "Que ne suis-je
> né en 1710, avec cinquante mille livres de rente!" (884)

This regret at not having been born into the best circles of
the eighteenth century points to the essential *ridicule* of the
Legitimists, and indicates why a social position among them
is finally boring and valueless. They are a perfect, voluntary

anachronism, living under the unamusing delusion that the past can be revived, that the present must be negated, that their genealogies are known beyond the confines of Nancy, that their society corresponds to some accepted reality. Even more than the bourgeois, they reveal themselves to be comically fixed, entrapped within their representative social roles; they are victims of their exclusive allegiance to a dead social order, and as a result they display, not the free and knowing mastery of men we associate with worldliness, but a purely representative style which calls attention to their narrowness and provinciality.[21] Stendhal's rendering of these figures finally reduces them to a gallery of social tics. There is, for instance, the Marquis de Sanréal, the richest landowner of the province:

> . . . cet héroïque marquis avait des inconvénients: il n'entendait jamais nommer Louis-Philippe sans lancer d'une voix singulière et glapissante ce simple mot: *voleur.* C'était là son trait d'esprit, qui, à chaque fois, faisait rire à gorge déployée la plupart des nobles dames de Nancy, et cela dix fois dans une soirée. (888)

And the three Counts Roller, retired from the army since 1830:

> Ludwig, Sigismond et André, braves officiers, chasseurs déterminés et fort mécontents. Les trois frères disent exactement les mêmes choses. (880)

And Comte Génévray:

[21] My discussion of "comic fixity" and "freedom" owes much to a similar use of terms by Richard Poirier in his remarkable study of Henry James, *The Comic Sense of Henry James* (London, 1960). One could relate these terms to Henri Bergson's classic analysis of the source of the comic in the contrast between mechanical rigidity and the movement of life, in *Le Rire* (Paris, 1900).

. . . petit bonhomme de dix-neuf ans, gros et trop serré dans un habit toujours trop étroit; moustaches noires, répétant tous les soirs dix fois que sans *légitimité*, il n'y a pas de bonheur pour la France. (880)

Responses to life in these and other similar figures are essentially inherited tropisms, the debris of an aristocratic pride and freedom which have atrophied into fear and hatred of the present and future, a rejection of reality which in no sense meets Lucien's demands for an elegant and viable social style.

Affectation of language, a verbal style of false and emphatic "nobleness," is the primary sign of these aristocrats' fixity. A good example is the style of the official representative of Henry V in the province, the Marquis de Pontlevé:

Quoi! ma fille, lui dit le grand M. de Pontlevé, avec le ton et les gestes d'Alceste *indigné*, dans la comédie: vos princes sont à Prague et l'on vous verrait à Paris! Que diraient les mânes de M. de Chasteller? Ah! si nous quittons nos pénates, ce n'est pas de ce côté qu'il faut tourner la tête de nos chevaux. Soignez votre vieux père à Nancy, ou, si nous pouvons mettre un pied devant l'autre, volons à Prague, etc. (905)

For this Stendhal provides his own stylistic commentary:

M. de Pontlevé avait ce parler long et figuré des gens diserts du temps de Louis XVI, qui passait alors pour de l'esprit.

To be considered among such puppets, Lucien quickly understands, one must adopt, not a style of true worldliness, but a comic and theatrical version thereof: "On ne peut trop charger un rôle avec ces gens-ci"(953). He learns to imitate some of the appropriate fixities of language, and to speak, as he puts it, provincial:

> Il lui eût semblé s'entendre jurer s'il leur eût dit d'une belle matinée: "C'est une belle matinée." Il s'écriait en fronçant le sourcil et épanouissant le front, de l'air important d'un gros propriétaire: "Quel beau temps pour les foins!" (954)

Such diverting stylistic parody points to the opposite of fixity: to Lucien's ability to manage others through a manipulation of their tropistic responses, and hence to the possibility of preserving his own uncommitted freedom in the search for a personal style. His sense of rightness of style is pointed up by his commentaries on the verbal mannerisms of others:

> —Ce courageux magistrat, disait M. de Serpierre, qui sut poursuivre ce malheureux La Chalotais, le premier des jacobins. On était alors en 1779 . . .
>
> Leuwen se pencha vers madame d'Hocquincourt et lui dit gravement:
>
> Quel langage, madame, et pour vous et pour moi! (1013)

The line of verse (it sounds like Corneille), forced into service as a commentary on M. de Serpierre's pomposity, reminds us of a real nobility of language, a true worldliness of style. A similar effect is obtained in the phrase which introduces Mme d'Hocquincourt as one of the few living creatures in a dead world, a phrase which juxtaposes the stylistic tics of M. d'Hocquincourt and the fresh beauty of his wife: "Tout en écoutant la parole lente, élégante, et décolorée de M. d'Hocquincourt, Lucien examinait sa femme" (869).

Throughout Lucien's experience at Nancy (Part One of the novel), Stendhal insists on the characteristic forms of expression of different milieux, social classes, and individuals. Challenges to Lucien, and his responses, are posed in terms of style—being a successful hypocrite is a matter of speaking *juste-milieu* at one point, the languages of religious devotion or *henriquinquisme* at others. By the range of his stylistic reproductions (as much as Flaubert, Stendhal is a master of capturing the inflection of the spoken word) and by his extensive casting of Lucien's story in dialogue (none of the other novels uses nearly so much), Stendhal, like a comic dramatist, forces us to distinguish between good and bad styles. Himself perpetually conscious of style, he repeatedly states all the issues of the book in terms of the ways in which style is used in the world. For example, when Lucien enters the Hôtel de Commercy, he discovers, in the narrator's formulation which makes conversational style the final measure of life, that "La conversation, comme l'ameublement, fut noble, monotone, lente, mais sans ridicule trop marqué"(867). Or the narrator gives this excuse for Lucien's exercise of hypocrisy to gain admission to Legitimist drawing rooms:

> Nous ferons remarquer, pour la justification de notre héros, que, depuis son départ de Paris, il ne s'était pas trouvé dans un salon; et vivre sans conversation piquante *est-ce une vie heureuse?* (864)

Consciousness of society's projected image, then, is seen as consciousness of society's styles, and all problems of ethics, class, politics, ambition, and comportment can be stated in the form which they assume in the dramatic interplay of society, the form of conversational style and personal manner. Stendhal thus posits a solution to the problem of molding different kinds of experience into the one experience of worldliness, the question of a person's total manner of being within the social medium.

This question, and Stendhal's responses, become more complex in the second part of the novel. At Nancy, Lucien has learned to regard others as mechanical entities easily manipulated through pressure applied to the appropriate foible, to produce the desired set response. But he is not yet a worldly master. His romance with Mme de Chasteller, a truly aristocratic *belle âme* whose natural sensibility has been suppressed and infringed by the teachings of the Convent of the Sacred Heart, is repeatedly thwarted by societal obstacles, and finally ends in débâcle as the plebeian hatchetman of the Legitimists, Dr. Du Poirier, fabricates a last, nearly incredible misunderstanding between Lucien and Mme de Chasteller, in the form of a simulated confinement and childbirth. Lucien deserts, flees to Paris, prostrate, irresolute, despairing, returned to his original state of emptiness and inertia. At this point, François Leuwen, the rich and witty father whom we glimpsed in the first chapters, takes over the destinies of his son, gives him a lesson of morality, and plans his future career. To save Lucien from misanthropy and the *ridicule* of becoming a utopian socialist and fleeing to America, he insists that Lucien sign his life over to his father for eighteen months, during which he will accept a solid position in the Bank, or the Ministry of the Interior. Lucien opts for the Ministry. Here, however, M. Leuwen feels obliged to pose a question: "Maintenant paraît une grande difficulté: serez-vous assez coquin pour cet emploi?" (1072). Lucien starts, then regains a measure of his father's urbanity:

    —Et que désirez-vous que je sois? demanda Lucien d'un air simple.

    —Un coquin, reprit le père, je veux dire un homme politique, un Martignac, je n'irai pas jusqu'à dire un Talleyrand. A votre âge et dans vos journaux on appelle cela être un coquin. Dans dix ans, vous saurez que Colbert, que Sully, que le cardinal de Richelieu, en un mot tout ce qui a été homme politique, c'est à dire *dirigeant les hommes,* s'est élevé au moins à ce premier degré de coquinerie que je désire vous voir. (1073)

François Leuwen is Stendhal's first successful creation of a worldly master on the eighteenth-century pattern—a figure who will return under the guise of Count Mosca in *La Chartreuse de Parme,* and who has another, quite different incarnation in the Doctor Sansfin of *Lamiel.* To M. Leuwen, the world is divided into the *coquins* and the *dupes*—the knaves and the fall-guys—and not to be the latter necessitates being the former. He takes as his ideal the kind of perfect control of others demonstrated by Versac or Valmont. Yet he realizes that the world has changed significantly since the eighteenth century, and that the manipulation of others has become an enormously more complicated affair. It no longer suffices to be an *homme à la mode;* one can no longer rely exclusively on a penetrating assessment of others, on manipulation of their psychological mechanisms and exercise of the social weapon of *ridicule.* As Ernest Dévelroy suggested at the outset, one needs the backing of certain constituent elements of this pluralistic society. Money is the primary force, and of this M. Leuwen is admirably possessed; the other most important factor is political power, for France with a constitutional monarchy and a Chamber is ruled through the ministries. Endowed with his creator's historical perspective, M. Leuwen understands that power has passed from the aristocracy of birth to that of wealth, from the aristocrat to a bourgeois banker like himself, from king and court to parliament and the bureaucrats. Hence Lucien must enter the Bank or the Ministry of the Interior (over which M. Leuwen has considerable control, since he helps the Minister to play the stockmarket and make huge profits from the secret economic information coming over the Ministry's telegraph system—a procedure given some sanction by the fact that

Louis-Philippe himself, whom Stendhal habitually named "le plus fripon des kings," does the same thing).

Yet financial and political control for M. Leuwen must always be absorbed into something else: into the power, of his own mind and social presence over the world. He is not simply a banker; he is the "Talleyrand of the Stock Exchange"(1111) whose wit is as famous as his probity, and whose epigrams are feared even in the Château. Georg Lukács once criticized Stendhal's portrait of M. Leuwen as not at all typical of a banker of the 1830's, and pointed to Balzac's Baron de Nucingen as a more accurate representation; Stendhal, according to Lukács, merely transplanted a figure from the Enlightenment into the nineteenth century.[22] But this is just the point: M. Leuwen's ideals are those of the eighteenth century, the ideals of worldliness; he understands that he must employ different methods to obtain these ideals, but he always insists that the methods serve worldliness, that political and financial manipulation work to guarantee one's social place and further one's social style. His proposal to Lucien is dictated by his acute consciousness of society's image, rules, and values. Lucien's career is not to be one of bureaucracy; rather, bureaucratic political power will assure him social consistency, the power to be at the center of drawing-room life. Hence the place in the Ministry is accompanied by season's passes to the Opéra and the Bouffes, with the clear command that Lucien spend at least a half-hour each evening in these *"temples du plaisir, particulièrement vers la fin des plaisirs, à onze heures"*(1102).

It is M. Leuwen who offers a solution to the problem of void left by the disappearance of the Old Régime. By perpetually conjugating the realities of economic and political power with the way one can exploit these realities socially, he makes

[22] Georg Lukács, "Balzac and Stendhal," *Studies in European Realism,* trans. Edith Bone (London, 1950).

us feel that his world can be a public stage for the enactment of social self-representations, that it can offer an image
which, mediated through the individual's consciousness, will
elicit and valorize the kind of systematic behavior found in
the *monde* of the eighteenth century. He is, to be sure, ever
exposing the bad taste, unintelligence, corruption, and
bourgeois platitude of his century. But this scorn and ironic
understanding of the decline of civilization rather contribute
to the impression that he has found a way to be a true *mondain* in the modern world. He can use his century's pomposities, give himself the inflated self-important manner of the
man known to control the destinies of others through his professional importance, yet he always remains at an ironic distance from this manner and transforms the ridiculous fixities
of his age into the play of his own wit. Like Valmont, he
shows his control of reality by his mastery of the manner and
expressive style of others. When, for instance, Lucien proposes resignation from the army, he replies:

> —Pas de démission, mon ami; il n'y a que les sots qui don-
> nent leur démission. Je prétends bien que vous serez toute
> votre vie un jeune militaire de la plus haute distinction at-
> tiré par la politique, une véritable *perte pour l'armée*, comme
> disent les *Débats*. (1074)

Here he uses the clichés of others as a guide to his own role-
playing, and his arrangement of the roles of others: he has
"cast" Lucien as "a real loss to the Army" because he fore-
sees that members of society will play their roles in relation
to this one. He is constantly aware of the duperies that can be
performed with slight perversions of language and, again
like Valmont, he is always on the verge of parody, travesty
of the expressive systems and roles of others. With Lucien,
for example, he inevitably turns their conversations into an
ironic play at a discussion between father and son. After

explaining to Lucien a particularly sinister ministerial action, he asks:

—Ah! diable, *mon jeune ami*, comme disent les pères nobles, vous êtes étonné?
—*On le serait à moins*, répond souvent le jeune premier, dit Lucien. (1074)

The "pères nobles" are those of the theater, and Lucien picks up the part of "jeune premier" in response to the role selected by his father. The conversation concludes:

—Très bien. A ce soir réponse décisive, claire, nette, sans phrases sentimentales surtout. Demain peut-être je ne pourrai plus *rien pour mon fils*.
Ces mots furent dits d'une façon à la fois noble et sentimentale, comme eût fait Monvel, le grand acteur.

This love of exploiting a theatrical mode of expression points to M. Leuwen's understanding that theatrical expression is already a codification and to a degree a parody of representative social styles, the way people talk as determined by what they are or what they conceive themselves to be. His mastery of the world's languages is one of the principal reasons that we can accept Stendhal's ultimate presentation of M. Leuwen as a man who virtually controls the destinies of France.

When Lucien goes to work in the Ministry of the Interior, he discovers the style of bureaucracy—"l'éloquence vide et l'emphase plate"(1101)—and discovers also that the platitude and impersonality of this style are ways of masking, and refusing to take responsibility for, the methods by which men are controlled in the nineteenth century—bribery, corruption, rigged elections, and worse: France is spied on by no fewer than five different secret polices, there are *agents provocateurs* charged with creating "incidents" that will give the army an excuse to suppress the workers' movement, diplo-

matic assassination is not unknown. The manipulation of
men in the nineteenth century is a tainted profession; it no
longer possesses the purity it could have within the closed system of the Old Régime, where manners alone were weapons,
and superior worldliness the principle of dominance. One
can no longer rely on *ridicule*; there is no such thing in a
fragmented and factionalized world. Conversely, the old
hierarchy of values and rewards is dead. The Minister of the
Interior, for example, is forced to employ bribery, threat, pa-
tronage and blackmail where an Old Régime master could
have relied on the power of the supreme form of public notice,
recognition by the king. When he notes how little effect promise of a private audience with Louis-Philippe has on Lucien,
M. de Vaize, the Minister, laments:

> Malheureuse monarchie! . . . Le nom du roi est dépouillé
> de tout effet magique. Il est réellement impossible de gou-
> verner avec ces petits journaux qui démolissent tout. Il nous
> faut tout payer argent comptant ou par les grades . . . Et cela
> nous ruine: le trésor comme les grades ne sont pas infinis.
> (1183)

The stage has become too vast, society too uncentered and
pluralistic, the machinery of power too public and too im-
personal for the control of a Valmont. We begin to understand that at the center of his novel Stendhal is working out
a contrast between an Old Régime ideal of world mastery and
the fact of what world mastery has come to mean in the
modern age—the world we know, but which was for Stendhal
a new phenomenon, which he was one of the first of his
generation to understand. His historical perspective not only
governs the novel, it is to an important degree its subject, and
all the major characters at some point pose the question of their
role in historical terms: what that role used to be, and what
it has become.

It is Lucien's reactions that point up the sordid immorality of modern France: he responds spontaneously, with an instinctive nobility and morality, revulsion from the wrong and unclean. But he refuses to withdraw: he has indentured himself to his father's world, and must gain a position of mastery within it. Preservation of morality and personal integrity in this world becomes another kind of problem in style: Lucien must adopt a cold, punctilious personal manner which discourages the advances of the bureaucratic hangmen, which announces a refusal of complicity and a will not to be contaminated. He repeats, as a sort of catechism, the style he must maintain with M. de Vaize:

> . . . je serai froid, respectueux, en laissant toujours paraître, même fort clairement, le désir de voir se terminer la communication sérieuse avec un si grand personnage. (1113)

This coolness and refusal to let himself be seduced by the Minister's attentions and overtures of intimacy are the guarantee of Lucien's freedom and his escape from commitment to bureaucratic crime—which would also be commitment to fixity, to entrapment within one role for the rest of one's life. Lucien's style permits him to distinguish between the permissible corruption and impermissible crime, between the cowardice of not acting at all and the infamy of acting wrongly. The question of the uses of style is given a new significance: personal style becomes the basis and guarantee of personal integrity in opposition to the demands of society; style is the foundation of a personal heroism.

The major test of this heroism comes with Lucien's journey as a "commissioner of elections" to assure the victory of governmental candidates in two Departments by the various means put at his disposition by the Ministry: tobacco concessions, destitutions of unzealous local officials, threats, outright purchase of votes. Whereas in earlier episodes Lucien's reactions were juxtaposed to those of more worldly figures—his father, Dévelroy—here he is "doubled" by M. Coffe, an indigent ex-Polytechnicien whom Lucien has rescued from debtors' prison, a plebeian devoted to an unflinching articulation of the truth, who clearsightedly accepts his role of "lackey to the hangman" because his poverty leaves him with no other choice. Coffe's comments serve to polarize the questions of style and morality which pursue Lucien in his rather sordid mission. When the two are pelted with mud in the streets of Blois, Lucien's reaction of wounded pride and honor is contrasted to Coffe's more realistic assessment:

> —Cette boue, c'est pour nous la noble poussière du champ d'honneur. Cette huée publique vous comptera, ce sont les actions d'éclat dans la carrière que vous avez prise, et où ma pauvreté et ma reconnaissance me portent à vous suivre. (1192)

The analysis cruelly exposes the nature of the battlefield on which Lucien is engaged, and it provokes what is more and more becoming his stock response, to gallop to Rochefort and embark for America under an assumed name.

But Coffe's ironic military analogy in fact implies what Lucien's mode of action should be: Coffe extends the metaphor by telling Lucien that although he may be engaged in a tainted mission, to desert, "like the Saxons at Leipzig," would not be morally beautiful. A model of the proper style is provided by the forthright General Fari, commander of the military post at Caen, who talks of the anti-governmental candidate—an honest and intelligent republican—as he would of a "Prussian general commanding the town to which he was laying siege" (1225). When the battle of Caen becomes a minor epic struggle with the defeat of the Government's man imminent, Lucien audaciously offers the Government's votes and 100,000 francs to the local Legitimists if they will produce an innocuous candidate and the country gentlemen to vote for him. In another military metaphor, he sees himself as a cavalry general in a losing struggle who, forgetting his self-interest, makes his troops dismount to fight with the infantry. The disengaged Coffe himself is caught up in the heroics of the moment, and this is our measure of the rightness of Lucien's manner: when the ministerial telegram giving them full powers to act arrives too late, Coffe declaims "Un peu moins de fortune, et plus tôt survenue"(1264). Once again Corneille (*Polyeucte*, slightly misquoted) serves to point up Lucien's heroism of style.[23]

But, while Lucien is able to conclude, in a final military metaphor, "Quoique la bataille fût perdue, j'ai fait donner mon régiment"(1263), heroics are not bureaucratic style. Coffe predicts that at the Ministry they will have expected only a series of long letters written in platitudinous and bombastic style; Lucien is guilty of showing "zeal," a quality utterly opposed to the bureaucratic virtues, and his colleagues will always consider him mad because of the way he has jeopardized his personal position. And of course Coffe is right: receiving Lucien in Paris, the Minister can only talk of the "astonishment" caused by Lucien's audacity. Hence Lucien's attempts to find a personal style capable of preserving freedom and a measure of heroism in the modern world isolate him from the element of social structure that was to provide his social "consistency."

The style of M. Leuwen operates differently, and, within its own terms, is more totally effective. He sees the immorality and the sordidness of France under the Citizen King, but refuses to react with moral shock; to do so would be unworldly, an admission to the same rigidity and fixity that characterize the bureaucrats or the aristocrats of Nancy. Next to the

[23] "Un peu moins de fortune, et plus tôt arrivée." *Polyeucte*, ii, i, 449.

detailed picture of governmental corruption, next to Lucien's moral responses and his effort to forge a style on their basis, we have the voice of M. Leuwen insisting that the serious ethical reaction is banal and boring, that all questions of morality and politics are really purely questions of style, that the former can be transmuted into the latter through the power of intelligence and wit. When Lucien's serious, misanthropic air has given credence to the insidious rumors that he is a socialist who secretly dreams of founding a new society in America, M. Leuwen's solution is to have Lucien conceive a passionate attachment for a socially prominent lady (Mme Grandet, as it turns out); this will explain Lucien's appearance by a suitably frivolous cause. But as his father tactfully reveals the plan, Lucien reacts with horror:

—Quoi! mon père, une grande passion! Avec ses assiduités, sa constance, son occupation de tous les moments?
—Précisément.
—*Pater meus, transeat a me calix iste!*
—Mais tu vois mes raisons.
   Fais ton arrêt toi-même, et choisis tes supplices.
   J'en conviens, la plaisanterie serait meilleure avec une vertu à haute piété et à privilèges, mais tu n'es pas ce qu'il faut, et d'ailleurs le pouvoir, qui est une bonne chose, se retire de ces gens-là et vient chez nous. Eh bien! parmi nous autres, nouvelle noblesse, gagnée en écrasant ou en escamotant la révolution de Juillet ...
—Ah! je vois où vous voulez en venir!
—Eh bien! dit M. Leuwen du ton de la plus parfaite bonne foi, où veux-tu trouver mieux? N'est-ce pas une vertu *d'après* celles du faubourg Saint-Germain?
—Comme Dangeau n'était pas un grand seigneur, mais *d'après* un grand seigneur. Ah! elle est trop ridicule à mes yeux; jamais je ne pourrai m'accoutumer à avoir une

grande passion pour Mme Grandet. Dieu! Quel flux de pa-
roles! Quelles prétentions! (1161-62)

This exchange, in the manner of the letters of Valmont and
the Marquise in *Les Liaisons dangereuses*, creates the illusion
of an intellectually superior medium in which we dominate
the actions of men through a kind of intellectual intoxication
with what words and style can do to reality. Jean Prévost once
characterized Stendhal's novels as "a feast of the intellect,"[24]
and it is to this feast that we are here superbly convoked. M.
Leuwen and, following his lead, Lucien, create in us a
sense of domination of the world through a total knowledge
of the forms and terms of social intercourse, and a total ability
to manipulate them. They play with the public's language
("une grande passion," "une vertu," "*d'après* celles du faubourg Saint-Germain"); they parody the roles they are assuming (Lucien quotes from the Vulgate Christ's words to his
Father during the Agony in the Garden, and M. Leuwen
from the role of the Emperor Augustus in Corneille's *Cinna*);
they give proof of a witty overview of society and history
("le pouvoir, qui est une bonne chose," "nouvelle noblesse,
gagnée en écrasant ou en escamotant la révolution de Juillet");
they are unfailingly good-humored and urbane in treating
an essentially scabrous proposition as a tedious but necessary social duty. There are evidently many ways in which a
father might discuss his son's taking of a mistress to further
his career. It might be a moral problem, a psychological problem, a drama of intrigue. Here it is simply a question of social
style—a problem in worldliness: that is, an intellectual system
in which all mundane, bourgeois and boring problems are sub-
sumed by and metamorphosed into a question of the manner
one cultivates to live in the world. To M. Leuwen as to an

[24] *La Création chez Stendhal* (Marseille: Éditions du Sagittaire, 1942),
p. 153.

eighteenth-century novelist, worldliness is one, a total way to be, a total style of life.

Stendhal is not content to stop with this kind of transmutation and this kind of illusion. He goes on to have M. Leuwen elected (through various minor corruptions) a deputy to the Assembly, then makes him a parliamentary power when he bands together thirty of the stupidest and most indigent newly-elected deputies into a bloc called the "Légion du Midi," feeds them dinner every night, and makes himself their spokesman. The Légion du Midi, with its thirty decisive votes, becomes the real, objective basis for M. Leuwen's exercise of wit against the Government; it allows Stendhal to create a new illusion, that his model of classical worldliness controls the destinies of modern France. All the ministers, and finally the king himself, are made to appear powerless before M. Leuwen and his thirty regimented imbeciles. The machinery of constitutional government is made to serve wit and intelligence; the maxim "Connaître les êtres pour agir sur eux" has been redefined and raised to a new dimension. The very "anachronism" of this character—to use Lukács' term—contributes to our sense that control is being exercised through superior worldliness, an intelligent manipulation of human weaknesses. M. Leuwen talks before the Chamber as he would in a *salon*; his arm is devastating extemporaneous satire and ridicule, the opposite of official parliamentary style. For him, the Chamber is a "fashionable plaything" (1312), and his exploitation of it demonstrates that a figure like Valmont can find a way to live in the nineteenth century.

Stendhal raises intellectual power to the dimensions of national political power, and transmutes the latter into the former. This sleight-of-hand is posited on what can only be called his conspiracy theory of history and politics: from the numerous political articles he wrote for English periodicals, and the analyses of power alignments in the Italian states he as consul sent to the Foreign Office, it is clear that Stendhal always thought of political power in the terms of M. Leuwen, as the maneuvers of a few powerful knaves who control the dupes.[25] In *Lucien Leuwen*, we are taken into Government councils, where we witness Louis-Philippe and his ministers struggling with the problems posed by M. Leuwen's disruption of the normally placid assembly. The grass roots of democracy, the people, in so far as they were enfranchised under the July Monarchy, exist only to furnish the equivalents of the Légion du Midi to those masters of men whom the narrator obviously so admires.

More and more, in this second part of the novel, Stendhal's comedy of manners becomes the comedy of politics. His concern to dramatize worldliness, we suggested, makes this inevitable: the fragmentation and factionalization of the modern world has also meant its politicization. The only medium which now really permits an exercise of the power sought by a Valmont is politics, and the only true world masters are those who can wield political influence. At the center of his *monde*, then, Stendhal has necessarily placed a caste of professional manipulators. Yet political manipulations are constantly seen to be sordid, wrong, ludicrous, unless transcended by their social use—the way M. Leuwen makes them act upon the interplay of persons in the social medium. In this impingement of politics upon sociability in the modern world, and the ways in which the impingement can be used, we have an important element in Stendhal's answer to the loss of *le monde*.

This interdependence is given a final and lucid representation when M. Leuwen reaches the point of provoking the fall

[25] See the articles collected in *Courrier Anglais*, ed. Henri Martineau (5 vols.; Paris: Le Divan, 1935-36); see, in the *Correspondance*, the letters of April 5 and 8, 1835, to the Duc de Broglie.

of the Government. He suddenly discovers that he is on the verge of falling into a disastrous *ridicule*: to accept a ministry in the new Government would be to destroy his freedom of movement, to force himself into a representative function; to demand nothing for himself, however, would be to make himself appear weak and inconsequential. He must operate through Lucien. Lucien is too young to be a minister, but if the idiotic M. Grandet is made Prime Minister, and Lucien becomes his clever wife's lover (she has not yet fallen to Lucien's halfhearted attack), it will be apparent to the knowing public that the head of state is controlled by his wife, who is in turn controlled by her twenty-six-year-old lover. This will create a final illusion that Lucien is master of the nation and that politics depend, as in true Old Régime fashion they should, on the salon and even the boudoir.

M. Leuwen's plan moves smoothly (the ambitious Mme Grandet, who likes to think of herself as a new Mme de Staël, accepts his proposition) until it encounters an unexpected obstacle in the fact that M. Grandet's stupidity is too patent even to the other ministers, and he is rejected. Mme Grandet accuses M. Leuwen of having acted in bad faith. In despair at this unfounded suspicion, he in turn tells Lucien the whole story of the bargain with Mme Grandet. This proves a major tactical error, for Lucien's vanity has in fact been flattered by what he considers his *mondain* success, his conquest without love of this socially prominent "virtue." He is seriously enjoying playing the role of a good roué; he is indeed most nearly at a point of being entrapped by his worldly position, on the verge of really becoming the social being M. Leuwen hoped to fashion. With the revelation of this final element in his father's manipulations of his career, his arrangement of reality, Lucien revolts. In a long monologue, appropriately pursued in a box at the Opéra, he

weighs the seductions of worldliness against his instinct to behave like Alceste:

> Un avancement merveilleux pour mon âge, mes talents, la
> position de mon père dans le monde, m'a-t-il jamais donné
> d'autre sentiment que cet étonnement sans plaisir: *n'est-ce
> que ça?* (1356)

This repeated reaction of all Stendhalian heroes, variously directed toward love, war, and all reputedly enviable sensations
and sentiments, here is aimed at the whole of the *monde* expounded by his father, its ideals, code, rewards. From a point
at which he was nearly entrapped by his worldly success,
Lucien abandons the search for a social style and all his *mondain* responsibilities: he refuses to make the requisite appearance in Mme Grandet's drawing room, and instead
takes an hotel room under an assumed name, and immediately
feels a sense of release and freedom; then he abandons Paris
altogether and flees to Nancy, to seek reunion with the one
woman for whom he had a real "great passion," the one
person with whom there was a possibility of communication
outside the social context, Mme de Chasteller.

The trip to Nancy was never written, but we do know
that Lucien was to be reunited with Mme de Chasteller, and
Stendhal's sketch of this scene vibrates with the discreet
emotion of all his final reunifications of lovers.[26] Leaving
several blank pages for the Nancy episode, Stendhal picks up
again with Lucien's return to Paris on learning of his father's
sudden death, which is followed by the bankruptcy of the
House of Van Peters & Leuwen, loss of the family fortune,
and fall from *le monde.* Lucien and his mother are no longer
received; Lucien obtains as a last favor from his father's old

---

[26] See, in the notes of the Pléiade edition, p. 1527. These notes contain
all Stendhal's marginalia, sketches, outlines, etc. for the novel, and I
will simply refer to them as to the text.

friend the Minister of War a post as second secretary in the French Embassy at "Capel" (Rome). The entire experience of worldliness goes smash: the master *mondain* is killed off, and Lucien is apparently supremely happy to leave Paris and journey through Switzerland—where the Lake of Geneva evokes for him memories of *La Nouvelle Héloïse*—and northern Italy, where, like his creator some thirty years earlier, he discovers the arts and music. When he arrives at the embassy in Rome, the narrator tells us, he must struggle to suppress his newly liberated sensibility and assume the appropriate bureaucratic "dryness" of manner. Since it is quite clear that Stendhal had abandoned the idea of making *Une Position sociale* into a last section of *Lucien Leuwen*, this must be the last view of Lucien he intended to give us: withdrawn from the *cursus honorum*, liberated from worldliness, moving in a new medium of sensibility. Like many of Stendhal's endings, this one rapidly, brusquely, elliptically opens up new possibilities, projects new and oblique illumination on the whole subject and manner of the novel, and, in this case, throws into question the experience of worldliness.

Stendhal's ultimate attitude toward the experience of worldliness cannot be gauged without close attention to the narrative voice and the kind of presence it creates in the novel, and the narrator's relation to his hero. This relation is both like that which we found in the eighteenth-century novel and considerably more complex. There is the same distance between the voice of a worldly, experienced narrator and the reactions of a young, impulsive protagonist. The narrator is ever exposing the gap between what Lucien knows and what a truly worldly hero would know, suggesting the realms of experience unknown to his protagonist. In a characteristic procedure (very perceptively analyzed by Victor

Brombert[27]), he opens in the middle of his narrative sentences written in the conditional or the hypothetical subjunctive suggesting that if only Lucien had done such and such, he would have obtained the results he was so foolishly missing by his unworldly behavior. For example, when Lucien walks in the street outside Mme de Chasteller's closed shutters at Nancy, the narrator comments:

> Si, dans ce silence profond et universel, Leuwen eût eu le génie de s'avancer sous sa fenêtre et de lui dire à voix basse quelque chose d'ingénieux et de frais, par exemple:
> "Bonsoir, madame. Daignerez-vous me montrer que je suis entendu?"
> Très probablement, elle lui eût dit: "Adieu, monsieur Leuwen." Et l'intonation de ces trois mots n'eût rien laissé à désirer à l'amant le plus exigeant. (951)

From his fund of worldly experience, the narrator weighs possibilities and decides that "very probably" Mme de Chasteller would have replied to Lucien's greeting, and in accents that showed her suppressed passion.

This worldliness of tone and knowledge is constant, yet the narrator's ironies toward his young, impulsive hero often cut several ways: when, for instance, he comments during a tender moment between Lucien and Mme de Chasteller, when the two are exchanging confidences while listening to Mozart in the Bois de Burelvillier, "Tel est le danger de la sincérité, de la musique et des grands bois" (967), his barb is directed as much against himself, and his urbane reader, as against his hero. His relation to his protagonists, whom he calls both ironically and tenderly "notre héros," is in fact always a blend of harsh judgment and affection, distance and

[27] *Stendhal et la voie oblique* (Paris and New Haven: Yale University Press, 1954); for his analysis of the quotation *infra*, see p. 145.

closeness.[28] In this novel the relation seems to be most significantly an educative one. If the narrator does not hesitate to intervene to judge his hero's actions and social manner, it is because he is concerned to estimate his hero's progress, to measure the evolution of his style, to debate his "rightness." His paternalism is not limiting; it is not comparable to the interventionism of a Thackeray, a Dickens, or a Mauriac concerned to define, limit, and prescribe their reader's moral reactions, and his ironies do not have the arid, reductive quality of Flaubert's. He does not pose himself as God to his characters; on the contrary, he becomes an independent personal voice, even a character in the novel, and engages the reader in a well-mannered, urbane conversational debate about his hero—a debate that convinces us that he believes in the reality and autonomy of his created life.

This conviction is reinforced by another debate about Lucien carried on by Stendhal in the margins of his manuscript. His marginal notes show the extent to which the novel was, even more than his other books, literally improvised: its rapid "self-engendering" tone and narrative manner derive in part from the fact that Stendhal was working without any outline or armature, without even the anecdotes which underlie *Le Rouge et le noir* and *La Chartreuse de Parme*, but from the slender givens of a character and a social situation. He projected the future as he wrote, and we find him searching to define his hero on the basis of the dramatization he has thus far given him. Well into the second part, for instance, he asks himself, "Quel caractère a Lucien?" (1575). He wants to avoid definition that precedes the hero's

---

[28] This relationship has been the object of some of the best Stendhalian studies: see Prévost, *La Création chez Stendhal*; Brombert, *Stendhal et la voie oblique*; and Georges Blin, *Stendhal et les problèmes du roman* (Paris, 1954).

self-definition in dramatized social encounters. His constant questionings about Lucien and his own attitudes toward him indicate most importantly a desire to let the hero develop his own reality according to his own virtualities. A curious image in the marginal notes expresses this concern:

> *For me.* Le meilleur chien de chasse ne peut que passer le gibier à portée du fusil du chasseur. Si celui-ci ne tire pas, le chien n'y peut mais. Le romancier est comme le chien de son héros. (1537)

This analogy has specific reference to Lucien's inability to profit from circumstances permitting seduction, but it also is a general, and remarkable, affirmation of the hero's independence from his creator. While the novelist creates the circumstances, the tests, the "obstacles," as Stendhal often calls them, which will provide a dramatization of the hero, the hero must be allowed to respond to them according to his own virtualities and must be given the freedom to forge his own being in his encounter with the world. Stendhal's dialogue with and about his creation indicates not a control of novelistic life by the novelist, but rather a concern to preserve its freedom, to give his characters—in the words Henry James once used contrasting Balzac to Thackeray—"the long rope, for acting [themselves] out."[29]

This relation between novelist and hero is in fact inversely dramatized within the frame of *Lucien Leuwen*. When Lucien returns from Paris to Nancy after his débâcle with Mme de Chasteller, at the end of the first section of the novel, he signs himself over to his father, and his father's conception of what his career and style should be, for eighteen months. M. Leuwen becomes almost literally the novelist of his son's destinies, forcing him to play out a role in a world

---

[29] "The Lesson of Balzac," *The Future of the Novel*, ed. Leon Edel (New York: Vintage Books, 1956), p. 115.

from which he had tried to withdraw. By transferring this question of control within the novel, Stendhal brilliantly solves a problem posed by his theme: how to keep an uncommitted, passionate, misanthropic hero (whose instinctive reaction is to quit the *cursus honorum* and flee to America), in *le monde*, struggling with questions of social position and style, without violating this hero's freedom. These different exigencies—similar to demands Stendhal felt in his own life—are satisfied when Stendhal shifts responsibility for Lucien's worldly career from novelist to father-as-novelist. The relationship of father and son is both like Stendhal's relation with his hero, and ultimately a metaphor of what he wants to avoid: too much interference, manipulation, and control.

These instances of Stendhal's concern to protect Lucien's freedom are important because Lucien's story is finally centrally *about* freedom. Lucien's ultimate revolt against his father's arrangements of his life comprehends a rejection of social position and a refusal of the role of manipulator. For M. Leuwen, as for Versac or Valmont, freedom is essentially the freedom to control, to assert his own liberty through his mastery of others. But Lucien at the end asserts another kind of freedom: disengagement, freedom from commitment to any social role or any exclusive interpretation of life. He posits the morality of non-commitment and the right to be governed by sensibilities other than the social. He arrogates to himself the right to follow his natural impulses where they will lead him and develop himself into all he may become. If Stendhal is so careful to grant Lucien the freedom to develop his own reality, it is because this reality must be the least committed in the novel: Lucien is, by the end, the most nearly free agent, and his freedom is his essence, the final example he offers us of a "way to be," and Stendhal's final comment on social styles.

Lucien's ultimate personal style is both the result of and
the reason for Stendhal's institution of freedom as a novelistic
stance. Throughout the novel Lucien's choices are dramatized as choices between styles of freedom and styles of
fixity, verbal styles that point toward a free mastery of social
life or an exclusive allegiance to some representative position and entrapment within a predetermined social role.
At the level of comedy of manners, the question of freedom is a question of style, and Stendhal cast this work as much
as possible into dialogue in order to preserve a free interplay
of voices representing and enacting the profound questions
of the novel. In his marginal notes, we find him defining his
method in this fashion: "*For me*. Scène (poésie dramatique):
C'est un dialogue qui amène un grand changement dans la
position d'un ou de plusieurs des interlocuteurs"(1556). That
is, scenic drama rather than exposition defines and modifies
the characters' relationships. We, like Lucien, form our judgments on the basis of the voices we hear; these lead us directly to the inner moral being. When, for example, we listen to M. de Vaize excusing the Rue Transnonain massa-
cres, his vocabulary of moral pomposities points to the ethical
atrophy of a bureaucrat who has sold out to the exercise of
governmental power:

> —Je gémis comme vous des accidents terribles qui peuvent
> arriver dans l'emploi trop rapide de la force la plus légitime.
> Mais vous sentez bien qu'un accident déploré et réparé
> autant que possible ne prouve rien contre un système. (1184)

Stendhal's marginalia show a constant, meticulous attention
to nuances of personal verbal style: in a passage where he at
first had M. de Vaize speak of "de bas coquins," he changed
the phrase to "hommes douteux," noting in the margin:
"Style. *Bas coquins*, c'est l'auteur qui parle; *hommes douteux*, c'est M. Cuvier ou M. de Vaize qui parle"(1559). A

striking example is Dr. Du Poirier, originally the parasitical
defender of Legitimist interests in Nancy, who was to perform a volte-face in the second half of the novel and become
a champion of the people in the Assembly. His role in the second part of the novel is only sketched out; all that was
actually written is his *stylistic* conversion: Stendhal has left
the draft of a speech he was to make in the Chamber, re-
plete with imitation Lamennais and populistic pieties. In
other words, Du Poirier, like all the other members of the
supporting cast, was to the novelist at first a voice, a problem
in verbal style, since Stendhal was in fact conceiving all the
questions of life in terms of style.

In contrast to the bad taste and bad faith of these characters
who are given over, bound and gagged as it were, to social
institutions or classes, to conformity and imitation, we have
the voice of M. Leuwen insisting that the only way to be,
the truly admirable manner, is a distanced, Olympian mastery
of the fixities and foibles of others. Take, for instance, his
description of his successful electoral campaign in the
Avéyron:

> —L'air est chaud, les perdrix excellentes, pleines de goût, et
> les hommes plaisants. Un de mes honorables commettants
> m'a chargé de lui envoyer quatre paires de bottes bien
> confectionnées; je dois commencer par étudier le mérite des
> bottiers de Paris, il faut un *ouvrage* élégant, mais qui pour-
> tant ne soit pas dépourvu de solidité. Quand enfin j'aurai
> trouvé ce bottier parfait, je lui remettrai la vieille botte
> que M. de Malpas a bien voulu me confier. J'ai aussi un em-
> branchement de route royale de cinq quarts de lieue
> de longueur pour conduire à la maison de campagne
> de M. Castanet, que j'ai juré d'obtenir de M. le ministre de
> l'Intérieur; en tout cinquante-trois commissions, outre cel-
> les qu'on m'a promises par lettre. (1274)

This shows marvellously comic nonchalance toward his own mastery of a system he knows to be utterly corrupt and disreputable. His good-humored condescension toward the country gentleman who made his vote contingent on four new pairs of boots (which permits M. Leuwen to imply that of course he has no knowledge of the relative merits of different boot makers, and to insinuate that the product he seeks must be built to stand up under long and rustic use), the excessive politeness of the phrase "a bien voulu me confier" applied to an old boot, the casual mention of the outrageous proposition of the road, and the final revelation of the fifty-three favors to be obtained—all remind one of the kind of comic transmutation of reality found in an eighteenth-century satirist like Voltaire. Intelligence and wit, in their verbal presence alone, prove their claim to mastery of reality, and provide a model of an enviable way to be.

Yet we feel to a degree that M. Leuwen, like M. de Vaize, can never be anything other than what he is: his style, however masterful and free from the fixities of others, marks a social commitment that limits his range of free development—a limitation that Lucien senses and rejects in his final refusal of his father's role. Nonetheless, while the voice of M. Leuwen unquestionably marks a commitment to the system of Old Régime worldliness into which he was born, his account of his electoral campaign, like his conversations with Lucien, should have indicated that his perspective on modern society and what it has become—no longer a pure, enclosed theater, but an uncertain aggregate of the Bank, the Exchange, the Chamber, the ministries, and salons both clever and pretentious, a mixture of capitalistic "democracy" and a world "*d'après* le monde" of the old order—creates an ironic remove from the practice of worldliness. He indeed to a degree even secretly admires the impetuous qualities he publicly deplores in his son. This distance from worldliness qualifies and complicates his position and our reaction to it: commitment to his voice and outlook seems less certain an allegiance, and leaves us disposed to respond to the other realms of being discovered by Lucien.

There are other models of "good style" in the book: the hard realism of the inexorable Coffe, the direct honesty of General Fari, the elegant simplicity of Mme de Chasteller, and the disengaged, heroic pride with which Lucien challenges the bureaucratic executioners, a style of moral heroism symbolized by the recurrent quotations from Corneille. Yet the moral reaction is not one we can rely on; we are never allowed to regard it as a definitively satisfying response to reality because it is too limited in its scope, too rigid and unintelligent. We are constantly forced back to a greater worldliness of outlook, to the position of M. Leuwen. An instance is the scene at Caen where Lucien is trying to wring coöperation from the local magistrate, the Président Donis, and decides it might be useful to accuse the judge of having let the opposition win too many trials; the truth uncovered by Lucien's acting horrifies him:

—Dernièrement, votre cour a fait gagner tous leurs procès aux anarchistes, aux républicains . . .
—Hélas! je le sais bien, dit le président en l'interrompant, les larmes presque aux yeux et du ton le plus piteux. Son Excellence le ministre de la justice m'a écrit pour me le reprocher.

Leuwen tressaillit.

"Grand Dieu! se dit-il en soupirant profondément et de l'air d'un homme qui tombe dans le désespoir, il faut donner ma démission de tout et aller voyager en Amérique. Ah! ce voyage-ci fera époque dans ma vie. Ceci est bien autrement décisif que les cris de mépris et l'avanie de Blois."
(1241)

Lucien's reaction of moral shock is "right," but it is made to appear rigid, even mechanical, and our reaction is one of sophisticated amusement. We may be as horrified as he is by the corruption of justice and the maneuvers of the rogues, but the presentation of the scene, the revelation of the minister's letter through Lucien's acting a "tough" role, the subsequent misunderstanding and doubletake, complete with the worthy magistrate's tears and Lucien's tropism of flight to America, moves us rapidly beyond the moral response. We witness the transformation of the crude matter of politics into comedy, and the effect of the transformation is to align us with the irony of the Olympian, M. Leuwen.

A resolution to this orchestration of different responses and different styles is to be found ultimately only in the voice of the narrator himself. Substantially, as we have seen, the narrator echoes M. Leuwen's tone, his wit, his play with the stylistic fixities of others to indicate his own free mastery of reality. Rejecting what was "Roman" in the tone of *Le Rouge et le noir*, Stendhal took as his model in this novel the stylish urbanity and wit of Fielding.[30] Like M. Leuwen, the narrator refuses to be shocked by the world's rogueries, constantly views them as the matter of comedy. Yet he also reserves the capacity to respond with vibrance and immediacy to Lucien when he is being most unworldly. Describing the first meeting between Lucien and Mme de Chasteller, he says that they talked together with

> . . . cette nuance de familiarité délicate qui convient à deux âmes de même portée, lorsqu'elles se rencontrent et se reconnaissent au milieu des masques de cet ignoble bal

[30] In a marginal note, Stendhal writes: "Style *of Dominique*—sensation sur les premières vingt-sept pages du cinquième volume de *Rouge et Noir*: vrai, mais sec. Il faut prendre un style plus fleuri et moins sec, spirituel et gai, non pas comme le *Tom Jones* de 1750, mais comme serait le même Fielding en 1834" (1528).

masqué qu'on appelle le monde. Ainsi des anges se parle-
raient qui, partis du ciel pour quelque mission, se rencontre-
raient, par hasard, ici-bas. (923)

This moment of truth amidst hypocrisy, this instinctive accord of two souls, elicits from the narrator his most elegiac
notes; it establishes a mood in which he can condemn the society which has formed his voice and manner, and align himself with the sublimity of Rousseau. Typically, in the middle of his attention to worldliness, Stendhal opens an alternative reality, another freedom that has nothing to do
with social manipulation, an impulse in opposition to any
concern with the manners of the world. The narrative voice
maintains a range and inclusivity of response that allows it
to embrace divergent, even contradictory attitudes. It responds
to the liberation of Lucien's sensibility as he leaves Paris for
the Alps and the cities of Lombardy and Tuscany; it makes
us feel the rightness of Lucien's choice, the superior morality
of his disengagement. Yet it does so without ever renouncing
the high, comic, Olympian overview of M. Leuwen, without violating urbanity and distance. The narrator can perhaps
best be characterized as a M. Leuwen freed of any social ob-
ligations, one who preserves his perfect understanding and
mastery of *le monde*, but no longer feels obliged to operate
in it. He maintains a sense of virtuality, diversity, and free
choice for his hero and for us to suggest that true urbanity
in the modern world is finally an attitude of freedom from
the world, freedom both to play with and leave it, to master it,
and to unfold one's sensibility outside it.

In this novel possibly more than in any other, Stendhal
demonstrates his ability to represent several points of view,
each represented dramatically with cogency and force,
which are resolved, but by no means cancelled out, in the
overview of the man of the world who knows the world so
well that he is not reluctant to turn his back on it. *Lucien*

Leuwen has been called the most "Balzacian" of Stendhal's novels,[31] but in fact its tone and outlook have little to do with Balzac. One can imagine what this subject would have become in Balzac's hands: the "human comedy" of politics would have become a dramatic and villainous plot, Lucien would have turned into an arriviste called upon to sacrifice morals to power, and any laughter would have been satanic. This may suggest why a *Lucien Leuwen* written by Balzac, while it would have been more of a novel of initiation than Stendhal's, more of a *Bildungsroman*, would not have been a novel of worldliness. Our sense that Stendhal's book is a novel of worldliness is a matter of the total outlook that shapes the subject and its form. Stendhal transforms his raw material into a question of "how to be" within a publicly defined system, an interplay of different social styles effectively dramatized by his constant use of dialogue. Finance and politics become tokens in a game played for social prominence and control. The narrative tone and style, this voice of good company with its knowing ironies and conversational ease, reflects an indulgent paternalism toward the hero— a relation transferred within the novel and dramatized by the introduction of the father-controller—and a comic distance from the immoralities of worldly behavior, an ability to regard social pretension and political viciousness as evidence of comic fixity, lack of worldliness. We are forced to consider the life recorded in the novel in a similar manner, to be ironical, knowing, distanced, and inclusive, to regard Lucien's experience not as an experience of politics, or morality, or love, or social place alone, but as something which

[31] René Boylesve, *Réflexions sur Stendhal* (Paris, 1929), p. 56; see also Maurice Bardèche, *Stendhal romancier* (Paris, 1929), p. 67; Albert Thibaudet, *Stendhal* (Paris, 1924), p. 163; and Georges Blin, "Sur une rencontre de Stendhal avec Honoré de Balzac: *Lucien Leuwen* et *La Femme abandonnée, Aurea Parma,* "Omaggio a Stendhal," July-December 1950, pp. 110-123.

includes, transforms, shapes, and gives meaning to these discrete elements: the experience of worldliness.

Stendhal's final judgment on this experience, we suggested,
is not simple: compared to that of the eighteenth-century
writers we have discussed, even Laclos, it is complex, ambivalent, and curiously balanced. Responding to M. Leuwen, we
feel an exhilarating intellectual domination of the world
through a commitment to the power of intelligence and
wit, a control of men through our easy apprehension of their
weaknesses and representative fixities. This commitment is
social and worldly, if also ironical about the world on which
it depends. At the same time, through the hero a more moralistic,
spontaneous, and heroic response is suggested; we are led to
appreciate Lucien's disengaged style and to respond to his
withdrawal. The narrator's own voice constantly reminds us
that the experience of worldliness can only be discussed by
the supremely witty voice of the man of the world, but one
who finds a superior worldliness in the ability to reach beyond the limits of the worldly sensibility. We, the "happy
few" to whom Stendhal dedicated all his novels, are defined and brought into being by the free interplay of styles
in the novel, by the transmutations of reality worked by the
intelligence of the worldly master, and most of all by the vibrant voice of the narrator himself, which is our final standard of judgment, our ultimate model of the most admirable
way to be. Like the dandy Stendhal affected to be in real life,
we enlist ourselves with the world, but remain *disponible*,
ready to move into whatever realms of sensibility life may
offer. Stendhal's complex attitude toward worldliness finally enlists us most of all with a concept of freedom: liberty
of action, freedom to follow our bent through the world to
wherever it will take us. What at last matters is not *what* one
is, but *how* one is; the former implies imprisonment within

a given social role—representative fixity—while the latter is the style of freedom.

Lucien Leuwen seems to me Stendhal's richest, most complex exploration of the conditions and consequences of the pursuit of worldliness in modern society; hence it by implication contains his most interesting commentary on the ethos and novelistic tradition we have been discussing. But *Lucien Leuwen* is not of course Stendhal's last word on worldliness: this is the role of *La Chartreuse de Parme*. Its finality is a product of its purity, and this purity makes *La Chartreuse* less significant a text for investigating Stendhal's problems in writing a modern novel of worldliness. What he has in fact done in *La Chartreuse* is to abandon the recalcitrant realities which he was forced to shape and transform in creating the world of *Lucien Leuwen*; he has solved the problem by abandoning some of its terms, by narrowing the extent of his stage, and returning worldliness to its original form, courtliness. No longer working to define and dramatize the modern social theater, he has chosen a conscious anachronism, a nineteenth-century absolute monarchy dedicated to the proposition that the French Revolution—the destroyer of *le monde*, its system and literature—never took place. He is hence no longer forced to locate his drama of worldliness within the comedy of national politics; it can once again be a drama of court intrigue within a perfect enclosure.

This solution would be too fantastic, the authorial sleight-of-hand too apparent, were it not rooted in historical truth. The vast opening movement of the novel describes how the Court of Parma came into being: the voluntary narrowing and limiting of the stage on which the novel is to be enacted is an historical fact, and one of the subjects of the novel. We move from the joyous triumphant entry of Bonaparte's young army into Milan in 1796, through the heroic vicissi-

266

tudes of the Cisalpine Republic, to the collapse of the Grand Army at Waterloo. Finally, surrounded by Austrian spies, forced into various disguises, with Fabrice we arrive at the court of His Most Serene Highness Ranuce-Ernest IV. The movement is backwards in time, with the European reaction, and inwards in space: the vast, total geographical view of the first chapters is progressively narrowed until it focusses on Parma. And if this narrowing means the advent of the prison—Spielberg, the Citadel of Parma—symbolic of the limitations upon life in the Europe of the Holy Alliance, it also brings the victory of the high comic view of life: the rifle barrels strewn on the plains of Lombardy since 1796 by European politics are gathered up by Italian peasants and made into *mortaretti*, giant firecrackers. The end of the epic brings not only the reign of the petty and restrictive, but also the necessity of the detached and happily ironic viewpoint.

In Parma, Stendhal's historical perspective, his ironical understanding of the European reaction, has produced a miniature, pseudo Old Régime, a state complete with its Versailles and its courtly ceremony, its courtiers, statesmen, and intriguers, a recreation of that lighted stage we found to be indispensable for any true dramatization of manners.[32] It is a world of conscious make-believe, from the sovereign's imitation Louis XIV on down, where courtly marionettes powder their hair to prove that the nineteenth century never dawned. Almost all the cast is fixed in roles dictated by historical necessity; their gestures and words are part of a theatrical idiom purified by their rejection of history and contemporary realities. Life has been refined into etiquette, as in Saint-Simon,

---

[32] My interpretation of the court of Parma, and my view of the whole novel, has been influenced by Harry Levin's chapter, "A Pistol Shot at a Concert," *The Gates of Horn*, pp. 129-49; also J. D. Hubert's "Notes sur la dévaluation du réel dans "La Chartreuse de Parme," *Stendhal Club*, 2e Année, No. 5 (1959), pp. 47-53.

and the interplay of persons and forces in society is constantly seen in terms of theater—*commedia dell'arte* is the courtiers' favorite occupation—and gaming: the most coveted honor of the court is to be asked to join *le whist du prince*.

Those who dominate Parma are the actress most in command of her theatricality, the Duchess of Sanseverina, and the most artful gamer, Count Mosca. The Sanseverina's great moments are all "acts," played with the Prince, or Ferrante Palla, or her servant Ludovico; she secures her ends through a perfect improvisation of the role demanded by a given "canvas," as in *commedia dell'arte*. In the Duchess, the conjunction of naturalness and artificiality is such that they cannot be distinguished: her theatricality is her nature; the style she deploys is hence utterly free of any social fixity and elicits our free response to it. Less moving, but more consistently successful than the Duchess, Mosca bases his control on his perfect knowledge of the rules of all the games. As he explains to a Fabrice about to embark on his very worldly career in the Church:

> Crois ou ne crois pas à ce qu'on t'enseignera, *mais ne fais jamais aucune objection.* Figure-toi qu'on t'enseigne les règles du jeu de whist: est-ce que tu ferais des objections aux règles du whist?[33]

To reduce life to a game of whist, transmute reality to the conventional moves of conventional tokens, is to be utterly worldly, more perfectly polished, urbane, and specious even than Valmont, who compared himself to Turenne and life to the art of war.

Like M. Leuwen, but without that character's necessary basis in solid cash and political power, hence more purely, Mosca rules men by knowing them. As was the case with

[33] *La Chartreuse de Parme,* in *Romans et Nouvelles,* II, 137.

M. Leuwen, or Valmont, our awareness and acceptance of his mastery are a product of his style. He dupes others, rearranges reality and rewrites history through witty twistings of language: at the moment of political paroxysm in Parma, the abortive revolution is turned into an "unfortunate event," the executed rebels are all "travelling abroad." Although his "liberal" opponents paint him as a sinister figure, Mosca in fact operates almost exclusively by the classical arm of ridicule. Fear of ridicule and fear of Jacobins dominate the Prince equally, and Mosca's indispensability derives from the elegance of style with which he performs the nightly function of looking under the Prince's bed for hidden liberals. His master stroke of domestic policy is the appointment of the titular head of the liberal party to governorship of the political prison: whatever move Fabio Conti may make in this hamstrung situation, he will appear damagingly absurd. Mosca's celebrated remark, "Avec ces propos de république, les fous nous empêcheraient de jouir de la meilleure des monarchies" (412), is fair enough: in a Parma run according to his principles, there would be only mock-executions, as mock everything else. He knows that it is not usually necessary to hang people because it is so easy to manipulate them in other ways, and this constitutes a sort of morality.

But "morality" in this novel is completely redefined. While all the "real" issues of ethics and comportment in *Lucien Leuwen* were transformed into questions of style, here they have become even more purely a matter of stylishness, expressions within an artificial and theatrical medium. The villains of the novel—Fabrice's father and brother, Rassi, Fabio Conti, Giletti—are notable for their unstylishness, their grotesque, mechanical ugliness and tastelessness. The heroes and heroines are remarkable not for any stricter morality (which in terms of this world would be a rather ludicrous fixity), but for the theatricality and free virtuosity with which they indulge in the "higher immorality," as Harry Levin characterizes it.[34] Mosca, the Duchess, Ferrante Palla all express themselves in an extravagant idiom of high comedy or opera; they are aristocratic, intelligent, handsome; their acts, words, and gestures announce an exhilarating freedom from questions of morality, and they create for themselves a medium in which our responses to life, our judgments, and our appreciations are almost purely esthetic. Clearly, *La Chartreuse* is one of the most worldly novels ever written because it does so redefine our responses and makes any simply moralistic or pragmatic reaction to a given act or word appear banal, irrelevant, provincial, evidence of unworldliness and lack of freedom. Mosca and the Sanseverina finally enlist our unhesitating assent to a realm beyond good and evil where all the qualities we associate with worldliness have an absolute value and irresistible force.[35]

But the nominal hero of *La Chartreuse* repeatedly eludes the intellectual grasp to which we are trained by the voices of Mosca and the Duchess. Our reactions to Fabrice are, throughout much of the novel, characterized by a certain opacity and even bafflement. After the destruction of his Napoleonic dream, Fabrice seems to adapt easily to the Parmesan order: he follows Canon Borda's rules for reconciliation with the Holy Alliance, including the taking of an ultra mistress without any of the protest Lucien exhibited when ordered to

---

[34] *The Gates of Horn*, p. 142.

[35] Giuseppe Tomasi di Lampedusa, in his interesting "Notes sur Stendhal," *Stendhal Club*, 2ᵉ Année, No. 6 (1960), pp. 153-68, observes that the narrator transforms the blood, violence, and immorality of the novel by assuming the viewpoint of an "homme de bonne société"; but he seems to me in error in identifying this point of view as Fabrice's— Fabrice is of good society, but does not represent and express its attitudes; that is Mosca's role. Recently, Louis Kronenberger, in "Stendhal's Charterhouse," *Encounter*, Vol. xxvii, No. I (July 1966), pp. 32-38, has argued that *La Chartreuse* is more a novel of worldliness than a political novel, as much in the spirit of Castiglione as of Machiavelli.

pay court to Mme Grandet; he accepts an ecclesiastical career because theology is an appealingly complicated game; he pursues actresses in a manner that fulfills all the social forms; he mouths without reflection the reactionary dogmas he is taught. When he returns from the Seminary, he astounds the Prince by his ultra-jesuitical replies; upon questioning, he announces he believes that:

> . . . tout ce qui a été fait depuis la mort de Louis XIV, en 1715, est à la fois un crime et une sottise. Le plus grand intérêt de l'homme, c'est son salut, il ne peut pas y avoir deux façons de voir à ce sujet, et ce bonheur-là doit durer une éternité. Les mots *liberté, justice, bonheur du plus grand nombre*, sont infâmes et criminels: ils donnent aux esprits l'habitude de la discussion et de la méfiance. . . .
> (147)

When we are ready to conclude with the Prince that Fabrice is a perfect hypocrite who has well learned his aunt's lessons, the narrator upsets our expectations by remarking,

> Fabrice croyait à peu près tout ce que nous lui avons entendu dire; il est vrai qu'il ne songeait pas deux fois par mois à tous ces grands principes. Il avait des goûts vifs, il avait de l'esprit, mais il avait la foi. (148)

The passage illustrates the kind of bafflement we feel with this hero: the narrator never allows us to judge him clearly as either *coquin* or *dupe*; his thought processes, both conventional and highly idiosyncratic, elude us. For a great part of the novel, we are inclined to agree with Mosca's judgment that he is "primitive."

Fabrice feels that he is worth something only in moments of exaltation. The forms of worldliness leave him unsatisfied, but his exaltation remains undirected during much of the novel. We do have suggestions of the kind of emotion that will fill his sense of void, first in the description of the Italian Lakes, a natural setting which for him as for Rousseau's protagonists seems a reality rediscovered, something hard and substantial to set against the system of *le monde* (and Stendhal's prose, evoking a non-intellectual, pre-verbal rapport with a certain landscape, suggests that the novel will exploit techniques other than the penetrating glance directed toward others). This description is a prelude to Fabrice's visit to the Abbé Blanès, whom he discovers—and the implicit alternative is Mosca—to be his "real father"(170). The message of the old astrologer is both a prediction and a lesson of morality: Fabrice is prepared for prison, warned against crime, even when it seems justified by the code of worldly honor, and told that he will die on a hard wooden bench, far from luxury, disillusioned with luxury. His force, the Abbé finally affirms, will one day be in his conscience. We are forced to contrast this statement to Mosca's explication of the rules of whist: at a distance from the worldly, cynical, witty, and self-interested voices of the court arises a dark, profound moral utterance. A new range of sensibility is discovered in the Abbé's tower, where Fabrice refinds happiness in an elevated visual perspective on the world, watching the religious procession in the village and listening to the comic explosions of the *mortaretti*.[36]

Fabrice's real being only begins to work toward clarity when he reascends a tower, this time the tower of a prison. Upon entering his cell, he is immediately drawn to the "sublime beauty" of the moon rising over the Alps. His altitude, his separation from the courtly intrigues of Parma, produces a purity of vision and an emotional purity which enable him to look, not down on men, but above and beyond

---

[36] See Proust's remark, that one always finds in Stendhal "un certain sentiment de l'altitude se liant à la vie spirituelle." *A la recherche du temps perdu* (Paris: Bibliothèque de la Pléiade, 1954) III, 377.

them. This aerial solitude is the precondition of his first and only real human contact. Setting Fabrice's romance with Clélia Conti next to Lucien's courtship of Mme de Chasteller, another *belle âme*, we again remark the purity and simplicity of the later novel, its less "realistic," more mythical mode. The social obstacles that separated Lucien and Mme de Chasteller have become physical obstacles: real space—the twenty-five feet between the two windows—and the actual barrier of the *abat-jour*. Communication has been stripped of its social forms, reduced to the simplicity of letters drawn on the hand with charcoal or marked on leaves of paper, and hence it is far more real, a direct communication without the misunderstandings that the interposition of social manners always implies for Stendhal's lovers. Because the obstacles between them are physical, not verbal and social, the lovers move toward a union which seems predestined in Rousseauian fashion—for it began, we vaguely realize, near the start of the novel when they were adolescents, in a chance encounter complete with mistaken identities, where Fabrice decided that Clélia would make a charming prison companion.

Chance may be a form of predestination, and *La Chartreuse* has a rich texture of prediction, foreshadowing, and rationally fortuitous encounters. The characters' gestures have a significance they do not consciously understand, but instinctively accept. When Archbishop Landriani gives Clélia his pastoral ring as token of his protection of Fabrice, she doesn't know how to keep it safely: "Mettez-le au pouce, dit l'archevêque; et il le plaça lui-même"(278). This symbolic marriage, slightly awkward but all the more binding for the characters' unconsciousness of what they are doing, finds its consummation at the end of Clélia's heroic, inspired dash up the tower to save Fabrice from poison. Such spontaneous, uncalculated action, and the whole realm of unconscious or obscurely motivated gestures exploited in the novel—the realm of the "primitive"—form a significant contrast to the voluntary, controlled, self-conscious moves of Mosca. The novel keeps suggesting other ways to be, and it deliberately avoids resolution.

The last chapters of *La Chartreuse* move through scenes in the palace drawing rooms, at the Prince's whist, through Fabrice's sermons, "touched with a perfume of profound melancholy," to Clélia's word of fulfillment spoken in the dark garden: "Entre ici, ami de mon coeur"(488). Courtliness and a deeper emotional reality impinge upon one another, and interfere with each other, without any viable relation between the two having been suggested. Both Fabrice's sermons and Clélia's ruse for preserving her vow with her love possess an uneasy and slightly comic mixture of worldly casuistry and spiritual sincerity. In some measure, the novel seems to repudiate such compromise solutions: Sandrino dies, and this sure sign of celestial wrath entails the death of Clélia; Fabrice retreats to that Charterhouse announced in the novel's title, which seems to have been waiting for him throughout his career. But the narrator's final comment on his hero is less than decisive:

> Fabrice était trop amoureux et trop croyant pour avoir recours au suicide; il espérait retrouver Clélia dans un meilleur monde, mais il avait trop d'esprit pour ne pas sentir qu'il avait beaucoup à réparer. (493)

The sentence preserves and perpetuates all the ambiguities surrounding Fabrice. The proportion of sacred and profane loves is not specified; the hope of refinding Clélia in a better world is balanced against the intellectual calculation of what remains to be repaired. I think we are entitled to view Fabrice's desire for a better world without irony: it corresponds to his emotional logic, and it is an inevitable reaction to what the politics of the best of monarchies have done to his life. Yet the novel does not close with mention of

Fabrice in the Charterhouse; the last sentence reminds us of the worldly happiness of Mosca, the Prince, and, ostensibly, all the Parmesans, since the prisons are empty. Stendhal's attitude is seemingly more divided here than at the end of *Lucien Leuwen*. There, we finally felt most strongly that Stendhal enlisted us with a human quality of freedom, freedom both to master the world and to deny it, freedom to be unbound to any representative system. *La Chartreuse* is at the same time happier, more detached and comic, and darker and more pessimistic.

The primary cause of the double vision we find at the end of the novel is the difference between Stendhal's treatment of the Duchess and Mosca, and his treatment of Fabrice and Clélia. With the pair of worldly controllers, the masters of social life, his attitude is luminous, hard-headed, gay, and urbane. With the two young lovers, however, there is reticence and a certain opacity: they resist the clear penetrating knowing directed at Mosca and the Sanseverina, and directed by them to other characters. When Fabrice reconstitutes himself prisoner at the Citadel, Mosca admits to Gina that Fabrice is the one being who constantly escapes his understanding and control: "Grand Dieu! chère amie, j'ai la main malheureuse avec cet enfant"(432). Fabrice passes beyond his ideal parents, to another realm of being where, in true romantic fashion, death and the maiden are inextricably intertwined, where not only society, but life itself becomes shaded. The darkened lovemaking of Fabrice and Clélia and the sound of her phrase "Cher Fabrice ... combien tu as tardé de temps à venir!" (453) generate a response foreign to Mosca's vocabulary, and which even the sublime Duchess seems never to have known.

We might be tempted to say that we are left, as at the end of *Les Liaisons dangereuses*, with two realities of a different order, one luminously, comprehensively articulated, the other suggested, pointed to, left as a mystery. But this is not quite accurate: like Laclos' novel, *La Chartreuse* is both a *summa* and a critique of worldliness, but it differs from *Les Liaisons dangereuses* in its movement beyond the terms of worldliness, toward something else—symbolic romance, a poetic vision of experience where predictions, chance meetings and mistaken identities, towers, rings, and darkened gardens are as real as anything acted out under the brilliant lights of the salon.[37] It not only suggests the realms lying outside the terra cognita of worldliness, it suggests ways to apprehend and represent them—modes of perception and representation unlike anything found in that literature which derives exclusively from the *moraliste* tradition. If, as Mosca argues, the vile Sancho Panzas will always be victorious over the sublime Don Quixotes, the dons have found within the novel a province for their poetic victory by compensation.

The complexities of *La Chartreuse* are finally given vibrant reality in a voice, an attitude, and a presence: that of the narrator. In relation to his world of miniatures, he has provided himself with an Olympian vantage from which, like Mosca, he controls life: managing a large cast, staging rapid changes of scene, moving geographically with ease among the states of Italy, looking backward and forward in history, he impresses us with his wide vision and the totality of his created world. Wide vision implies altitude and distance; this distance is gained by and for the ironical and comic perspective, the attitude which comes to us in the amused and urbane voice of a man who has lived European history for nearly sixty of its most exciting and disillusioning years. And this distant, broad, and total view implies not only the ability to look down on the immediate, but to look beyond it to something else: like Fabrice in the Farnese Tower, Stendhal discovers the

[37] See Gilbert Durand, *Le Décor mythique de la Chartreuse de Parme* (Paris, 1961).

realities beyond Parma, the "sublime beauty" to be found in nature, in myth, and in vision itself.

La Chartreuse de Parme both exemplifies and goes beyond the terms of this study. Compared to *Lucien Leuwen*, it provides a less direct exploration of Stendhal's novelistic response to worldliness because it abandons the attempt to confront the ethic of worldliness and the realities of the modern world, and because it also opens up new, otherworldly realms of habitation. Yet at the last one should emphasize the extent to which all of Stendhal's fiction tends to define itself in relation to the great worldly tradition we have sketched in preceding chapters. Mme de Lafayette, Crébillon, Duclos, Marivaux, Laclos, the classical moralists and the memorialists of the eighteenth century, these authors who nourished his youth always remained vital and relevant to Stendhal: they seemed to him eminently to have known what life was about.

When the system in whose terms they knew life was destroyed, their stance of worldliness became problematical. That is, from being the only intelligent response to one's consciousness of the image projected by society, it became simply one possible response to a fragment of society. In this manner, it became a stylistic problem: whereas eighteenth-century society assumed and demanded a certain style, the nineteenth century permitted many styles and authorized none. The assumption of the stance of worldliness meant the self-conscious affirmation of social stylishness. Stendhal's pose as dandy is the style of someone who feels himself wandering between two worlds; it is the stylistic affirmation of certain worldly values despite their uncertainty in reality.

But it would be a mistake to see this stylization of self as mannerist: with ever-increasing rigor, the dilettante Stendhal sought to institute a literary manner of "fact" and "truth" which alone could free one's message from the cant of one's age and bring it through intact to the "happy few" of succeeding generations. The lack of any sure correspondence with the sensibility of one's public can be made into a liberation: as he states in *La Vie de Henry Brulard*, the book he most explicitly directed to an audience of 1880 or 1930:

> Parler à des gens dont on ignore absolument la tournure d'esprit, le genre d'éducation, les préjugés, la religion! Quel encouragement à être *vrai*, et simplement *vrai*, il n'y a que cela qui tienne.[38]

The message to the future would in fact be this style. And by "truth," Stendhal in talking about his protagonists' personal styles essentially means freedom, freedom from the hypocrisies and representative fixities of one's age, freedom to deploy the wit and mastery of Valmont, Mosca, or M. Leuwen, yet freedom also to reject when necessary any commitment to sociability, to forge a more radically personal style. The destinies of Stendhal's characters are posed in terms of style; and by his own narrative style he shows his protagonists and his readers how they must be: sociable, worldly, ironic, and free.

[38] *La Vie de Henry Brulard*, p. 11.

EPILOGUES TO WORLDLINESS

STENDHAL cuts a somewhat anachronistic figure among the writers of his time. He was, of course, considerably older than the authors of the Generation of 1830 who fought and won the battle of Romanticism, then became the literary orthodoxy of the mid-nineteenth century. His tastes were old-fashioned, and on their basis he rejected the representative styles of his epoch as pretentious, inelegant, and hypocritical. While Balzac was extolling the invention of the modern novel by Scott, Stendhal was indicating his preference for Mme de Lafayette.[1] To contrast his views of such authors as Marivaux, Chamfort, and Laclos with those of Sainte-Beuve—for whom these were dead figures, worth only an antiquarian's interest and temporary resurrection—is to understand that Stendhal was the last major novelist to have a direct and important relationship to the French eighteenth century. Any later writers nourished from this source—the Goncourts, Proust, Radiguet—will have returned to it consciously and artificially, whereas Stendhal's sensibility was directly and primarily formed by it.

It would not be useful or meaningful to call most of the subsequent novelists of the nineteenth century "worldly"; they may embrace some of the attitudes and techniques of worldliness, but their basic stance has necessarily been displaced, forced from *le monde* to one of the fragmentary realities which constitute the modern world, from the model of sociability to some individual interpretation of life. Moving from Stendhal's two world masters and exponents of worldliness, M. Leuwen and Mosca, we come to Balzac's Vautrin, convict, homosexual, general of the underworld, chief of police, a master intelligence who starts outside society and be-

---

[1] See "Walter Scott et *La Princesse de Clèves*," *Mélanges de littérature*, II, 305-311.

neath it, in the shadow society known as the underworld, to work on its weaknesses, to conquer it like a plague, and finally to control it from the underside up. Urbanity and social manner are not and need not be a part of Vautrin's leverage on the world. Required now is an intelligent perception of what Marx would soon call the contradictions of society, its fissures and zones of ambiguity, the lack of correspondence between given conventions and economic realities —the way everything, whatever its apparent distance from the marketplace, can be given a price tag and bought, sold, or somehow appropriated. Such contradictions did not exist within *le monde*; or rather, the system of *le monde* had relegated them to unconsciousness—until they violently asserted their reality in Revolution.

Theoretically, Balzac's world includes and contains all subworlds, but least convincingly *le monde* and most vividly the *demi-monde*. His view is most effectively that of the outsider, the arriviste, the criminal, and the detective. His scenes of sociability are always threatened by his vision of the totality of society: behind and beneath Anastasie de Restaud's diamonds, worn at the Vicomtesse de Beauséant's ball, we are made to see Père Goriot dying on his filthy bed in the Pension Vauquer. Rather than a fine attention to the interplay of manners, Balzac at his most powerful gives us a number of summary metaphorical juxtapositions of social superstructure and substructure. Yet he is unquestionably committed to the social medium as the necessary framework, providing the necessary terms, for his representations of human relations. This ceases to be true for Flaubert and the Naturalists. Flaubert in fact is at least a symbolic turning point in the development of the novel, for his works continually denounce the falsity of an attention to human social relationships. *Madame Bovary, L'Éducation sentimentale, Bouvard et Pécuchet* progressively demonstrate the meaninglessness of sociable contacts

among people, the strangulation of communication, the irrevocable loneliness of man in society—and hence the impossibility of a novel of manners. And it may in large measure
be because of Flaubert's message that most modern novelists
have regarded "manners" with suspicion, and have attended
to them, if at all, only to unmask their frivolity and hypocrisy.

There are evidently some twentieth-century writers to
whom the idea of a novel played out exclusively in a medium
of sociability, where the characters know one another, and
are known to the reader, through their socially conscious
gestures on a public stage, has exercised a continuing attraction, or indeed seemed necessary to a representation of
their vision of social relationships. There is the example of
Raymond Radiguet's ambition to write a novel "où c'est la
psychologie qui est romanesque,"[2] which led him consciously
and artificially to recreate a theatrical *monde* in his brilliant
récit, *Le Bal du Comte d'Orgel*. Psychology can furnish the
novel's drama most effectively in a circumscribed, enclosed
medium where psychological signs have an accepted value as
code, and operate as gestures in a system of manners. Without
any self-conscious relationship to the eighteenth century, Scott
Fitzgerald was forced by the theme of *The Great Gatsby*
to create a system of sociability whose awareness of its own
image provided the gestures to dramatize its interrelationships: the scene where Gatsby piles before Daisy his super-
fluous imported shirts is an impressive example of how Fitzgerald makes his world yield the terms he needs to make a
drama of manners. More recently, the very specialized and refined psychological dramas of Nathalie Sarraute turn on her
actors' hypersensitized consciousness of others, of the image
projected by a social milieu, where all gestures, even the un-

[2] The phrase was discovered by Jean Cocteau in the papers of Radiguet. See *Oeuvres complètes de Raymond Radiguet* (Paris: Grasset,
1952), p. 180.

articulated verbal gesture, can ultimately be referred to the individual's imagination of the social group.

These novelists, and of course many others, often remind us of the seventeenth and eighteenth-century tradition of worldliness, and renew our sense of the drama inherent in it. These are only isolated and fragmentary examples; there are, however, at least two novelists subsequent to Stendhal whose total manner and enterprise are importantly related to the tradition of worldliness: Henry James and Proust. James is formed by both English and French traditions. His English inheritance was mainly Jane Austen and George Eliot, and through them an eighteenth-century English novel of manners. F. R. Leavis indicates this line of influence in a comment on the passage from Richardson to Austen:

> The social gap between them was too wide . . . for his work to be usable by her directly: the more he tries to deal with ladies and gentlemen, the more immitigably vulgar he is. It was Fanny Burney who, by transposing him into educated life, made it possible for Jane Austen to absorb what he had to teach her. Here we have one of the important lines of English literary history—Richardson—Fanny Burney—Jane Austen.[3]

With James, a cosmopolitan with a Puritan conscience, the moral-rural-protestant-country-gentlemanly tradition of Jane Austen and George Eliot is rendered more urbane by French influences. These included Flaubert and Maupassant, whom he admired for the perfection of their artistry but censured for their failure to deal with subjects that permitted an exploration of the refined and civilized, that allowed development of complex social and psychological interrelationships; and Balzac, whose massive, coherent interplay of characters in society

---

[3] *The Great Tradition* (4th edition; London: Chatto and Windus, 1960), p. 4.

was a lesson to him. He read Stendhal—he must have been one of the very few Anglo-Saxons to do so at that time—and appreciated the "amiable" worldly irony of *La Chartreuse de Parme*.[4] Like all his contemporaries (except for few bibliophiles) he was undoubtedly completely ignorant of the eighteenth-century French novel. Yet from the models of a novel of manners he did possess, equipped with his hypersensitivity to questions of social comportment and psychology, ways of acting and knowing, he wrote novels that often seem the true posterity of the novel of worldliness.

This is first of all a product of his imagination of society. Dr. Leavis remarks that:

> It is doubtful whether at any time in any place [James] could have found what would have satisfied his implicit demand: the actual fine art of civilized social intercourse that would have justified the flattering intensity of expectation he brought to it in the form of his curiously transposed and subtilized ethical sensibility.[5]

Probably only eighteenth-century France could have offered a social reality answerable to this demand (and it would of course have been repugnant to James in other ways). He sought such a society in contemporary Parisian salons and English country houses, but he probably only found it in the created worlds of his novels, in his own efforts to impart meaning to social intercourse. Sometimes to an almost pathological degree, his fictional world is one where no word or gesture is insignificant, where penetrating observation of social manners is necessary to control others and preserve one's own freedom, where management of life depends on an abil-

---

[4] See "Henri Beyle," *The Nation*, xix, 17 September 1874, reprinted in Henry James, *Literary Reviews and Essays*, ed. Albert Mordell (New York, 1957), pp. 151-56.

[5] *The Great Tradition*, p. 11.

ity to manipulate social forms. Yet, as Dr. Leavis suggests, James' social imagination and his "ethical sensibility" are finally one, engaged with the same material and asserting the same values, and this effectively makes his drama of manners also an ethical ordeal.

If *The American* most forcibly reminds us of Balzac, and *The Europeans* of Jane Austen, from *Portrait of a Lady* on James is engaged on a terrain almost identical to that of the novel of worldliness. *The Wings of the Dove*, for example, turns on the questions of false social representation as protection of self and illegitimate control of others; the drama of disguises and penetrations is played out within a small, mannered society of cosmopolites, and in the enclosed, controlled settings of Lancaster Gate and a Venetian palazzo. *The Sacred Fount* can almost be seen as a rewriting of *Les Liaisons dangereuses*: a novel about the dangerous cruelty of sociability run wild, where the spying attempt to penetrate social relationships and to profit from one's discoveries for the control of others is both attractive and destructive. In these novels, worldliness is both a necessary manner and a temptation into immoral manipulation of others. Like Stendhal, James gives his allegiance to freedom; his "villains" are those characters who attempt to control life too much, to deprive others of their freedom, who systematize rather than idealize. Both manipulation and the maintenance of freedom are rendered extraordinarily complex and subtle by the equivocal nature of the *monde* in these novels: standards of conduct are not clearly demarcated (Kate Croy could not handle Merton Densher the way she does if they were), there are no universally accepted models of rightness of manner, which must finally be achieved by an individual sacrifice to the ideal. It is, finally, notable that James's most perfectly worldly woman, his answer to Mme de Merteuil and the Duchess of Sanseverina, Mme de Vionnet of *The Ambassadors*, is ultimately seen as a pathetic figure, entrapped by the code and demands of her society.

Proust resembles James in his fascinated attention to forms of social comportment, in his psychological refinement, and in his position in the history of the novel. With Proust, there is of course a very direct relationship to the literature of worldliness, especially to Mme de Lafayette, Mme de Sévigné, Saint-Simon, Stendhal; one can feel the way the *moraliste* tradition informs the glance that narrator and protagonist turn toward the Faubourg Saint-Germain in an effort to comprehend individual roles and to master social structure. The game of penetration and unmasking reaches an apotheosis not unlike that found in Saint-Simon: at the center of the novel is the protagonist-as-voyeur. Action, experience in the normal sense of the term, is transferred to the others, and the experience of Marcel is most importantly one of social epistemology: finding out, discarding and revising erroneous first impressions, penetrating to the truth of the others, which eventually allows one to posit a personal truth.

Proust's world is of course notoriously factitious, a society where titles, privileges, and codes have an existence no longer recognized outside its limits. *Mondanité*, reality and sentiment, is placed in a double temporal perspective. The narrator's story is one of enchantment and disenchantment with the image of society; the gilded aura of the Guermantes gives way to a sense of their vulgarity and atrophied capacity for personal relationships. And in the larger perspective, the historical, this sterile world, like the cities of the plain, is moving toward annihilation, and after the World War will never be anything but a travesty of itself (the War indeed sounds throughout European literature as a second French Revolution, a social cataclysm which effectively liquidates what is left of *le monde*). The artist alone can confer on it a dignity which is not inherent to it, but to art. Proust records the passing, and the self-destruction, of the last vestiges of the Old Régime, and he is evidently another real point of terminus in a study of the novel of worldliness: he was perhaps the last major novelist to have a vital relationship to a structured, systematic society which, at least in its own terms, provided an image of society which shaped the individual consciousness and comportment.

The twentieth century has rediscovered the eighteenth. But the French eighteenth century that has known a brilliant revival among contemporary novelists, moralists, sociologists and historians is in a sense the inverse image of that which has concerned us here. The "invention of liberty" (Jean Starobinski's phrase) is a movement from closure to openness, from absolutism to freedom, from unity to pluralism. All the novels we considered dramatize an issue of freedom, but essentially (until the new world of Stendhal) to bear witness to its strict limitations in the world, the close bounds within which we are held by the image projected by society within the enclosure of *le monde*. For Crébillon, Duclos, Marivaux, even Laclos, as for Mme de Lafayette and the *moralistes*, while life within the enclosure may be an ordeal for the personal consciousness, life outside is unthinkable—obscured, desolate, unnameable, literally inexpressible.

Why should one bother at all with a literature concerned with what Julie, with considerable accuracy, describes to Saint-Preux as the "little mannerisms of a few coteries of *précieuses* and bored gentlemen"? It is clear that our century has, despite or perhaps because of its "rage for order," valued the elastic, inclusive and open form as the only way of remaining truthful to its realities (and the eighteenth-century French writer who probably commands the greatest prestige today is Diderot, for the diversity of his audacities). Roman Jakobson's remarks about the style of Realism and Naturalism could, I think, apply to the general trend of modern esthetics: art, especially the novel, continues to seek the kinetic form, to create movements, slidings, from one contiguous particular to another, to construct the whole out of a complex and dynamic tension of particulars. The novel of worldliness is situated at the opposite pole, the pole of arrest, generality, and metaphor. It seeks to know and to express totally and clearly through the imposition of certain limits and the arrest of life in a stasis which permits summary, definition, and evaluation. Its process of penetration, definition, evaluation, and control works at all only because its field of operation is so eminently closed, and dominated by a coercive image of society which shapes the individual consciousness.

The limitations of this closure are obvious: so much of life is left out, to reassert its claim to attention only in violent revolutionary upheaval. Yet there is also a value to closure, in the image of man it permits and elicits, in the kind of behavior it valorizes, and the kind of literary analysis it creates. *La mondanité*, as Roland Barthes pointed out, exists only in function of this closure, and it provides a correspondence of reality and literary stance rarely attained. The individual's imagination of society makes him a voluntary, artistic self-creation called upon to play a self-representation in a tense, concerted manner before the eyes of others who are constantly trying to master his role through their own, to reduce him to less enviable positions, to fix and control him. Within the limits of this stage which is both closed to the outside and utterly public to its members, the question of right social manner, of "how to be," is vital, and all the talents of the individual and the group are directed to defining, preserving, and furthering an agreed-upon image. This means that the literature which responds to this image and behavior itself is vitally concerned with the drama of "how to be." It exists within the ethos of the enclosure, within a medium which embraces writer

287

and reader, gives them the terms of their mutual assessments and permits a witty, subtle commerce between them. And as the ethos values penetration, lucidity of perception and clarity of enunciation of signs within a code which is finally a systematization of life in language, so its literature is finally dedicated with remarkable force and skill to the right uses of language: in life and in art, mastery of the world is mastery of language.

Baudelaire called *Les Liaisons dangereuses* a novel of "terrible sociability," and the phrase could be extended to all the novels of our study: they are concerned with the drama—comic, tense, cruel, potentially explosive—created by the fact that people must live together in an ordered way. The effort of any artist is to give meaning and significance to what would otherwise remain simply external reality, an "otherness" unappropriated to the self; the effort of the novelists of worldliness is directed toward giving meaning and significance to our sociability, to the commerce that, as Marivaux put it, we all, without exception, have with one another: to our "being together." As Henry James's extreme imaginative social constructions may indicate, this effort is most successful and most telling when the imagination of society has the richest medium for its deployment. The sociability of seventeenth and eighteenth-century France was rich because of social closure; it produced one of the most elaborately systematized orders of "being together" the world has ever known, and the writers who turned their attention to it occupy a privileged position in the range of the novel.

INDEX

Acceto, Torquato, 46
Addison, Joseph, 95
Alexander the Great, 53
Allem, Maurice, 172n
Ancients and Moderns, Quarrel
of the, 59
Argens, Jean-Baptiste de Boyer,
Marquis d', 36
Aristotle, 58
Arland, Marcel, 104, 138, 139
Arnauld, Angélique, 66
Auerbach, Erich, 47, 62, 82,
158, 227n
Austen, Jane, 34, 90, 282, 284

Balzac, Jean-Louis Guez de, 46,
58n
Balzac, Honoré de, 35, 90, 91-92,
97-98, 158, 162, 167, 169, 228,
240, 256, 264, 279-80, 282, 284
Bardèche, Maurice, 265n
Barthélémy, Edouard de, 48n, 58n
Barthes, Roland, 5n, 15, 16n, 42,
78ff, 92, 287
Baudelaire, Charles, 187, 192, 215,
216, 288
Bénichou, Paul, 67
Bergson, Henri, 234n
Bernardin de Saint-Pierre,
Jacques-Henri, 217
Bersani, Jacques, 71n
Besenval, Pierre Victor, Baron de,
222
Besterman, Theodore, 146n
Blin, Georges, 190, 204n, 227n,
255n, 264n
Boase, Alan, 46n
Boileau-Despréaux, Nicolas, 53,
142
Bone, Edith, 240n
Bossuet, Jacques-Bénigne, 142

Boudhors, Charles-H., 46n
Bourgogne, Marie-Adélaïde de
Savoie, Duchesse de, 82
Boylesve, René, 264n
Bray, René, 47n
Broglie, Léonce-Victor, Duc de,
250n
Brombert, Victor, 85n, 253-54, 255n
Brontë, Charlotte, 138
Brosses, Charles de (Président
de), 219
burlesque novel, 88
Burney, Fanny, 282
Byron, George Gordon, Lord,
192, 228, 231

Caesar, C. Julius, 53f
Carré, H., 6n
Castiglione, Baldesar, 44-45, 53,
54, 270n
Cervantes Saavedra, Miguel de,
88, 222, 276
Chamfort, Nicolas-Sébastien
Roche de, 222, 279
Chapelain, Jean, 54
Chapman, George, 54
Charron, Pierre, 164
Chateaubriand, François-René,
Vicomte de, 223, 228
Cherpack, Clifton, 36n
Chevigni, 63n
Cicero, Marcus Tullius, 53, 54
Cocteau, Jean, 281n
Colbert, Jean-Baptiste, 238
Corneille, Pierre, 54, 67, 72n, 76,
94, 96, 132, 181, 190, 209, 236,
246, 248, 261
Cousin, Victor, 48n, 51, 67n
Crébillon, Claude-Prosper-Jolyot,
3, 11-36, 40, 42, 43, 48, 62, 64,
65, 80, 82-91 passim, 96, 101,

INDEX

Louis XV, 6
Louis, XVI, 209, 235
Louis, Le Grand Dauphin, 81, 82
Louis-Philippe, 233, 234, 240, 243, 246, 250
Lukács, Georg, 240, 249

Macchia, Giovanni, 46n, 69
Machiavelli, Niccolo, 46, 270n
McKenna, Ethel, 165n
Magendie, Maurice, 46n, 48n, 63n
Magne, Émile, 70n
Malraux, André, 176
Manheim, Ralph, 47n
Marguerite de Navarre (Marguerite d'Angoulême), 45
marivaudage, 105-107, 110-15, 132, 139
Marivaux, Pierre Carlet de Chamblain de, 3, 85, 87, 88, 90, 93, 94-141, 148, 158, 162, 174, 179, 187, 218, 222, 277, 279, 286, 288; *Le Cabinet du Philosophe*, 95; *L'Indigent Philosophe*, 95; *Le Jeu de l'amour et du hasard*, 105, 136; *Le Paysan parvenu*, 135, 139-40; "Pensées sur la clarté du discours," 104-105, 106-107, 113; "Réflexions sur l'esprit humain à l'occasion de Corneille et de Racine," 94; *Le Spectateur François*, 95; *La Vie de Marianne*, 93, 96-141, 222, 230; *The Virtuous Orphan* (English trans. of *Marianne*), 97; "Le Voyageur dans le nouveau monde," 95.
Marmontel, Jean-François, 6, 112, 222, 223
Martignac, Jean-Baptiste Gay, Vicomte de, 238
Martineau, Henri, 219n, 220n,

225n, 226n, 230n, 250n
Marx, Karl, 280
Matucci, Mario, 94n
Maupassant, Guy de, 282
Mauriac, François, 255
May, Georges, 3n, 87n
Meister, Paul, 37n
memoirs, novels as, 11, 32, 40, 87, 100
Méré, Antoine Gombaud, Chevalier de, 46, 53-55, 58, 60
Molière (Jean-Baptiste Poquelin), 60, 61-62, 92, 97, 113n, 134, 143-46, 160, 219-21, 225, 252
Mongrédien, Georges, 6n, 47n
Montaigne, Michel de, 46, 164
Montesquieu, Charles de Secondat, Baron de, 7, 84, 85
Montpensier, Anne-Marie-Louise d'Orléans, Duchesse de, 57, 58, 65, 66
moralistes, 6, 41, 43, 56, 60-68 passim, 72n, 76-77, 78, 82-91 passim, 95, 101f, 110, 112ff, 139, 142, 145, 149, 151, 154, 155, 164, 174, 179, 203, 206, 218, 222, 223, 276, 277, 285, 286
Mordell, Albert, 283n
Mornet, Daniel, 3n, 162n, 163n
Mozart, Wolfgang Amadeus, 254
Mylne, Vivienne, 4n, 32n, 90n

Napoléon, 225, 266
Naturalism, 91, 280, 286
Nerciat, Andréa de, 84, 222
Nervèze, Antoine de, 46
Nicole, Pierre, 164
nouvelle historique, 68-69, 87

Orléans, Philippe III d', 6

Papin, Claude, 46n
Pascal, Blaise, 66, 67, 104

292